Speech and Voice Science Workbook

FOURTH EDITION

Speech and Voice Science Workbook

FOURTH EDITION

Alison Behrman, PhD, CCC-SLP
Donald Finan, PhD

PLURAL
PUBLISHING
INC.

5521 Ruffin Road
San Diego, CA 92123

e-mail: information@pluralpublishing.com
Web site: https://www.pluralpublishing.com

Typeset in 12/14 Garamond by Flanagan's Publishing Services, Inc.
Printed in the United States of America by Integrated Books International

ISBN-13: 978-1-63550-193-3
ISBN-10: 1-63550-193-8

Contents

About This Workbook   vii
Reviewers   ix

Part I. Questions

1 Introduction Questions   3

2 Describing and Explaining Motion Questions   5

3 Sound Waves Questions   17

4 Breathing Questions   57

5 Phonation I: Basic Voice Science Questions   99

6 Phonation II: Measurement and Instrumentation Questions   133

7 The Production and Perception of Vowels Questions   155

8 The Production and Perception of Consonants Questions   193

9 Prosody Questions   227

10 Theories and Models of Speech Production Questions   237

11 Theories of Speech Perception Questions   251

12 Instrumentation Questions   261

Part II. Answers

2 Describing and Explaining Motion Answers   285

3 Sound Waves Answers   287

4 Breathing Answers   291

5 Phonation I: Basic Voice Science Answers   297

6 Phonation II: Measurement and Instrumentation Answers   304

7 The Production and Perception of Vowels Answers   309

8 The Production and Perception of Consonants Answers   319

9 Prosody Answers   331

10 Theories and Models of Speech Production Answers   336

11 Theories of Speech Perception Answers   341

12 Instrumentation Answers   346

About This Workbook

Welcome to the *Speech and Voice Science Workbook, Fourth Edition*! Our intention in creation of this workbook is to offer you a tool for learning. The contents can be used for review, self-study and exam preparation, to highlight areas of confusion, to learn concepts, to connect ideas, and to spark new questions and thoughtful discussions. We believe that all faculty who teach this course, from novice instructors to well-established speech scientists, will find at least some portion of this workbook to be an asset to teaching and learning. We hope that students will feel the same.

This workbook is divided into chapters that correspond to the chapters in the textbook *Speech and Voice Science, Fourth Edition*. Within each chapter, you will find four sections: *Foundational Knowledge* questions, *Conceptual Integration* questions, TRY IT! activities, and *Clinical Application* questions. (Exceptions are Chapter 1, which contains only TRY IT! activities, and Chapters 2 and 3, which contain no clinical questions.)

The *Foundational Knowledge* questions in each chapter are organized by major section and reference the first page of their respective sections in the textbook. Therefore, the questions in this section follow the order of the material presented in the chapters. These questions are in the format of multiple choice, true/false, matching, figure identification, and complete the statement/fill-in-the-blank. The purpose of these questions is to allow students to assess their basic knowledge of factual information obtained from their reading and to highlight information that they need to review.

The *Conceptual Integration* questions demand that the student pull together diverse information and interrelate that information into a coherent structure. It asks the student to delve deeper into the material and demands understanding rather than memorization. Thus, the questions in this section do not follow a specific order within the chapter or relate to a single page number in the textbook. Furthermore, some of these questions address similar information to that found in the *Foundational Knowledge* section, but with greater complexity. The questions in this section are presented in a variety of formats, including many questions that require a few sentences or short paragraph in response.

The TRY IT! activities are fun (we hope), short activities that students can use to explore concepts presented in the chapter. These activities can be assigned as homework or they can be in-class activities that students can work through in pairs or small groups or online within virtual break-out rooms. We believe that, through this opportunity of experiential learning, new insights will be attained, and new questions will arise that could spark good classroom discussions or online discussion board topics.

The *Clinical Application* questions are designed to help guide students in the usefulness of speech and voice science. Hopefully, these questions will help to answer the common student query, "Why do I have to take this course?" Some of the questions are taken directly from the Clinical Case questions in the textbook. (Answers are not provided in the textbook, but they are provided here in this workbook.) Other questions in this section address clinically relevant topics that were not part of the textbook clinical cases.

The first half of this workbook contains all of the questions. The second half of the book contains the answers. We separated the answers from the questions to encourage students to try (and perhaps to struggle) to answer the questions before looking at the answers. Quickly checking the answers defeats the purpose of learning. Strongly encourage your students to resist the temptation to glance at the answers too quickly.

Unlike many workbooks in speech-language pathology and audiology, we did not include blank lines for students to write their answers. It takes up much space and it can prevent students from returning and trying a second (or third) time to answer questions. We encourage students to answer questions on their computer or with old-fashioned paper and pencil.

Some of the questions have accompanying illustrations, particularly the *Conceptual Integration* questions. A few of the illustrations come directly from the textbook with labels removed. Most of the illustrations, however, were created specifically for this workbook to give students a new look at concepts.

You will find that topics of particular importance, or topics that often confuse students, are addressed in multiple questions within the *Foundational Knowledge* and *Clinical Integration* sections. We have found, and we're sure you have as well, that students can be misled into thinking they understand a concept because they can answer a single question on the topic. However, a rephrasing of the questions, or addressing the concept from a different approach, reveals fundamental confusion.

We hope that you find this workbook a useful teaching and learning tool. Please let us know your thoughts—what you like, what you don't, and suggestions for additions and changes.

Alison and Don
Alison.Behrman@lehman.cuny.edu
Donald.Finan@unco.edu

Reviewers

Plural Publishing and the authors would like to thank the following reviewers for taking the time to provide their valuable feedback during the manuscript development process. Additional anonymous feedback was provided by other expert reviewers.

Stephen Enwefa, PhD, CCC-SLP, ND
Professor
Southern University A&M College
Baton Rouge, Louisiana

Alice Henton, SLPD, CCC-SLP
Associate Professor
Harding University
Searcy, Arkansas

Daniel J. Hudock, PhD, CCC-SLP
Associate Professor
Idaho State University
Pocatello, Idaho

Nandhu Radhakrishnan, PhD, CCC-SLP
Associate Professor
Lamar University
Beaumont, Texas

Part I
QUESTIONS

1

Introduction Questions

1. Read over the list of 18 study techniques discussed in the textbook. Identify the top three suggestions that you believe could work for you and that you might be willing to try. Next, you will use a scale of 1 to 10, with 1 being least confident that you could use the technique and 10 being most confident that you could use the technique. With that scale, for each of the three techniques you have chosen, assign a number on the 1-to-10 scale that reflects your confidence that you could employ the technique this semester. Very likely, the number of the scale that you choose will be different for each of three techniques. Now ask yourself, why did you choose each number—why didn't you choose one lower number? Finally, ask yourself, what would it take to move each number up one higher on the scale?

2. Now select the bottom three techniques that you believe would not work for you and that you do not want to try to apply. Using the same 1-to-10 scale, again assign a confidence number to each of the three techniques, and determine why each number isn't one number lower and what it would take to move each number one higher.

Note that both exercises 1 and 2 are designed to help you better understand your study habits and to reveal impediments to improved studying that you may not realize exist!

2

Describing and Explaining Motion Questions

Foundational Knowledge

2.1 Systems of Measurement (p. 12)

1. In the "MKS" system of measurement, "M," "K," and "S" stand for
   A. Meters, Kilograms, Seconds
   B. Miles, Kilometers, Seconds
   C. Meters, Kilometers, Sound
   D. Miles, Kings' Foot, Sound

2. Which of the following are used in the English system of measurement?
   A. Meter
   B. Gram
   C. Quart
   D. Liter

3. The liter is a measurement of
   A. Volume
   B. Time
   C. Length
   D. Sound intensity

4. Which of the following is the International System of measurement?
   A. The standard system
   B. The metric system
   C. The English system
   D. The foot, yard, minute system

5. The MKS system of measurement is also known as the _____ system.

6. There are _____ centimeters in a meter.

2.2 Describing Motion: Speed, Velocity, Acceleration, and Deceleration (p. 13)

7. "Uniform motion" occurs when a moving object's
   A. Position is unchanging.
   B. Speed is constantly increasing.
   C. Speed is unchanging.
   D. Speed changes randomly.

8. If an object's speed is increasing over time, that object is undergoing
   A. Uniform motion
   B. Deceleration
   C. Constant velocity
   D. Acceleration

9. Velocity may be defined as
   A. An object's speed and direction of movement
   B. An object's total distance moved
   C. An object's maximum acceleration
   D. The force applied to an object

10. "Speed" defines the relationship between an object's changing distance over _____.

11. "Speech rate" can be described as the speed of _____.

12. True/False   "Velocity" and "Speed" are synonymous terms.

2.3 Newton's Laws Explain Motion (p. 14)

13. The physical law stating that an object at rest will remain at rest unless acted on by an external force is known as
    A. Newton's first law of motion
    B. Newton's second law of motion
    C. Newton's third law of motion
    D. Gravity

14. In the equation of Newton's second law of motion, F = m*a
    A. "m" stands for mass and "a" stands for angle.
    B. "m" stands for mass and "a" stands for acceleration.
    C. "m" stands for movement and "a" stands for acceleration.
    D. "m" stands for movement and "a" stands for angle.

15. "Force" can be described as
    A. An object's weight
    B. The change in direction of movement of an object
    C. An object's inertia
    D. A "pull" or "push" on an object

16. Newton's first law of motion suggests that the only way for an object to accelerate or decelerate is by application of
    A. Gravity
    B. An outside (unbalanced) force
    C. Uniform motion
    D. Balanced forces

17. Newton's third law of motion states that for every action (force), there is an equal and opposite
    A. Mass
    B. Inertia
    C. Reaction (force)
    D. Motion

18. The unit of "force" is named after
    A. Sir Alec Guinness
    B. Heinrich Hertz
    C. Sir Isaac Newton
    D. James Watt

19. Newton's first law is often called the law of _____.

20. The tendency of an object to resist change in its motion is called _____.

21. The amount of matter that an object contains is known as its _____.

2.4 Momentum and Energy (p. 15)

22. Momentum is defined as an object's mass multiplied by its _____.
    A. Inertia
    B. Velocity
    C. Size
    D. Distance from where it started to move

23. The ability to do work is termed
    A. Force
    B. Speed
    C. Momentum
    D. Energy

24. Work is defined as force exerted over
    A. Distance (when an object is moved or displaced)
    B. Time
    C. Energy
    D. Mass

25. The amount of work completed over time is termed
    A. Inertia
    B. Momentum
    C. Power
    D. Speed

26. The unit for power is
    A. Distance/second
    B. Joules
    C. Newtons
    D. Watts

27. The formula for work is
    A. Force / Energy
    B. Energy * Time
    C. Power / Energy
    D. Force * Displacement

28. Power is the relationship between
    A. Energy and distance
    B. Force and distance
    C. Work and time
    D. Displacement and velocity

29. The law of conservation of energy states that
    A. An object's potential energy always equals its kinetic energy at any time.
    B. An object's kinetic and potential energy can be exchanged, but the total energy (kinetic and potential) will remain the same.
    C. Potential energy is the same as momentum.
    D. The amount of work done equals the momentum of the object.

30. The type of energy that is "stored" and can be used in the future is known as _____ energy.

31. True/False   Momentum is another term for "inertia."

2.5 Three States of Matter (p. 18)

32. The way that the molecules are arranged within a substance is related to the
    A. Amount of mass of an object
    B. Three states of matter (solid, liquid, gas)
    C. Amount of inertia of an object
    D. Amount of potential energy within that object

33. Which state of matter contains the lowest level of kinetic energy of its molecules?
    A. Solid
    B. Liquid
    C. Gas
    D. All are the same

34. Surface tension of a liquid is generated because
    A. The molecules are of greater mass at the surface of the liquid.
    B. The liquid molecules do not exert an attraction force to the molecules at the surface.
    C. The molecules at the surface are being pulled sideways and down, but not upward, due to attraction from the other molecules in that liquid.
    D. The molecules at the surface are in the "solid" state of matter.

35. In which state are the molecules not able to move and slide relative to each other?
    A. Liquid
    B. Gas
    C. Solid
    D. None of the states of matter allow the molecules to move.

36. The density of an object is defined as
    A. The mass of the object divided by its volume.
    B. The volume of the object divided by its potential energy.
    C. The inertia of the object.
    D. The mass of the object multiplied by its acceleration.

37. An object's resistance to a deformation in its shape is termed its
    A. Inertia
    B. Stiffness
    C. Density
    D. Elasticity

38. Which substance has the highest density (at room temperature and at sea level)
    A. Gold
    B. Lead
    C. Air
    D. Water

39. An object's ability to return to its original shape or position after being deformed is termed its
    A. Inertia
    B. Stiffness
    C. Density
    D. Elasticity

40. The force of air molecules exerted on the walls of a container is termed
    A. Pressure
    B. Inertia
    C. Density
    D. Mass

41. Pascals, kilopascals (kPa), cm H_2O, N/m^2, and pounds per square inch are all units of
    A. Mass
    B. Weight
    C. Pressure
    D. Momentum

42. In the MKS system of measurement, which unit of pressure is used?
    A. The pascal
    B. N/m^2
    C. Pounds per square inch
    D. Microbar

43. True/False   Barometric pressure is a measure of the pressure of air in the atmosphere.

Conceptual Integration

1. The force of gravity on the mass of an object is that object's
   A. Length
   B. Weight
   C. Duration
   D. Volume

2. If I push on a stationary object, that object will exert a force
   A. Equal in magnitude and opposite in direction to my applied force
   B. Equal in magnitude and in the same direction as my applied force
   C. Lower in magnitude than my applied force
   D. Greater in magnitude than my applied force and in a random direction

3. An object that is not moving (that is, its velocity is zero) can be said to have
   A. No momentum
   B. No inertia
   C. No mass
   D. No weight

4. In order to produce momentum of an object, we first have to overcome that object's
   A. Inertia
   B. Weight
   C. Size
   D. Velocity

5. Consider that you have two moving objects, both with the same velocity. The object with greater mass will have greater
   A. Speed
   B. Acceleration
   C. Momentum
   D. Size

6. Using your knowledge of Newton's second law of motion, a greater force applied to an object will yield
   A. Greater acceleration of that object
   B. Greater mass of that object
   C. Lower inertia of that object
   D. Lower speed of that object

7. If I exert a force on an object over a longer distance (vs. exerting force on that object over a short distance), I have increased
   A. The momentum of the object
   B. The work done
   C. The inertia of the object
   D. The reaction force from that object back to me

8. I pick up a pencil and move it 4 inches to the right. Next, I pick up the same pencil and move it 4 inches to the left, but in half the time as the first movement. What can you say about these two situations?
   A. The velocity of the pencil was greater when moving to the right, but the momentum of the pencil was greater when moving to the left.
   B. The amount of work done was greater when moving the pencil to the left, and the momentum of the pencil was greater when moving to the left.
   C. The momentum of the pencil was the same when moving to the right or to the left, but the power used was greater when moving the pencil to the left.
   D. The momentum of the pencil was greater when moving to the left, and the power used was greater when moving the pencil to the left.

9. An object with greater momentum than another object can be described as having greater
   A. Potential energy
   B. Kinetic energy
   C. Velocity
   D. Inertia

10. The force generated by molecules moving within the air as they collide with each other is called
    A. Air pressure
    B. Surface tension
    C. Work
    D. Air density

11. Blowing more and more air into a balloon will
    A. Increase the density of air molecules and increase the pressure inside the balloon
    B. Increase the density of air molecules but decrease the pressure inside the balloon
    C. Increase the mass of each individual air molecule and therefore increase the density of air molecules
    D. Decrease the mass of each individual air molecule but maintain the same air pressure inside the balloon

12. Consider 1 cubic centimeter (cm^3) of the following substances. Which will have the most weight?
    A. Silver
    B. Water
    C. Iron
    D. Concrete

Table 2–1. Conversion of Pressure Measurements

1 kilopascal (kPa) = 10.197 cm H_2O = 10^4 dyne/cm^2 (microbars)
1 dyne/cm^2 (microbar) = 1.0×10^{-4} kPa = 1.0197×10^{-3} cm H_2O
1 cm H_2O = 0.098 kPa = 980.68 dyne/cm^2 (microbars)

13. Using Table 2–1, 1.5 kPa (kilopascal) = _____ cm H_2O.

14. Using Table 2–1, 12 cm H_2O = _____ kPa.

15. Using Table 2–1, 0.43 cm H_2O = _____ dyne/cm^2 (microbars).

16. True/False   "Mass" is the same concept as "weight."

17. Speech rate is often measured as
    A. Syllables per minute
    B. Words per second
    C. Sentences per kilometer
    D. Phonemes per liter

18. Which of Newton's laws of motion explains why muscle force will produce movement of body parts?

    A. Newton's first law of motion

    B. Newton's second law of motion

    C. Newton's third law of motion

    D. None of Newton's laws of motion apply to human movements.

19. Which of Newton's laws of motion can show us how much force is necessary to move the articulators, based on their mass?

    A. Newton's first law of motion

    B. Newton's second law of motion

    C. Newton's third law of motion

    D. None of Newton's laws of motion apply to speech movements.

20. Physically smaller vocal folds will exert _____ inertia as compared to larger vocal folds.

    A. More

    B. Less

    C. The same

    D. Vocal folds don't have inertia.

21. Commonly used measurements of pressure for speech are

    A. "Kilopascal (kPa)" and "cm H_2O"

    B. "Millibar" and "pascal"

    C. "cm H_2O" and "pounds per square inch"

    D. "Millimeters of mercury" and "pounds per square inch"

3

Sound Waves Questions

Foundational Knowledge

3.1 Vibration (p. 28)

1. A "back-and-forth" movement of an object around a rest position is called
   A. Vibration
   B. Inertia
   C. Mass
   D. Random motion

2. A mass and a _____ can model a simple mechanical system that can oscillate.
   A. Spring
   B. Balloon
   C. Air molecule
   D. Wheel

3. Another term for "vibration" is
   A. Acceleration
   B. Inertia
   C. Equilibrium
   D. Oscillation

4. "Equilibrium" is the position where a system that can vibrate is
   A. Moving with its greatest acceleration
   B. Changing direction
   C. At rest and not moving
   D. Slowing down

5. What will cause an object to move from a position of equilibrium?
   A. Application of an outside force
   B. Removal of all energy
   C. Reduction of the object's power
   D. Elimination of all forces acting on the object

6. Stretching a spring builds up
   A. Potential energy
   B. Kinetic energy
   C. Both potential and kinetic energy
   D. Frictional energy

7. Releasing a stretched spring will yield
   A. Potential energy
   B. Kinetic energy
   C. Both potential and kinetic energy
   D. Frictional energy

8. The force that causes a stretched spring to recoil back to its equilibrium position is called
   A. Displacement force
   B. Restorative force
   C. Pressure force
   D. Equilibrium force

9. Forces that oppose the movement of an object are known as
   A. Restorative forces
   B. Displacement forces
   C. Frictional forces
   D. Oscillatory forces

10. For a spring, the restorative force is also known as

    A. Elastic force

    B. Inertia

    C. Frictional force

    D. Kinetic energy

3.2 The Nature of Waves (p. 28)

11. A wave is the movement of _____ between two points without moving an object from one point to the other.

    A. Force

    B. Mass

    C. Energy

    D. Pressure

12. The material that transports the energy of a wave is called the

    A. Mass

    B. Equilibrium

    C. Spring

    D. Medium

13. Sound, water waves, and vibration carried through solid structures are known as

    A. Mechanical waves

    B. Vacuum waves

    C. Air waves

    D. Electromagnetic waves

14. A single disturbance in a medium can be described as a _____ wave.

    A. Pulse

    B. Repeating

    C. Equilibrium

    D. Vacuum

15. A vibrating tuning fork produces

    A. A pulse wave

    B. Repeating waves

    C. Equilibrium

    D. Electromagnetic waves

16. As a sound wave travels through the medium of air, areas of _____ are produced.
    A. Compression and rarefaction
    B. Rarefaction and equilibrium
    C. Compression and inertia
    D. Friction and pulses

17. An area of compression in a sound wave is represented by
    A. An increase in the air pressure (density)
    B. A decrease in the air pressure (density)
    C. An increase in the inertia of the air molecules
    D. Maintenance of equilibrium position of the air molecules

18. Sound waves are carried as _____ waves.
    A. Transverse
    B. Longitudinal
    C. Water
    D. Electromagnetic

19. As an object is vibrating, the movement of the object's particles are perpendicular to the direction of movement of the wave energy. This is what type of wave? _____

3.3 Transfer of Energy in Waves (p. 32)

20. A wave in the air
    A. Transmits energy from molecule (or particle) to molecule
    B. Moves each air molecule a long distance, where it then stays
    C. Does not result in movement of air molecules
    D. Only disturbs the air particles that are in direct contact with the object that is vibrating

21. A water wave is what type of wave?
    A. Transverse
    B. Longitudinal
    C. Combination of transverse and longitudinal
    D. Waves do not occur in water

22. True/False   Throwing an object is an example of a wave of energy being transported.

3.4 Visualizing a Sound Wave (p. 35)

23. A simple mass-spring system produces
    A. Random motion
    B. Sound
    C. Simple harmonic motion
    D. Simple harmonic circles

24. A waveform is a graphical representation of a change of some phenomenon over
    A. Space
    B. Time
    C. Distance
    D. Area

25. Another term for "simple harmonic motion" is
    A. Uniform circular motion
    B. Waveform motion
    C. Graphical motion
    D. Compression motion

26. The peak (upward curve) of a sound waveform would represent _____, while the valley (downward curve) would represent _____.
    A. Rarefaction; compression
    B. Compression; rarefaction
    C. Pressure; displacement
    D. Equilibrium; displacement

27. The vertical axis of a sound waveform represents the _____ of the sound.
    A. Amplitude of the pressure
    B. Distance moved by each air molecule
    C. Time
    D. Acceleration of each air molecule

28. Mathematically, simple harmonic motion can be described as a _____.

3.5 **Properties of Sound Waves** (p. 35)

29. How often a wave pattern repeats itself is described as that wave's
    A. Amplitude
    B. Frequency
    C. Time
    D. Movement

30. One "cycle" of vibration is defined as
    A. One complete repetition of the waveform's pattern
    B. The maximum amplitude of the waveform
    C. The total number of repeated waveform patterns produced
    D. The total duration of the sound

31. Frequency is measured as
    A. The amplitude of compression and rarefaction
    B. The total time (duration) of the waveform
    C. The number of complete cycles per second
    D. The amplitude of one complete cycle

32. The unit for measuring the frequency of a waveform is
    A. Watts
    B. Hertz
    C. Cycles per second
    D. Either "hertz" or "cycles per second"

33. The frequency of a waveform is 302 hertz. How many cycles of the waveform will repeat per second?
    A. 1
    B. 151
    C. 302
    D. No way to determine this from the information provided

34. The measurement of the time it takes for one complete cycle of vibration is called the
    A. Frequency
    B. Intensity
    C. Phase
    D. Period

35. If you know the cycle period, the formula for calculating the frequency of a wave is
    A. Frequency = 1 / period
    B. Frequency = 1 × period
    C. Frequency = 2 × period
    D. Cycle period is not related to the frequency of the wave.

36. True/False   Another term for "cycle" is "phase."

37. The amount of energy carried by a waveform is determined by the vibrating object's
    A. Frequency of vibrations
    B. Mass
    C. Amplitude of vibrations
    D. Cycle period

38. The intensity of a waveform expresses that waveform's
    A. Power
    B. Frequency
    C. Phase
    D. Duration

39. The unit for measuring the intensity of a sound is
    A. W/m^2
    B. Seconds
    C. Hertz
    D. Degrees

40. The relationship between the amplitude of a sound's pressure wave and the resulting sound energy can be expressed by

    A. The intensity is increased as the square of the amplitude

    B. The intensity equals the amplitude

    C. The intensity is halved as the amplitude is doubled

    D. The intensity is doubled as the amplitude is doubled

41. Halving a sound pressure waveform's amplitude will result in

    A. Halving of that sound's intensity

    B. Doubling of that sound's intensity

    C. Quartering of that sound's intensity

    D. No change to that sound's intensity

42. True/False   As sound travels through a medium, the sound's intensity increases with greater distance from the sound source.

43. The relationship between sound energy and distance from the sound source is described as

    A. A reduction in frequency relationship

    B. An inverse square relationship

    C. An amplitude doubling relationship

    D. A hearing threshold relationship

44. The unit for sound intensity is

    A. Hertz (Hz)

    B. Degrees of phase (degrees)

    C. Milliseconds (ms)

    D. Decibel sound pressure level (dB SPL)

45. True/False   A sound's intensity is measured as the relative power of one sound as compared to another sound.

46. True/False   The decibel scale is a linear counting scale that allows us to express large numbers easily.

47. True/False   The decibel scale was named after the inventor of the telephone.

48. The lowest intensity sound that humans can typically hear at 1000 Hz is
    A. 10^{-12} W/m^2
    B. 10 W
    C. 20 hertz
    D. 20,000 hertz

49. A 10 times increase in a sound's intensity would equal
    A. An increase of 10 dB
    B. An increase of 100 dB
    C. A decrease of 10 dB
    D. No change to the dB of the sound

50. Wavelength is defined as
    A. The distance a single cycle of a wave travels through a medium such as air
    B. The amount of distance between a waveform's peak and valley, also called "amplitude"
    C. How far away you can hear a sound
    D. The change in a sound's intensity with distance

51. The unit for wavelength is
    A. Hertz
    B. Decibels
    C. Milliseconds
    D. Distance/cycle

52. True/False   A sound's wavelength is dependent on the velocity of the sound wave as it travels through a medium.

53. True/False   The relationship between wavelength and frequency is inverse such that an increase in wavelength would result in a decrease in frequency.

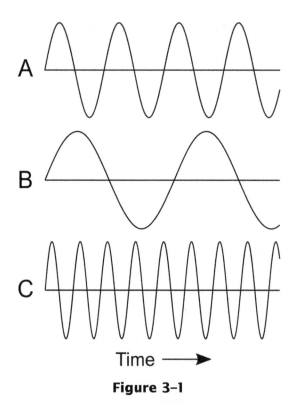

Time ⟶

Figure 3–1

54. Which of the waveforms in Figure 3–1 will have the longest wavelength as they travel through the air?

    A. A

    B. B

    C. C

    D. All of the waveforms will have the same wavelength.

55. Which of the waveforms in Figure 3–1 has the highest frequency?

    A. A

    B. B

    C. C

    D. All of the waveforms have the same frequency.

56. The speed of sound through the air is dependent on what properties?

    A. Sound wave frequency

    B. Air pressure and temperature

    C. Sound wave amplitude

    D. Sound wave wavelength

57. The speed of sound in the air at room temperature and at sea level is
    A. 340 meters/second
    B. 110 dB
    C. 20 meters
    D. 20,000 hertz

58. True/False   Sound speed is highest in the air and slowest through liquids.

59. True/False   Sound speed is the same as sound wave frequency.

3.6 The Perception of Sound Waves (p. 46)

60. Match the term on the left with the descriptor on the right. Descriptors may be used more than once or not at all.

    _____Fundamental frequency   1. Perceptual

    _____Loudness   2. Acoustic or physiologic

    _____Intensity   3. Both perceptual and acoustic/physiologic

    _____Pitch

    _____Difference limen

61. The psychoacoustic phenomena of loudness can be measured using the
    A. Bark scale
    B. Phon or sone scales
    C. Bark or semitone scales
    D. Phon, sone, or Bark scales

62. The difference limen is usually
    A. 1 dB
    B. 2 dB
    C. 5 dB
    D. 0 dB

63. If a sound is 60 phons, then
    A. It is as loud as a 60-Hz pure tone produced at 60 dB.
    B. The sound is 60 times as loud as a 1000-Hz pure tone produced at 100 Hz.
    C. It is as loud as a 1000-Hz pure tone produced at 60 dB.
    D. Its loudness level depends upon the frequency of the pure tone.

64. Audiometric zero is

    A. The point at which the 10-phon line intercepts the 1000-Hz line at 10 dB

    B. The average minimum audibility curve for adults under 65 years of age

    C. The normal binaural minimum audible field for adults 18 to 25 years of age

    D. The sound pressure level in decibels for a given frequency

65. For the average adult with normal hearing, perception of the difference in frequencies between 120 Hz and 220 Hz

    A. Is easier than the perception of the frequency difference between 1000 and 1100 Hz

    B. Is harder than the perception of the frequency difference between 1000 and 1100 Hz

    C. Is equal in difficulty to the perception of the frequency difference between 1000 and 1100 Hz

    D. Is not possible without amplification

66. The semitone scale

    A. Is a psychoacoustic scale representing linear differences between frequencies

    B. Reflects human's linear perception of pitch

    C. Consists of 24 tones separated from each other by one semitone interval

    D. Consists of 12 tones separated from each other by one semitone interval

67. The formula used to determine the semitone difference between two frequencies is

    A. $39.86 \times \log_{10}(\text{lower frequency} / \text{higher frequency})$

    B. $39.86 \times \log_{10}(\text{higher frequency} / \text{lower frequency})$

    C. $39.86[\log_{10}(\text{lower frequency} / \text{higher frequency})]$

    D. $39.86[\log_{10}(\text{higher frequency} / \text{lower frequency})]$

68. The Bark scale is a nonlinear transformation such that

    A. Equal distances on the Bark scale correspond to equal distances in pitch

    B. Equal distances on the Bark scale correspond to semitone distances in pitch

    C. As the Bark scale proceeds from low to high frequency, the distances between the scale units increase to match the human nonlinear perception of pitch

    D. As the Bark scale proceeds from low to high frequency, the distances between the scale units decrease to match the human nonlinear perception of pitch

69. The study of the relationship between the physical properties of a stimulus and our subjective experience of it is called _____.

70. The minimal difference between two sounds that can be perceived as having different loudness levels is called the "just noticeable difference" or _____.

71. A synonym for the minimum audibility curve is _____.

72. The human ear is [less/more] sensitive to lower frequency compared to high frequencies.

73. The human ear is [less/more] sensitive to differences in frequency at lower frequencies compared to higher frequencies.

74. A linear psychoacoustic scale of loudness that is based upon orchestral music is called the _____ scale.

75. The difference in frequency between octaves of the semitone scale reflects the human [linear/nonlinear] perception of pitch.

76. The Bark scale converts the [acoustic/psychoacoustic] phenomenon of frequency into the [acoustic/psychoacoustic] of pitch.

77. True/False   The human ear is equally sensitive to frequency changes at all intensity levels.

78. True/False   In the semitone scale, an octave represents the $\log_{10}$ of the frequency.

3.7 Pure and Complex Tones (p. 52)

79. True/False   A graphical representation of a pure tone is the sine wave.

80. A pure tone consists of how many separate frequencies?
    A. Zero
    B. One
    C. Two
    D. Three or more

81. Which of the following is NOT an example of simple harmonic vibration?
    A. Tuning fork
    B. Pendulum (or someone on a swing)
    C. Mass-spring system
    D. The human voice

82. A complex wave
    A. Is created by a single simple harmonic oscillator
    B. Consists of two or more sine waves of different frequencies added together
    C. Is produced by a tuning fork
    D. Is impossible for humans to hear

83. A wave that has a pattern that repeats over time is termed
    A. Simple
    B. Complex
    C. Periodic
    D. Without a wavelength

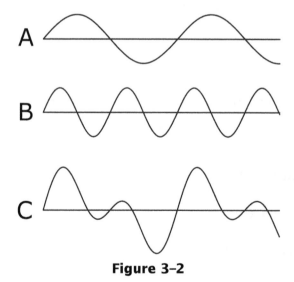

Figure 3–2

84. In Figure 3–2, wave "A" has a frequency of 100 hertz and wave "B" has a frequency of 200 hertz. Wave "C" is the result of adding waves "A" and "B" together. What is the fundamental frequency of complex wave "C"?
    A. 100 hertz
    B. 200 hertz
    C. 300 hertz
    D. There is no way to determine the frequency of wave "C."

85. A power spectrum is produced with the mathematical process called
    A. Fourier analysis
    B. Time analysis
    C. Waveform addition
    D. Logarithmic scaling

86. A line spectrum of a sine wave will show how many vertical lines to indicate frequency?
    A. Zero
    B. One
    C. Two
    D. More than two

87. True/False   A waveform plot is a frequency domain plot.

88. What parameter of a waveform is NOT shown on a power spectrum plot?
    A. Frequency
    B. Amplitude
    C. Time

89. A sine wave has an amplitude of 40 dB. What will the amplitude be shown as on a power spectrum plot?
    A. 0 dB
    B. 20 dB
    C. 40 dB
    D. 120 dB

90. A complex wave has two frequencies. The amplitude of one frequency is 25 dB and the amplitude of the other frequency is 35 dB. What will the amplitude(s) show on a power spectrum plot?
    A. Amplitude of 25 dB for the first frequency, amplitude of 35 dB for the second frequency
    B. Amplitude of 35 dB for both frequencies
    C. Amplitude of 10 dB
    D. Amplitude of 60 dB

91. A sound that doesn't have a repeating wave pattern (aperiodic) can be described as

    A. A pure tone

    B. A sine wave

    C. A noise wave

    D. A high-amplitude wave

92. True/False   An aperiodic waveform is typically displayed on a line power spectrum plot.

93. True/False   The frequencies that comprise a noise waveform are not necessarily all at the same amplitude.

94. Which of the following waveforms does not have a fundamental frequency?

    A. Sine wave

    B. Simple periodic wave

    C. Complex periodic wave

    D. Noise wave

95. When two sound waves in the same space at the same time meet and generate a higher-amplitude resulting wave, this is termed

    A. Constructive interference

    B. Fundamental frequency

    C. A transverse wave

    D. Periodicity

96. Two sound waves that meet and are opposite in phase with each other will result in

    A. A transverse wave

    B. Increased compression or rarefaction

    C. Destructive interference

    D. Aperiodicity

97. A sound wave traveling through the air may encounter another medium, such as a wall. The wall would be termed

    A. Destructive interference

    B. A boundary

    C. A transverse wave

    D. Noise

98. A sound wave that encounters a boundary and bounces backward is called
    A. A reflected wave
    B. An incident wave
    C. A diffracted wave
    D. An aperiodic wave

99. If sound traveling through a medium encounters a medium (boundary) with very different physical properties, what will happen?
    A. Most of the sound energy will transmit through the boundary.
    B. Most of the sound energy will be reflected, but some will transmit through the boundary.
    C. No sound energy will be reflected or diffused at the boundary.
    D. Nothing will change, as all of the sound energy will transmit through the boundary.

100. True/False   For speech, the vocal tract causes sound waves to reflect between the lips and the vocal folds.

3.8 Behavior of Sound Waves (p. 56)

101. Pushing someone on a swing at the same frequency of vibration as the swing naturally moves and with appropriate timing can result in
    A. An increase in the amplitude of the swing's vibration
    B. An increase in the frequency of the swing's vibration
    C. A decrease in the frequency of the swing's vibration
    D. A reduction in the amplitude of the swing's vibration due to friction

102. The frequency that an object can vibrate at once set into motion is called that object's
    A. Amplitude frequency
    B. Periodic frequency
    C. Natural frequency
    D. Frequency of friction

103. For a mass-spring system, the natural frequency is based on the amount of mass in that system as well as
    A. The stiffness of the spring
    B. The temperature of the mass
    C. The length of the spring
    D. The density of the material

104. True/False   An incident and a reflected wave confined to the same medium can interfere to produce a standing wave.

3.9 Resonance (p. 59)

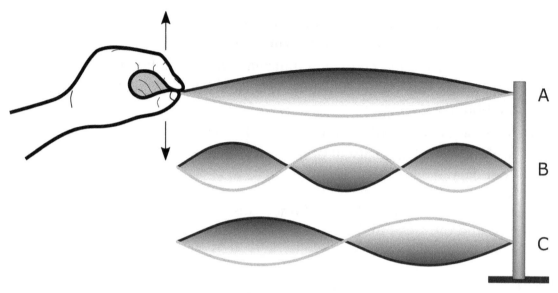

Figure 3–3

105. Figure 3–3 shows three standing waves formed by vibrating the string at different frequencies. Which string was vibrated at the highest frequency?

    A. String A
    B. String B
    C. String C
    D. All were vibrated at the same frequency.

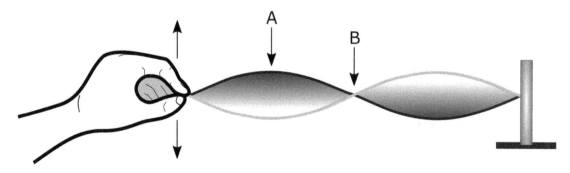

Figure 3–4

106. For the standing wave in Figure 3–4, location "B" is called
    A. An antinode
    B. A node
    C. A period
    D. A cycle

107. True/False   For the standing wave in Figure 3–4, location "A" indicates an area of maximal wave energy.

108. True/False   Objects that vibrate can have many natural frequencies.

109. A harmonic relationship between frequencies can be expressed by the following expression
    A. Harmonics have twice the amplitude as other frequencies.
    B. The harmonic frequencies are expressed by a logarithmic function with the unit "dB."
    C. The harmonic frequencies are not related mathematically.
    D. Each harmonic frequency is an integer multiple of the fundamental frequency.

110. The harmonic frequencies at which standing waves will form in a vibrating system are called
    A. The natural frequencies
    B. Aperiodic waves
    C. Pulse waves
    D. Destructive interference

111. When an object is disturbed and allowed to vibrate freely, the resulting vibration is called
    A. Displaced vibration
    B. Free vibration
    C. Forced vibration
    D. Aperiodic vibration

112. True/False   When a system vibrates freely, it vibrates at its natural frequency as determined by that system's mass and stiffness.

113. If one system sets an adjoining or connected system into vibration, it is termed
     A. Forced vibration
     B. Free vibration
     C. Noise
     D. A pulse wave

114. True/False   Resonance occurs when one system forces another system to vibrate at its resonant frequency.

115. The condition of "resonance" produces
     A. An aperiodic waveform
     B. A periodic waveform
     C. Destructive interference with a waveform amplitude of zero
     D. A frequency that does not equal the natural frequency

116. The air chamber inside acoustic instruments acts like a/an
     A. Tuning fork
     B. Compression wave
     C. Acoustic resonator
     D. Free vibrating system

117. True/False   The resonant frequency of the air chamber inside an acoustic resonator is determined by the size of the air chamber.

118. True/False   The vocal tract acts like a mechanical resonator.

Conceptual Integration

1. If a mass-spring system is at its equilibrium position and not acted on by an external force, why won't it move?
   A. Newton's first law states that an object at rest will remain at rest unless acted on by an external force.
   B. Newton's third law states that for each force, there is an equal and opposite reaction force.
   C. At equilibrium, the mass will have no inertia.
   D. At equilibrium, the spring exerts kinetic energy.

2. When a mass-spring system is vibrating, what causes the mass to pass through ("overshoot") the position of equilibrium and keep moving?
   A. The inertia of the mass
   B. The restorative force
   C. The displacement force
   D. The frictional forces of the system

3. Which of Newton's laws of motion explains why releasing a stretched spring will cause it to recoil toward its equilibrium position?
   A. Newton's first law
   B. Newton's second law
   C. Newton's third law
   D. None of Newton's laws relate to this scenario.

4. The farther we stretch a spring, the greater the amount of _____ that is created.
   A. Restorative force
   B. Displacement force
   C. Mass
   D. Inertia

5. The interplay between what two forces explain the back-and-forth movement of vibration?
   A. Inertia and restorative force
   B. Restorative force and frictional force
   C. Equilibrium and inertia
   D. Frictional force and restorative force

6. Increasing what force will result in an increase in the restorative force of a spring?
   A. Inertia
   B. Displacement force
   C. Frictional force
   D. Air pressure

7. Which of Newton's laws of motion help to explain the process of vibration?
   A. First and second laws
   B. First and third laws
   C. Second and third laws
   D. Only the first law

8. Why won't a mass-spring system vibrate indefinitely once it has been set into motion?

   A. Frictional forces will result in the loss of energy within the system.

   B. The potential energy will be used up.

   C. Too much kinetic energy will build up, causing the system to stop vibrating.

   D. Vibration cycles never repeat unless more displacement force is applied to the system.

9. As sound passes through the air

   A. Air particles move completely from the object that is vibrating to your eardrums.

   B. Air particles vibrate back and forth, carrying a wave of energy from the object that is vibrating to your eardrums.

   C. All of the air particles move in the same direction simultaneously.

   D. The air particles stay at equilibrium.

10. These forces produce compressions and rarefactions as the sound wave travels through the air

    A. Compression and pulses

    B. Inertia and friction

    C. Restorative force and momentum

    D. Displacement force and friction

11. For sound waves, the air particles move _____ to the direction of the wave movement.

    A. Parallel

    B. At right angles (perpendicular)

    C. In a circular fashion

    D. Air particles do not move when a sound wave goes through them

12. In terms of air molecules, sound can be defined as a wave of _____ changes.

13. True/False   A wave requires a medium through which energy can be transferred from place to place.

14. True/False   Air is the only medium that can transport sound vibrations.

15. True/False   Mechanical waves can't occur without a physical medium.

16. The frequency of a sound waveform is 1200 hertz. How many compressions and rarefactions will be produced per second for this sound?

    A. 12 compressions, 6 rarefactions

    B. 600 compressions, 600 rarefactions

    C. 1,200 compressions, 1,200 rarefactions

    D. No way to determine this from the information provided

17. Sound wave "A" has a frequency of 200 Hz, while sound wave "B" has a frequency of 400 Hz. What can you say about these two waveforms?

    A. Sound wave "A" will have twice as many compressions and rarefactions in the same amount of time as sound wave "B."

    B. Sound wave "B" will have twice as many compressions and rarefactions in the same amount of time as sound wave "A."

    C. Both sound waves "A" and "B" will have the same number of compressions and rarefactions per second, but the amplitude of sound wave "B" will be greater.

    D. Sound wave "B" will have fewer complete cycles per second than sound wave "A."

18. Sound "A" has a frequency of 100 Hz and sound "B" has a frequency of 400 Hz. What can you say about sounds "A" and "B"?

    A. Sound "A" will repeat its pattern four times more than sound "B" per second.

    B. Sound "A" will have a longer cycle period than sound "B."

    C. Sound "B" will have a longer cycle period than sound "A."

    D. Sound "B" will repeat its pattern every 400 seconds, while sound "A" will repeat its pattern every 100 seconds.

19. A sound has a cycle period of 17 milliseconds (0.017 seconds). What is the frequency of this sound?

    A. 58.82 Hz

    B. 125 Hz

    C. 250 Hz

    D. Not enough information provided to be able to answer the question

20. True/False   The beginning point of waveform's cycle is always measured from the maximum amplitude of the waveform crest.

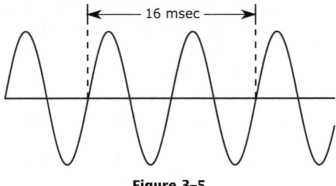

Figure 3–5

21. What is the frequency of the waveform shown in Figure 3–5?
    A. 16 hertz
    B. 32 hertz
    C. 62.5 hertz
    D. 125 hertz

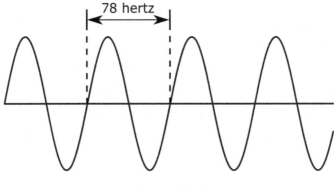

Figure 3–6

22. Can you find the error in Figure 3–6?
    A. The measurement shown is of cycle period, but the unit reported is for frequency.
    B. The measurement shown is of amplitude, but the unit reported is for cycle period.
    C. The measurement shown is of cycle period, but the unit reported is for intensity.
    D. The measurement shown is of frequency, but the unit reported is for phase.

23. The amplitude of a sound pressure waveform is increased by 4 times. What is the relative change in the sound's intensity?

    A. Increased by 4 times

    B. Increased by 16 times

    C. Decreased by half

    D. Increased by 4 hertz

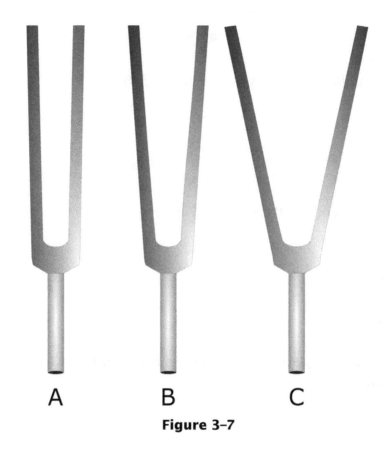

Figure 3–7

24. For the tuning forks shown vibrating in Figure 3–7, which will produce the greatest amplitude of sound pressure?

    A. A

    B. B

    C. C

    D. All will produce the same level of sound pressure amplitude.

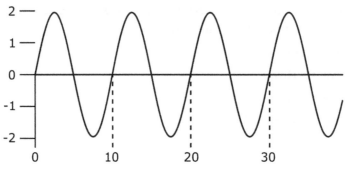

Figure 3–8

25. What is the amplitude of the wave in Figure 3–8?

    A. 2 units

    B. 4 units

    C. 10 units

    D. 30 units

26. What is the frequency of the wave in Figure 3–8 if the cycle period is measured in ms?

    A. 4 hertz

    B. 33.33 hertz

    C. 100 hertz

    D. 250 hertz

27. The highest frequency sound that humans can hear has a cycle period of

    A. 20,000 ms

    B. 20 hertz

    C. 0.00005 s

    D. 0 ms

28. A sound's intensity has increased by 100 times. This will produce

    A. An increase in the sound's dB level by 10 dB

    B. An increase in the sound's dB level by 20 dB

    C. An increase in the sound's dB level by 100 dB

    D. A decrease in the sound's dB level by 100 dB

29. A sound has a sound pressure level that is 1,000 times greater than another sound. What is the difference between these two sounds in decibels?

    A. 10 dB

    B. 30 dB

    C. 60 dB

    D. 1,000 dB

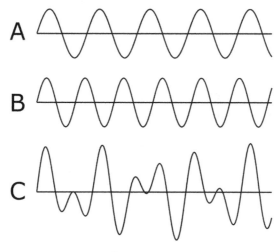

Figure 3–9

30. In Figure 3–9, wave "A" has a frequency of 100 Hz, wave "B" has a frequency of 170 Hz, and wave "C" is the complex wave resulting from adding waves "A" and "B" together. What can we conclude about wave "C"?

    A. Wave "C" has a fundamental frequency of 270 Hz.

    B. Wave "C" is a pure tone.

    C. Wave "C" is a periodic waveform, because its constituent components (waves "A" and "B") are both periodic sine waves.

    D. Wave "C" is not a periodic waveform, because the frequency of wave "B" is not an integer multiple of the frequency of wave "A."

31. True/False   The human voice produces a complex sound wave, although it is not a purely periodic waveform.

32. A graphical representation of a sound's energy and how it changes over time is the _____.

33. A graphical representation of a sound's power and the frequencies of that sound is the _____.

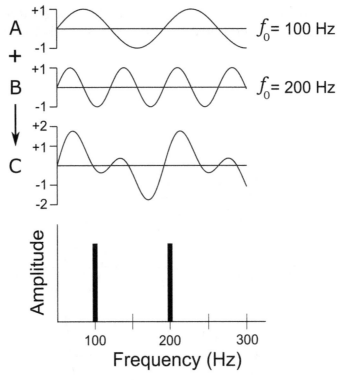

Figure 3–10

34. For the plot shown in Figure 3–10, sine waves "A" and "B" have been added to produce wave "C." The power spectrum of wave "C" is shown at the bottom. What amplitude values should be represented for the frequencies shown on the power spectrum plot?

    A. −2

    B. +1

    C. +2

    D. +4

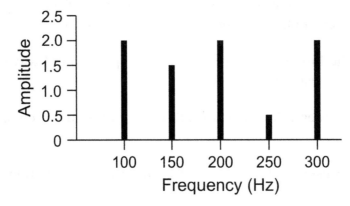

Figure 3–11

35. For the power spectrum plot in Figure 3–11, how many frequencies are present in the sound that is represented?

    A. One

    B. Five

    C. Eight

    D. The number of frequencies can't be determined from this plot.

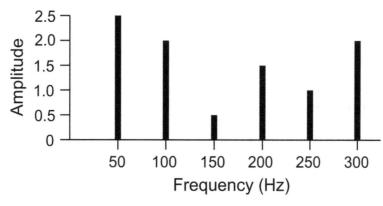

Figure 3–12

36. For the power spectrum plot in Figure 3–12, what type of wave is represented?

    A. A simple wave (a pure tone) that is not periodic

    B. A simple wave (a pure tone) that is periodic

    C. A complex wave that is not periodic

    D. A complex wave that is periodic

37. What is the fundamental frequency of the sound represented in the power spectrum plot shown in Figure 3–12?

    A. 0 Hz

    B. 50 Hz

    C. 100 Hz

    D. 300 Hz

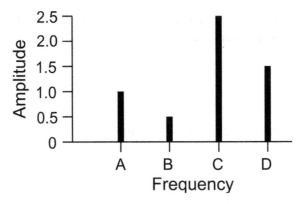

Figure 3–13

38. For the sound shown in the power spectrum plot from Figure 3–13, what frequency will have the shortest wavelength?

    A. Frequency A

    B. Frequency B

    C. Frequency C

    D. Frequency D

39. For the sound shown in the power spectrum plot from Figure 3–13, what frequency will have the longest cycle period?

    A. Frequency A

    B. Frequency B

    C. Frequency C

    D. Frequency D

40. True/False   All complex periodic waveforms consist of a series of sine waves that are harmonically related in terms of frequency.

41. Which of the following sounds may be described as "noise"?

    A. Sine wave

    B. A complex sound where the frequencies are not harmonically related

    C. A complex periodic sound

    D. All speech sounds (phonemes)

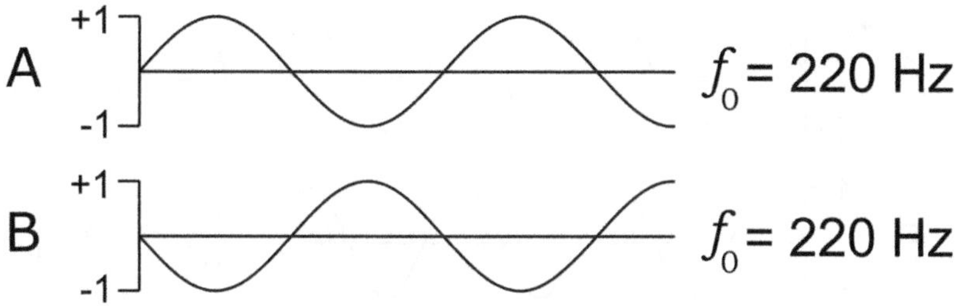

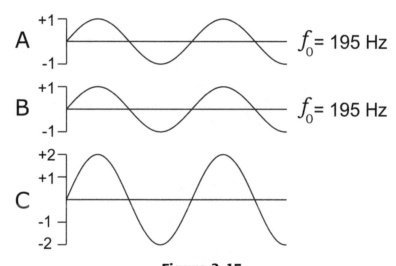

Figure 3–14

42. In Figure 3–14, waves "A" and "B" each have an amplitude of 2 units. The waves are equal in frequency but are opposite in phase. What will the resulting amplitude be if these waves are added together?

    A. 0 units

    B. 1 unit

    C. 2 units

    D. 4 units

Figure 3–15

43. In Figure 3–15, the waves "A" and "B" meet in the same place at the same time, resulting in the creation of wave "C." Why is the amplitude of wave "C" greater than either wave "A" or wave "B"?

    A. Constructive interference

    B. Destructive interference

    C. Wave "C" is aperiodic.

    D. Wave "B" is out of phase with wave "A."

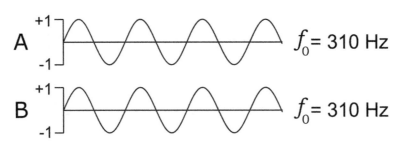

Figure 3–16

44. In Figure 3–16, wave "A" and wave "B" meet at the same place in the same time to create a new wave. What will be the fundamental frequency of the resulting wave?

   A. 155 Hz

   B. 310 Hz

   C. 620 Hz

   D. The new wave will be aperiodic and will not have a fundamental frequency.

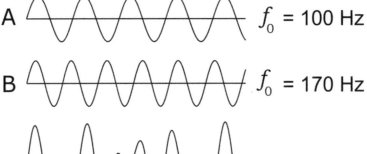

Figure 3–17

45. In Figure 3–17, wave "A" and wave "B" meet in the same place at the same time, creating wave "C." What is the fundamental frequency of wave "C"?

   A. 100 Hz

   B. 170 Hz

   C. 270 Hz

   D. There is no fundamental frequency, as the resulting wave is aperiodic.

46. For the waves shown in Figure 3–17, what physical principle(s) can explain the resulting shape of wave "C"?

    A. Constructive and destructive interference

    B. Compression and longitudinal waves

    C. Wave "C" is periodic.

    D. Wave "C" is a sine wave.

47. In your house or apartment, you may hear sound generated in another room that passes through the wall. This can be termed

    A. Sound transmission

    B. Sound reflection

    C. Incident wave

    D. Sound diffraction

48. The sound that passes through the wall is lower amplitude than the original sound wave. The wall causes some of the sound energy to be

    A. Reduced in frequency

    B. Increased in sound pressure level

    C. Reflected

    D. Increased due to constructive interference

49. Considering the vocal tract as a tube, the lips and the vocal folds can both be considered

    A. Boundaries that can alter the sound wave

    B. Boundaries that cannot alter the sound wave

    C. The same medium as the air inside the vocal tract

    D. Incident waves

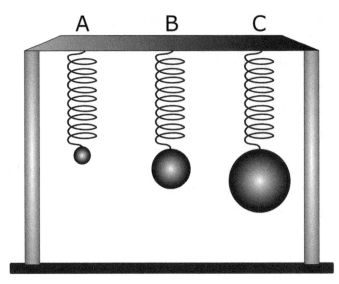

Figure 3–18

50. For the three mass-spring systems shown in Figure 3–18, the mass of system A is the lowest and the mass of system C is the greatest amount. The spring stiffness is equal across all systems. Which mass-spring system will have the highest natural frequency of vibration?

A. System A

B. System B

C. System C

D. There is no way to determine the relative difference in natural frequency for the three systems.

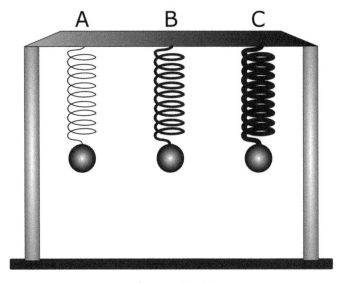

Figure 3–19

51. For the three mass-spring systems shown in Figure 3–19, the spring stiffness of system A is the lowest and the spring stiffness of system C is the greatest amount. The mass is equal across all systems. Which mass-spring system will have the highest natural frequency of vibration?

    A. System A

    B. System B

    C. System C

    D. There is no way to determine the relative difference in natural frequency for the three systems.

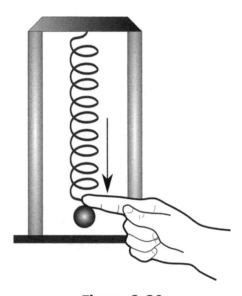

Figure 3–20

52. The spring on the mass-spring system in Figure 3–20 has been stretched downward by pulling on the mass. What will happen if the mass is released?

    A. The mass will return to its equilibrium position and stop.

    B. The mass will stay in its current position.

    C. The mass will move upward, beginning a series of up-and-down vibration cycles.

    D. The mass will move to the highest point and stop there.

53. When stretching the spring downward in the mass-spring system of Figure 3–20, what happens as the spring stretches further?

    A. The restorative force is increased with increased stretch.

    B. The resulting frequency of vibration increases with increased stretch.

    C. The amplitude of vibration decreases with increased stretch.

    D. The mass is reduced with increased stretch.

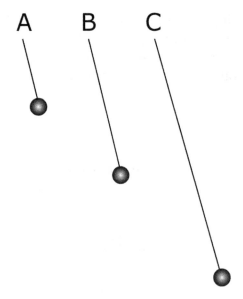

Figure 3–21

54. For the pendulums (consider someone on a swing) in Figure 3–21, which will vibrate at the highest frequency?

    A. A
    B. B
    C. C
    D. They will all vibrate at the same frequency.

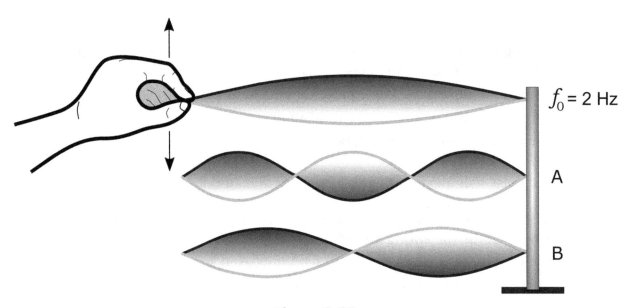

Figure 3–22

55. Consider the three standing waves shown in Figure 3–22. What frequency will string B need to be vibrated at in order to produce the standing wave shown here?

    A. 1 Hz

    B. 2 Hz

    C. 4 Hz

    D. 8 Hz

56. For the three standing waves shown in Figure 3–22, what frequency will string A need to be vibrated at in order to produce the standing wave shown here?

    A. 1 Hz

    B. 2 Hz

    C. 4 Hz

    D. 6 Hz

57. For the standing waves shown in Figure 3–22, how many nodes does the standing wave on string A have?

    A. 2

    B. 3

    C. 4

    D. 7

58. A standing wave is formed from an incident wave and its

    A. Transmitted wave

    B. Diffused wave

    C. Reflected wave

    D. Aperiodic wave

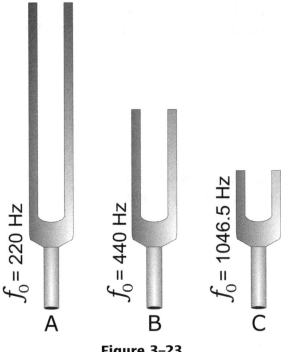

Figure 3–23

59. In Figure 3–23, there are three tuning forks with different natural frequencies. Striking which tuning fork will cause another to resonate?

A. Striking "A" will cause "B" to resonate.

B. Striking "A" will cause "C" to resonate.

C. Striking "B" will cause "C" to resonate.

D. None of the tuning forks can set any other into resonance.

60. In Figure 3–23, how can you express the harmonic relationships between the tuning forks?

A. Tuning fork "A" is the second harmonic of tuning fork "C."

B. Tuning fork "A" is the third harmonic of tuning fork "B."

C. Tuning fork "B" is the second harmonic of tuning fork "A."

D. Tuning fork "C" is the first harmonic of tuning fork "B."

61. True/False   Forced vibration always produces maximum amplitude of vibration in the system that has been forced to vibrate.

62. True/False   The vocal tract acts like an acoustic resonator, similar to the air inside an acoustic musical instrument.

63. When an acoustic resonator is forced to vibrate at its resonant frequency
    A. The amplitude of the vibration increases.
    B. The frequency of the vibration decreases.
    C. The vibration changes to noise.
    D. Only a single sine wave is produced.

64. Which of the following phonemes would be considered a "pulse" wave?
    A. /i/
    B. /s/
    C. /r/
    D. /p/

65. Which of the following phonemes would produce a wave that has a pattern that repeats over a long time?
    A. /t/
    B. /g/
    C. /a/
    D. /j/

TRY IT!

1. Tie a rope to a chair or other immoveable object (such as a bored friend), pull to produce a small amount of tension (don't pull your friend over), and shake the rope to generate a standing wave like a jump-rope. Can you produce the second or third standing wave by vibrating the rope faster? If you can't vibrate the rope fast enough, reduce the tension on the rope a bit and try again.

2. Have a friend hold the end of a rope (try for 8–10 feet long) while you hold the other. Pull lightly to generate a small amount of tension in the rope. Produce simultaneous upward "pulses" of the rope that are in phase by both of you rapidly raising your end of the rope and then lowering it back to where you started. When the pulses meet in the middle of the rope, did you see the evidence of constructive interference? Try producing destructive interference by producing pulses that are out of phase with each other, too!

3. Attach two objects of different mass (one at a time, please) to a long rubber band or a Slinky™ spring. Set each mass-spring system into vibration and observe the resulting frequency of vibration.

4. Tie a mass to a string and let it swing like a pendulum. Shorten or lengthen the string and observe the resulting change in vibration frequency.

4

Breathing Questions

Foundational Knowledge

4.1 Introduction (p. 72)

1. Speech breathing is
   A. Breathing in before speaking
   B. The regulation of breathing for voice and speech production
   C. Breathing while talking
   D. The adaptation of speaking to meet the body's need for respiration

2. The terms *inhalation* and *exhalation*
   A. Are equivalent to the terms *inspiration* and *expiration*, respectively
   B. Refer to inspiration and expiration, respectively, when used in the context of speech breathing
   C. Refer to breathing in and breathing out, respectively, in the absence of speaking
   D. Refer to breathing in and out, respectively, while inspiration and expiration refer to gas exchange in the lungs at the cellular level

3. Respiration
   A. Is the type of breathing performed during speech production
   B. Is the type of breathing performed in the absence of speech production
   C. Generally, refers to the process of gas exchange at the cellular level
   D. Is the type of breathing performed during intensive physical activity

4. The regulation of inhalation and exhalation for purposes of speech production is called _____.

5. Synonyms for *inhalation* and *exhalation*, respectively, are _____.

6. Which one of the following statements is true?
   A. Neurons represent a single nerve fiber.
   B. The central nervous system consists of the brain.
   C. The peripheral nerves that extend from the brainstem to organs outside of the central nervous system are called cranial nerves.
   D. The peripheral nervous system originates and terminates outside of the brain and spinal cord.

7. Efferent and afferent refer to
   A. Motor and sensory functions of nerves, respectively
   B. Sensory and motor functions of nerves, respectively
   C. Central and peripheral nerves, respectively
   D. Cranial and spinal nerves, respectively

8. A neurological pathway or tract refers to
   A. Bundles of nerve fibers in the peripheral nervous system that form an anatomical or functional unit
   B. A single nerve fiber in the peripheral nervous system that forms an anatomical or functional unit
   C. Bundles of nerve fibers in the central nervous system that form an anatomical or functional unit
   D. A single nerve fiber in the central nervous system that forms an anatomical or functional unit

9. Which one of the following statements about the somatic and visceral system is true?

   A. Peripheral nerves can be categorized as somatic—generally serving skeletal muscles, skin sensation, vision, and hearing—and visceral, which serve automatic functions such as the digestive system.

   B. Peripheral nerves all can be categorized as visceral—generally serving skeletal muscles, skin sensation, vision, and hearing—and somatic, which serve automatic functions such as the digestive system.

   C. Peripheral nerves are all somatic—generally serving skeletal muscles, skin sensation, vision, and hearing—and spinal nerves are all visceral, which serve automatic functions such as the digestive system.

   D. Spinal nerves can be categorized as somatic—generally serving skeletal muscles, skin sensation, vision, and hearing—and cranial nerves are all visceral, which serve automatic functions such as the digestive system.

10. The autonomic nervous system

    A. Is divided into the parasympathetic function (prepare the body for emergency activities) and the sympathetic function (rest and digest and conserve energy)

    B. Is divided into the sympathetic function (prepare the body for emergency activities) and the parasympathetic function (rest and digest and conserve energy)

    C. Consists of motor and sensory neurons that are all involved in nonvolitional, reflexive movements

    D. Consists of sensory neurons only that are all involved in nonvolitional, reflexive movements

11. Which one of the following statements about synaptic activity is true?

    A. An excitatory impulse has a greater electrical charge than an inhibitory impulse.

    B. Synaptic activity is always excitatory, but it can result in either excitation or inhibition of the connecting neuron or muscle fiber.

    C. An excitatory impulse facilitates firing of the connecting neuron or muscle fiber.

    D. Excitatory synapses connect to muscle fibers, while inhibitory synapses connect to other neurons.

12. The four major functional subdivisions of the neurological motor system are

    A. The somatic, visceral, parasympathetic, and sympathetic systems

    B. The central nervous system, the peripheral nervous system, the somatic nervous system, and the visceral nervous system

    C. The direct activation pathway, the indirect activation pathway, the central nervous system, and the peripheral nervous system

    D. The direct activation pathway, the indirect activation pathway, the control circuits, and the final common pathway

13. The neurological control circuits

    A. Connect directly with the final common pathway to coordinate and integrate only the excitatory impulses from the direct and indirect activation pathways

    B. Consist of the basal ganglia and cerebellum

    C. Consist of the direct and indirect activation pathways

    D. Are activated only during highly complex movements, such as speech production

14. The _____ nerves originate in the brainstem and terminate in organs in the head and neck.

15. Bundles of nerves that form a functional or anatomic unit are called a ___.

16. The sympathetic system is used for the ["fight or flight"/"rest and digest"] response, while the parasympathetic system is used for the ["fight or flight"/"rest and digest"] response.

17. The chemicals in the synapses that enable electrical activity to pass from one neuron to the next are called _____.

18. Another name for the lower motor neurons is the [final common pathway/ peripheral nervous system].

19. The area of neurons that is involved in regulation of arousal, attention, and awareness is called the [cerebellum/reticular formation].

4.2 **Respiration** (p. 76)

20. Our breathing is driven by our body's need to
    A. Remove carbon dioxide and obtain oxygen
    B. Obtain oxygen
    C. Circulate the air in our lungs so that the carbon dioxide and oxygen remain well mixed
    D. Keep our lungs moving

21. Diffusion is the process of movement of molecules of a fluid from
    A. Regions of high concentration to low concentration
    B. Regions of low to high concentration
    C. Regions that have equal concentrations
    D. One organ to another (such as from the lungs to the bloodstream)

22. Exhalation is a process that allows the body to rid itself of [carbon dioxide, excess oxygen].

4.3 **Balloons or Boyle's Law?** (p. 76)

23. Boyle's law states that, given a constant temperature,
    A. If the volume of a gas is increased, the pressure will increase.
    B. If the volume of a gas is increased, the pressure will decrease.
    C. If the volume of a gas is decreased, the pressure will increase.
    D. If the volume of a gas is decreased, the pressure will decrease.

24. Boyle's law describes
    A. A reverse relationship between volume and pressure
    B. A direct relationship between volume and pressure
    C. An indirect relationship between volume and pressure
    D. An inverse relationship between volume and pressure

25. Increased density of air molecules
    A. Results in increased pressure because the number of molecule collisions increases
    B. Results in increased pressure because molecule movement slows down so the number of molecule collisions decreases
    C. Results in decreased pressure because the number of molecule collisions increases
    D. Results in decreased pressure because molecule movement slows down so the number of molecule collisions decreases

26. The lungs expand in the following directions
    A. Forward (toward the front), lower (toward the bottom), and front-to-back
    B. Forward (toward the front), inferiorly-superiorly, and laterally
    C. Diagonally, laterally, and front-to-back
    D. Front-to-back, sideways, and lower-to-higher

27. The pressure differential between the atmosphere and our lungs is caused by
    A. Expansion or contraction of the lungs
    B. Expansion of the lungs only
    C. Contraction of the lungs only
    D. Holding our breath to build up the pressure in our lungs

28. We can expand our lungs in three directions lower to higher, laterally, and ___.

29. Negative pressure means that the pressure in the lungs is [greater/lesser/equal] to atmospheric pressure.

30. In order to exhale, the pressure in the lungs must be [positive/negative] with respect to the atmospheric pressure.

31. In order to inhale, we must be able to [increase/decrease] the volume of our lungs.

4.4 Anatomy of the Lower Airway (p. 78)

32. The pulmonary system is composed of the
    A. Lungs and thorax
    B. Trachea, bronchial tree, lungs, and thorax
    C. Trachea, bronchial tree, and lungs
    D. Trachea, bronchial tree, lungs, and diaphragm

33. The lungs are composed of
    A. Air, blood vessels, connective tissue, respiratory tissue, and muscles
    B. 90% air and 10% solid tissue
    C. Blood vessels, connective tissue, respiratory tissue, bronchial tree, and muscle
    D. Muscle

34. The thoracic cavity is made up of the
    A. Sternum and 12 pairs of ribs and it is bounded inferiorly by the diaphragm
    B. Sternum, 12 pairs of ribs, the lungs, and is bounded inferiorly by the diaphragm
    C. Sternum, the shoulder, the pelvis, and the lungs
    D. Rib cage, the spinal vertebrae, the sternum, the shoulder, and the pelvis

35. The ribs at rest
    A. Are angled downward slightly from posterior to inferior
    B. Are angled upward slightly from posterior to inferior
    C. Are level without angle upon expansion of the lungs, the ribs angle downward
    D. Are slightly twisted so that they move downward and outward upon inhalation

36. The bronchial tree
    A. Starts with the trachea superiorly and then divides within the left and right lungs, with each subdivision maintaining the same diameter
    B. Starts with the trachea superiorly and then divides within the left and right lungs, with each subdivision becoming wider in diameter
    C. Starts with the trachea superiorly and then divides within the left and right lungs, with each subdivision becoming smaller in diameter
    D. Starts with the trachea superior and then divides into the left and right bronchiole within the left and right lungs

37. The bronchial tree
    A. Contains 38 generations from the trachea to the terminal bronchiole
    B. Contains 18 generations (2 for the right lung and 2 for the left lung) from the trachea to the terminal bronchiole
    C. Is designed to transfer oxygen from the outside air to the tissues in a slow and orderly fashion
    D. Is designed to transfer oxygen to the upper part of the lungs first and then to the lower part of the lungs

38. The alveoli
    A. Expand upon inhalation and collapse upon exhalation
    B. Are always expanded and filled with air
    C. Are present in the first 9 generations of the bronchial tree only
    D. Are present in all generations of the bronchial tree

39. The pulmonary system is composed of the _____, _____, and the lungs.

40. The lungs are composed of approximately 90% _____ [tissue/muscle/air/blood] and about 10% _____ [tissue/muscle/air/blood].

41. The large muscle that forms the floor of the thoracic cavity is called the _____.

42. The ribs are attached to the spine in such a way as to allow the ribs to move upward and outward [separately and individually/in unison].

43. Each subdivision or branching of the bronchial tree is called a _____.

44. At the end of each terminal bronchiole are clusters of microscopic air-filled sacs called _____.

45. Pascal's law states that
    A. Air pressure decreases from the upper to the lower portion of the lungs.
    B. Air pressure increases from the upper to the lower portion of the lungs.
    C. Air pressure is equal everywhere within the lungs.
    D. Air pressure in the lungs is an absolute pressure, independent of the atmospheric pressure.

46. _____ law that states that change in air pressure is rapidly transmitted within an enclosed space such as the lungs, and the pressure does not decrease as it is transmitted.

47. Another term for lung pressure is _____.

48. Which one of the following statements is true?
    A. Yawning is an automatic reflex that occurs because we are tired or bored.
    B. Yawning is a semiautomatic reflex demonstrated by many different types of animals, including humans.
    C. The neurobiology of yawning has finally been fully explained within the past 10 years.
    D. Yawning occurs because we build up excess carbon dioxide in the blood.

49. Which one of the following statements is true?

    A. A motor unit is a single motor neuron branch and the muscle fibers it innervates.

    B. A motor unit generally consists of 50 to 100 muscles fibers.

    C. A motor unit permits the brain to stimulate an individual muscle fiber.

    D. In general, slower muscles require activation of a larger number of motor units than do fast muscles, in order to maintain accuracy of slow movements.

50. The combination of a single motor neuron branch and the muscle fibers it innervates is called a _____.

51. Muscles that are involved in high force and large movements have a [greater/lesser] number of fibers per motor unit than do muscles involved in precise, fine movements.

52. All of the following statements about muscles are correct except

    A. Elongation of a group of muscle fibers occurs through active and passive muscle fiber activity.

    B. Muscles generally function best when within 50% of their resting length.

    C. Muscle tone is characterized by the readiness of a muscle to contract.

    D. Healthy muscle tone is characterized by a high level of muscle contraction.

53. Isometric and isotonic refer to

    A. Whether or not muscle contraction results in shortening (unopposed contraction) or the absence of change in length (opposed contraction)

    B. Eccentric muscle contractions

    C. The amount of work achieved by a muscle

    D. The amount of passive elongation achieved by the muscle

54. Muscles generally function within __% of their resting length.

55. Muscle elongation occurs only by ___ [active/passive] stretching beyond their resting length.

56. Unopposed contraction of a muscle results in shortening of the muscle fibers, which is known as [isotonic/isometric] contraction.

57. Complete the following table of types of muscle movement by selecting one term from each choice.

Tension-Load Relationship	Muscle Length	Action
Tension less than load	Muscle [lengthens/ shortens/remains unchanged in length]	[Concentric/isometric/ eccentric]
Tension greater than load	Muscle [lengthens/ shortens/remains unchanged in length]	[Concentric/isometric/ eccentric]
Tension equal to load	Muscle [lengthens/ shortens/remains unchanged in length]	[Concentric/isometric/ eccentric]

58. Agonist and antagonist refer to

    A. The type of muscle fibers contained within a muscle

    B. The type of attachment of the muscle to the joint

    C. The degree to which a muscle is a prime mover or a synergist

    D. The roles played by each muscle in a pair to achieve a given movement

59. A muscle that opposes contraction of another muscle is called an [agonist/ antagonist].

60. A prime mover and a synergist are two categories of an [agonist/antagonist] muscle.

61. How is the muscle-joint-skeletal element best described?

    A. As a rigid bar that rotates about a fulcrum at one end

    B. As a rigid bar that rotates about a fulcrum at the midpoint like a seesaw

    C. As an energy-inefficient design but one that can generate tremendous force and velocity

    D. As an energy-efficient design but one that can generate only small amounts of force and velocity

62. True/False   The velocity and the force of a muscle exist in an inverse relationship If the velocity is maximized, the force is minimized.

63. The major muscle(s) of the lower airway that function in inspiration during all types of breathing is/are

    A. The diaphragm, the internal intercostals, and the external intercostals

    B. The diaphragm and the internal intercostals

    C. The diaphragm and the external intercostals

    D. The diaphragm and the abdominal muscles

64. The external intercostal muscles are

    A. A single sheet of muscle that covers the rib cage and is angled inferiorly and anteriorly

    B. A single sheet of muscle that covers the rib cage and is angled inferiorly and posteriorly

    C. A series of muscles between each pair of ribs that are angled inferiorly and anteriorly

    D. A series of muscles between each pair of ribs that are angled inferiorly and posteriorly

65. Contraction of the external intercostal muscles results in

    A. Upward and outward expansion of the rib cage, expanding the volume of the lungs

    B. Upward and outward expansion of the rib cage, compressing the volume of the lungs

    C. Downward and inward movement of the rib cage, expanding the volume of the lungs

    D. Downward and inward movement of the rib cage, compressing the volume of the lungs

66. The internal intercostal muscles are primarily active

    A. During inhalation

    B. During expiration

    C. During equilibrium of the breathing cycle

    D. During both inhalation and exhalation

67. The major muscles of the lower airway that function during inspiration are the _____ and the _____.

68. The major muscle of the lower airway that functions during exhalation is the _____.

69. At rest, the diaphragm is [convex/concave] shaped, and upon contraction, the muscle [flattens downward/is drawn upward].

70. Upon contraction of the rostral external intercostal muscles, the rib cage is [elevated/depressed] in an [upward and outward/downward and inward] movement.

71. The ability of individuals to achieve similar breath support during an activity by using different strategies of muscle activation is called motor _____.

72. True/False   The muscles of the neck, chest, back, and abdominal wall contribute to change in lung volume through expansion and contraction of the thoracic cavity and also help to stabilize posture.

73. True/False   The diaphragm is generally considered the primary muscle of inhalation.

4.5 The Biomechanics of Breathing (p. 87)

74. The lungs are mechanically attached to the thoracic by
    A. The visceral pleura, which encases the outside of the lungs, and the parietal pleura, attached to the inside of the thoracic cavity, and pleural fluid between the two membranes
    B. The visceral pleura, which is attached to the inside of the thoracic cavity, and the parietal pleura, which encases the outside of the lungs, and the blood between the two membranes
    C. The direct contact between the visceral pleura, which encases the outside of the lungs, and the parietal pleura, attached to the inside of the thoracic cavity
    D. The direct contact between the visceral pleura, which is attached to the inside of the thoracic cavity, and the parietal pleura, which encases the outside of the lungs

75. The intrapleural pressure
    A. Is negative with respect to the atmospheric pressure
    B. Is positive with respect to the atmospheric pressure
    C. Is negative with respect to the atmospheric pressure upon inhalation
    D. Is positive with respect to the atmospheric pressure upon inhalation

76. If the lungs and thorax were not biomechanically linked and were free to move on their own

    A. The thorax and lungs would remain at a size similar to when they are biomechanically linked.

    B. The thorax would contract to a much smaller size and the lungs would expand to a larger size.

    C. The lungs would contract to a much smaller size and the thorax would expand to a larger size.

    D. Inhalation would be easier, and exhalation would be more difficult.

77. During quiet breathing, a moment of equilibrium occurs

    A. At the end of inhalation, just prior to the start of exhalation

    B. At the end of exhalation, just prior to inhalation

    C. At approximately 50% of the inhalation cycle

    D. At approximately 50% of the exhalation cycle

78. When the diaphragm contracts

    A. It flattens downward, expanding the volume of the lungs.

    B. It flattens downward, reducing the volume of the lungs.

    C. It is drawn upward in a convex shape, expanding the volume of the lungs.

    D. It is drawn upward in a convex shape, reducing the volume of the lungs.

79. Upon contraction of the diaphragm

    A. The pressure on the abdominal contents is reduced, pushing the abdomen outward and helping to pull outward the lower ribs and increase the lung volume.

    B. The pressure on the abdominal contents is increased, pushing the abdomen outward and helping to pull outward the lower ribs and increase the lung volume.

    C. The pressure on the abdominal contents is reduced, pulling the abdomen inward and helping to pull outward the lower ribs and increase the lung volume.

    D. The pressure on the abdominal contents is increased, pulling the abdomen inward and helping to pull outward the lower ribs and increase the lung volume.

80. In quiet tidal breathing, the external intercostal muscles
    A. Contract slightly, which may help elevate the ribs outwardly and increase the transverse dimension of the lungs
    B. Contract slightly, which may help press the ribs downward and decrease the transverse dimension of the lungs
    C. Contract slightly, maintaining the equilibrium of the muscles of inhalation and exhalation
    D. Do not contract

81. In quiet tidal breathing, inhalation is achieved by
    A. Contraction of the lung volume, which results in a decrease in air pressure within the bronchi, resulting in an inward flow of air, per Boyle's law
    B. Expansion of the lung volume, which results in a decrease in air pressure within the bronchi, resulting in an inward flow of air, per Boyle's law
    C. Actively pulling air inward into the lungs, which increases the air pressure in the lungs, and pushes outward on the lung tissue, causing the lungs to expand, per Boyle's law
    D. Expansion of the upper airway in the lungs and compression of the lower airway in the lungs, thus resulting in a pressure differential and a flow of air into the lungs, per Boyle's law

82. In quiet tidal breathing, exhalation is achieved by
    A. Contraction of the muscles of expiration, resulting in decreased lung volume and outward flow of the air from the lungs
    B. Contraction of the muscles of inspiration, resulting in decreased lung volume and outward flow of air from the lungs
    C. Passive relaxation of the muscles within the lungs
    D. Passive relaxation of the elastic recoil force of the lungs

83. Two factors that enable lung volume changes are _____ and the _____.

84. The _____ pleura is a membrane that encases each lung.

85. The fluid-filled space between the visceral and parietal pleura is called a _____ space because it is not filled with air, but it is not a vacuum.

86. The forces that act upon the lungs and thorax to return them to their resting state after being stretched is called the _____ forces.

87. If the lungs were free to move on their own and were not linked to the thoracic cavity, the lungs would naturally [expand/contract].

88. During the breathing cycle, when the elastic recoil forces acting to expand the thoracic cavity and contract the lungs are equal, the forces are said to be at _____.

89. Resting lung volume is also called resting _____ level.

90. On average, during quiet tidal breathing, we take approximately _____ to _____ breaths per minute.

91. True/False   The lungs contain muscle tissue.

92. True/False   If the thorax expands or contracts, the lungs must similarly expand or contract due to the pleural linkage.

93. True/False   Equilibrium of the elastic recoil forces of the lungs and thorax occurs at the end of inhalation, just prior to the start of exhalation.

94. Which one of the following statements about pneumothorax is true?
    A. The difficulty breathing results from the surfactant and air between the pleural linings leaking into the lungs.
    B. In most cases, a pneumothorax results in the "collapse" of both the right and left lungs, resulting in the complete inability to inhale.
    C. It is difficult to breathe when a pneumothorax occurs because one or more ribs are broken inward, which mechanically blocks the lung from expanding.
    D. It results from the rupture of the biomechanical linkages between the visceral and the parietal pleura.

95. True/False   The presence of millions of air-filled alveoli in the lungs contributes significantly to the elasticity of the lungs.

96. In regard to lung volumes and lung capacities
    A. They both refer to the same quantity.
    B. Lung volumes refer to absolute values, depending upon the size of a person's lungs, while lung capacities refer to the health status of a person's respiratory system.
    C. Each of the four lung volumes is distinct with no overlap, while each of the four lung capacities describe two or more lung volumes.
    D. Both of the two lung volumes are distinct with no overlap, while both of the two lung capacities describe two or more lung volumes.

97. Which one of the following statements about tidal volume is true?

    A. Tidal volume is the volume of air exchanged during a single cycle of breathing and is approximately 15% of vital capacity in quiet tidal breathing.

    B. Tidal volume is the volume of air exchanged during a single cycle of breathing and is approximately 30% of vital capacity in quiet tidal breathing.

    C. Tidal volume is the amount of air inhaled during a single cycle of breathing and is approximately 15% of vital capacity in quiet tidal breathing.

    D. Tidal volume is the amount of air inhaled during a single cycle of breathing and is approximately 30% of vital capacity in quiet tidal breathing.

98. Which one of the following statements about total lung capacity is true?

    A. Total lung capacity is the maximum volume of air that the lungs can hold, and all of that air can be exhaled.

    B. Total lung capacity is the maximum volume of air that the lungs can hold, but about 25% of that air cannot be exhaled.

    C. Total lung capacity is the total volume of air that can be exchanged during a single maximal inhalation and exhalation.

    D. Total lung capacity is the total volume of air that remains in the lungs after all air is exhaled.

99. At resting lung volume

    A. An individual has just finished inhaling and is ready to exhale.

    B. An individual has just exhaled to residual volume.

    C. The tendency for the lungs to spring outward is balanced by the tendency for the thoracic cavity to recoil inward.

    D. The tendency for the lungs to recoil inward is balanced by the tendency for the thoracic cavity to spring outward.

100. Resting lung volume generally occurs at approximately

    A. 38% to 40% of vital capacity

    B. 20% to 50% vital capacity

    C. 50% to 75% vital capacity

    D. 80% to 100% vital capacity

101. Residual volume

    A. Is the same as functional residual capacity

    B. Is the volume of air that cannot be exhaled

    C. Is the volume of air that is used when a person speaks with an insufficient amount of air

    D. Is present only in individuals with respiratory disease

102. Forced inhalation occurs when
    A. A greater volume of air is inspired than during tidal breathing.
    B. The lung volume is above approximately 38% vital capacity.
    C. The muscles of inspiration are more relaxed.
    D. An individual is at rest or sleeping.

103. In quiet tidal breathing, tidal volume is approximately _____% of vital capacity.

104. Approximately 25% of total lung capacity that remains in the lungs upon complete exhalation is called _____ volume.

105. At _____ volume, the tendency for the lungs to recoil inward is balanced by the tendency for the chest wall to expand outward.

106. The point at which the elastic recoil forces of the lungs and thorax are balanced occurs between _____% and _____% of vital capacity.

107. True/False   Muscles of the neck, shoulder, abdomen, and back may become engaged and assist in breathing.

108. True/False   Lung capacity is determined by health of the individual, not by body size.

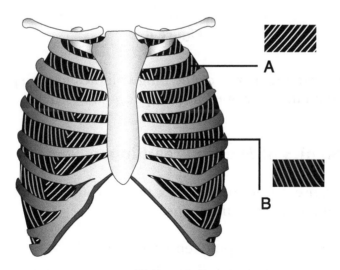

Figure 4–1

109. Label the muscles indicated in Figure 4–1.

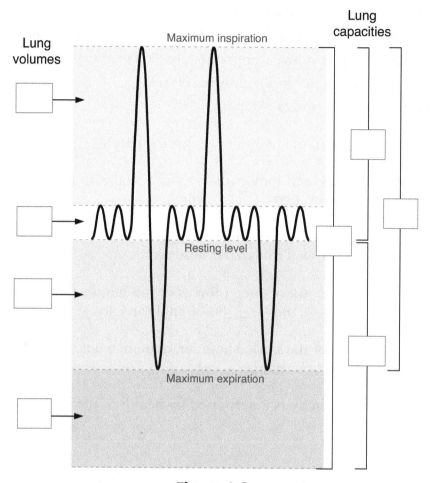

Figure 4–2

110. In Figure 4–2, write the names of the lung volumes in the spaces to the left and the names of the lung capacities in the spaces to the right.

4.6 The Biomechanics of Speech Breathing (p. 95)

111. Relaxation pressure is said to be (select one) [positive/negative] when the pressure is acting to expand the lungs.

112. The relaxation curve is a graphic representation of
   A. Elastic recoil forces of the lungs at different percentages of vital capacity
   B. Elastic recoil forces of the lungs at different percentages of total lung capacity
   C. Elastic recoil forces of the lungs and thorax together at different percentages of vital capacity
   D. Elastic recoil forces of the lungs and thorax together at different percentages of total lung capacity

113. The pressure difference between the atmosphere and the alveoli is called the _____ pressure.

114. Resting lung volume is located at approximately _____ % of vital capacity.

115. Relaxation pressure is sufficient to sustain phonation above approximately _____ vital capacity.

116. The braking action used to counteract relaxation pressure and provide for stable lung pressure for phonation is called _____.

117. The average rate of quiet breathing—12 to 20 breaths per minute—is typically

    A. Slower than breathing rate during speech

    B. Faster than the breathing rate during speech

    C. More variable than the breathing rate during speech

    D. Similar to the breathing rate during speech

118. Match the breathing phase and breathing type with the percentage of the total breathing cycle. Percentages may be used more than once or not at all.

Phase	Percentage
Inspiratory phase in tidal breathing	90%
Inspiratory phase in speech breathing	60%
Expiratory phase in tidal breathing	40%
Expiratory phase in speech breathing	20%
	10%

119. A phrase group (synonymously, breath group) is the number of words or syllables spoken during one _____.

120. True/False   Relaxation pressure alone is sometimes the solitary force that manages speech breathing.

121. As lung volume decreases

    A. Inspiratory muscle force decreases, and expiratory muscle force increases.

    B. Expiratory muscle force decreases, and inspiratory muscle force increases.

    C. Both inspiratory and expiratory muscle forces decrease.

    D. Neither inspiratory nor expiratory muscle forces decrease.

122. True/False   The lung volumes typically used for soft or quiet conversational speech are significantly greater than lung volumes used for quiet tidal breathing.

123. In comparing resting tidal breathing and breathing during physical exertion, one notes that
    A. Breathing cycles are similar from one cycle to the next.
    B. Breathing cycles are more variable in exertional breathing than in resting breathing.
    C. Both resting and exertional breathing are generally characterized by 40% inhalation and 60% exhalation.
    D. Breathing cycles are highly variable in both resting and exertional breathing.

4.7 The Work of Breathing (p. 106)

124. Variables that may influence speech breathing mechanics include cognitive-linguistic factors and
    A. Muscle mass
    B. Bone density
    C. Motivation
    D. Positive attitude

125. Speech breathing personality includes clavicular and _____ breathing styles.

126. Overall, as ventilatory demands increase, the length of the phrase breath group
    A. Becomes more variable
    B. Increases
    C. Decreases
    D. Is not affected

127. The difference in pressure between two points is called the _____ pressure.

128. The three types of resistance most important in breathing are airway resistance, elastic resistance, and _____.

129. Airflow through the breathing system is
    A. Directly proportional to resistance
    B. Inversely proportional to resistance
    C. Equal to resistance
    D. More variable as resistance increases

130. True/False   Airway resistance is high in the lower airways.

4.8 Instrumentation for Measuring Breathing Kinematics (p. 110)

131. The motor action unit potentials of muscle fibers can be measured by _____.

132. Inductance plethysmography measures
    A. The change in lung volume during breathing and the relative contributions of the abdomen and rib cage
    B. The change in lung volume during breathing and the relative contributions of the rib cage and lungs
    C. The change in lung volume during breathing and the relative contributions of the abdomen and the lungs
    D. The change in overall lung volume and the relative contributions of the upper and lower thoracic cavity (e.g., the extent of clavicula and diaphragmatic breathing)

Conceptual Integration

1. The lungs become stiffer at higher lung volumes.
    A. It is easier to inhale at high lung volumes.
    B. It is harder to inhale at high lung volumes.
    C. No change in ease of inhalation would be expected, all other factors being equal.
    D. Lung stiffness is not relevant to ease of inhalation.

2. Phonation is more efficient (requires less work)
    A. Above resting expiratory level up to approximately 60% vital capacity
    B. Between resting expiratory level and approximately 38% vital capacity
    C. Between approximately 38% vital capacity above and below resting expiratory level
    D. Between approximately 60% vital capacity above and below resting expiratory level

3. Recall that a force is a push or a pull. Forces require a relatively solid platform against which to act. What is used as a relatively solid platform against which the forces of lung volume work during speech breathing?
    A. Diaphragm
    B. Rib cage
    C. Abdominal wall
    D. Lungs

4. True/False   The concept of adaptive control means that a deeper inhalation will likely precede a longer phrase group.

5. Laminar airflow through the respiratory system requires lesser driving pressure than does turbulent airflow because laminar airflow
   A. Is less dense
   B. Occurs only in the largest diameter passages
   C. Contains circular movement called eddies
   D. Runs parallel to the axis of the airway

6. Breathing in very humid air requires more work, in general, than breathing in air with low humidity because
   A. Humid air is more viscous and generates greater frictional forces.
   B. The water in humid air allows the air molecules to slide against each other more easily.
   C. Humid air is in the airways at the same time that it is flowing through the bronchial tree.
   D. Low-humidity air dries out the tissues of the bronchial tree, making it more difficult to allow air molecules to slide by it.

7. The most important reason why breathing is not similar to blowing up a balloon is that
   A. Our lungs do not expand as much as a balloon.
   B. The air travels through tubes (the trachea and bronchi) and not directly into the lungs, while a balloon is blown up by air flowing directly into it.
   C. The air that we inhale does not press against the lung tissues.
   D. The air we inhale is not pushed into the lungs. Instead, we expand the lungs, which lowers the air pressure and draws in the outside air.

8. Boyle's law explains the [direct/inverse] relationship of [volume and pressure/ fluids and gases].

9. Lung pressure
   A. Is generally higher than subglottal pressure in a healthy person
   B. Is generally lower than subglottal pressure in a healthy person
   C. Is equivalent to subglottal pressure and higher than alveolar pressure
   D. Is equivalent to subglottal pressure and alveolar pressure

10. Positive lung pressure is achieved when the lungs
    A. Contract
    B. Expand
    C. Are at rest
    D. Positive lung pressure cannot be achieved in a healthy individual.

11. The term *motor equivalence*, when applied to breathing, refers to
    A. The ability of one muscle to perform in exactly the same manner as another muscle
    B. The ability of people to breathe easily without use of the diaphragm
    C. The fact that all muscle of inspiration and expiration contract with the same force
    D. The variability in muscle activity used by people to achieve inhalation and exhalation under similar conditions

12. The two factors that enable the lungs to change volume are
    A. Muscle contraction and passive elongation by the muscles of the lung
    B. The visceral pleura and alveolar surfactant
    C. The mechanical linkage between the lungs and the thoracic cavity, and the restorative force of the lungs
    D. The muscle contraction of the lungs to make them smaller and the restorative force of the lungs to allow them to regain their larger volume

13. Elastic recoil forces are
    A. Due to muscle contraction
    B. Muscular restorative forces
    C. Restorative forces acting upon the lungs and thorax to expand them from their resting state
    D. Restorative forces acting upon the lungs and thorax to return them to their resting state

14. Equilibrium of the forces of inhalation and exhalation means that
    A. A person can choose to inhale or exhale.
    B. A person is breathing comfortably and not "out of breath."
    C. The muscles of breathing are not contracted and the forces are balanced.
    D. The muscles of breathing are contracted and the forces are balanced.

15. During inhalation in quiet tidal breathing, when the atmospheric and lung pressure equalize, the restorative force of the lungs becomes greater than the force exerted by the thoracic cavity to expand, thus causing _____ to begin.

16. The elastic properties of the lungs come from two factors
    A. The millions of alveoli that make up the lungs and the elastin and collagen connective fibers of the lung tissue
    B. The flexibility of the muscles of the lungs and the elastin and collagen connective fibers of the lung tissue
    C. The elastin fibers of the visceral and parietal pleura and the millions of alveoli that make up the lungs
    D. The air in the trachea and bronchi and the elastin fibers of the lung tissue

17. Forced exhalation
    A. Occurs when the volume of air in the lungs is exhaled at a rate slower than during tidal breathing and/or a smaller volume of air is exhaled than during tidal breathing
    B. Occurs when the volume of air in the lungs is exhaled at a rate faster than during tidal breathing and/or a greater volume of air is exhaled than during tidal breathing
    C. Occurs when the internal intercostal muscles do not contract, thus forcing the external intercostal muscles to do all of the work
    D. Is a passive process

18. Passive forces that act upon our breathing include
    A. Gravity
    B. Muscle contraction
    C. Physical exertion
    D. All forces that act upon our breathing system are active.

19. If the transthoracic pressure is negative, the pressure in the alveoli is
    A. Equal to the atmospheric pressure
    B. Greater than the atmospheric pressure
    C. Lesser than the atmospheric pressure
    D. Absent

20. In the relaxation pressure curve, the top right quadrant represents
    A. Relaxation pressure working to decrease lung volume
    B. Relaxation pressure working to increase lung volume
    C. Muscle contraction pressure working to increase lung volume
    D. Muscle contraction pressure working to decrease lung volume

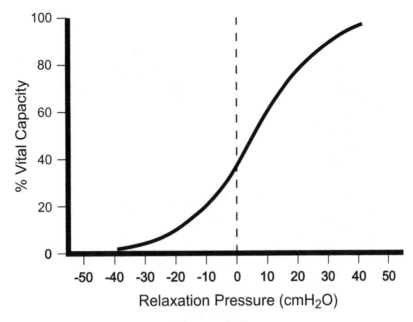

Figure 4-3

21. In Figure 4–3, why does the relaxation curve intersect the dashed line at 0 cmH$_2$O of alveolar pressure?

    A. The elastic recoil forces are equal and opposite at that intersection.

    B. The elastic recoil force of the lungs equals zero force at that intersection.

    C. The elastic recoil force of the chest wall equals zero force at that intersection.

    D. The vital capacity equals zero at that intersection.

22. In Figure 4–3, the intersection of the relaxation curve and the dashed line at 0 cmH$_2$0 represents

    A. Vital capacity

    B. Intrapleural pressure

    C. Tidal volume

    D. Resting lung volume

23. Boyle's law can be explained as

    A. An increase in the volume of a container will produce an increase in the pressure of the air inside it.

    B. A decrease in the volume of a container will produce an increase in the pressure of the air inside it.

    C. Pressure can be measured at any location within a container holding air.

    D. Air volume is produced by the force of air molecules within a container.

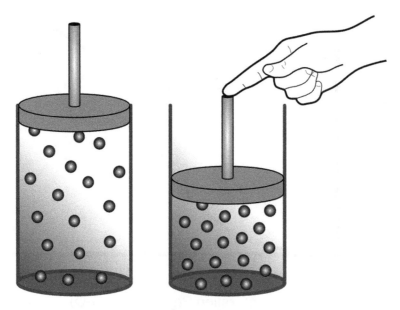

Figure 4–4

24. Figure 4–4 shows an air chamber with a plunger at the top. Pushing downward on the plunger (right) will produce

    A. An increase in air volume

    B. A decrease in air pressure

    C. A decrease in air volume and a decrease in air pressure

    D. A decrease in air volume and an increase in air pressure

25. In Figure 4–4, the air chamber's volume has decreased by 50%. What, if anything, has happened to the air pressure inside the chamber?

    A. Air pressure has decreased by 50%.

    B. Air pressure has increased by two times (it has doubled).

    C. Air pressure has not changed.

    D. Air pressure has gone from positive to negative.

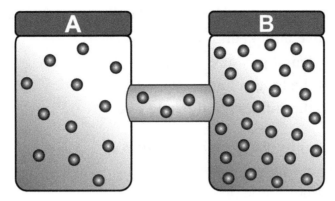

Figure 4–5

26. Figure 4–5 shows two air-filled jars connected by an open tube. What can we deduce about the air molecules in jars A and B?

    A. The air molecules in jar A will flow to jar B

    B. The air molecules in jar B will flow to jar A.

    C. The air molecules are moving randomly from jar A to B, with no net change in the number of air molecules in each jar.

    D. None of the air molecules will move at all between the jars.

27. In Figure 4–5, what will happen over time?

    A. The air molecule density will become equal in both jars.

    B. All of the air molecules will be collected in jar A.

    C. All of the air molecules will be collected in jar B.

    D. There will be no change, as the air molecules do not move between the jars.

28. Considering Pascal's law, to obtain a value of the air pressure in the lungs, we can measure air pressure at

    A. The alveoli of the lungs, nowhere else

    B. The intrapleural space

    C. The trachea (with the vocal folds open)

    D. The nasal passages (with the vocal folds closed)

29. As we expand the thoracic cavity during inhalation

    A. The pressure in the lungs increases, expanding the lungs.

    B. The pressure in the lungs decreases as the lungs expand.

    C. The pressure in the lungs stays the same as atmospheric pressure.

    D. The atmospheric pressure decreases.

30. Expanding the thoracic cavity during inhalation will also produce
    A. Greater negative intrapleural pressure
    B. Positive intrapleural pressure
    C. A decrease in the lung volume
    D. A decrease in the stiffness of the lung tissue

31. During inhalation, alveolar (lung) pressure is
    A. Higher than atmospheric pressure
    B. Lower than atmospheric pressure
    C. Equal to atmospheric pressure
    D. Continually changing from positive to negative

32. During exhalation
    A. Alveolar (lung) pressure is increased.
    B. Alveolar (lung) pressure is decreased.
    C. Lung volume expands.
    D. Lung volume does not change.

33. True/False   Air pressure determines the direction of airflow.

34. True/False   During inhalation, air is forced into the lungs from the atmosphere.

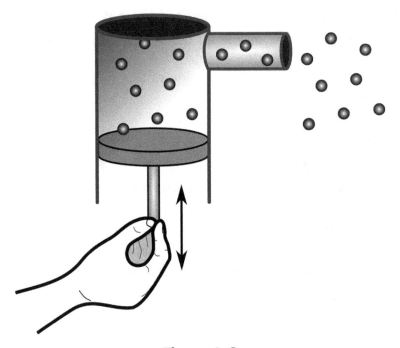

Figure 4–6

35. In Figure 4–6, an air chamber is shown with a plunger at the bottom. At the top right, there is a tube open to the atmosphere. The plunger can move up and down, changing the volume of the air chamber. What anatomical structure of the respiratory system would be analogous to the plunger in this figure?

    A. The alveoli of the lungs

    B. The trachea

    C. The diaphragm

    D. The lungs

36. In Figure 4–6, what will happen if the plunger is moved upward?

    A. The air molecules in the air chamber will flow out through the tube.

    B. The air molecules in the atmosphere will flow into the air chamber through the tube.

    C. Some air molecules will flow out of the tube, and an equal number will flow in through the tube.

    D. The air molecules will not be affected by the movement of the plunger upward.

37. In Figure 4–6, what will happen if the plunger is moved downward?

    A. The air molecules in the air chamber will flow out through the tube.

    B. The air molecules in the atmosphere will flow into the air chamber through the tube.

    C. Some air molecules will flow out of the tube, and an equal number will flow in through the tube.

    D. The air molecules will not be affected by the movement of the plunger upward.

38. Using Figure 4–6 as a model, what movement of the plunger would be analogous to movements produced during inhalation?

    A. Downward movement of the plunger

    B. Upward movement of the plunger

    C. Spinning movement of the plunger

    D. The plunger would not move

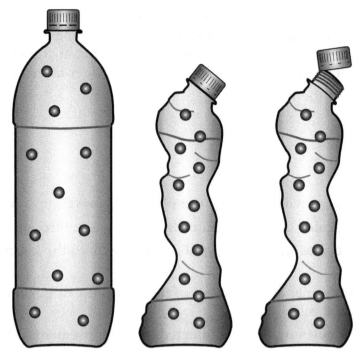

Figure 4–7

39. Figure 4–7 shows a 1-liter water bottle empty of water but filled with air molecules at atmospheric pressure. You crush the bottle, and your impressive hand strength was able to decrease the volume of the bottle from 1 liter to 0.5 liters (middle picture). If the atmospheric pressure is 1,033 cmH_2O before crushing the bottle, what would the pressure be inside the bottle after crushing it?

   A. −1,033 cmH_2O

   B. 0 cmH_2O

   C. 1,033 cmH_2O

   D. 2,066 cmH_2O

40. On the right side of Figure 4–7, you open the top of the water bottle after you've crushed it. What will happen?

   A. Air molecules will be pushed inward from the atmosphere, expanding the bottle.

   B. Air molecules will be pushed outward to the atmosphere.

   C. Air molecules will flow equally inward and outward.

   D. Air molecules will not move.

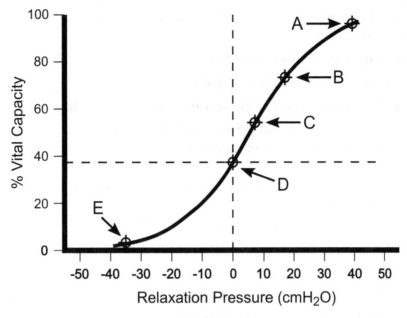

Figure 4–8

41. Figure 4–8 shows the relaxation pressure curve. At point D, the elastic recoil forces are
    A. Balanced: (equal in magnitude) inward for the lungs and outward for the chest wall
    B. Balanced: inward for the lungs and inward for the chest wall
    C. Unbalanced: inward for the lungs and zero elastic recoil force for the chest wall
    D. Unbalanced: outward for the lungs and maximal elastic recoil force for the chest wall

42. At which point on the relaxation pressure curve in Figure 4–8 will the inward-directed elastic recoil force be maximal for both the lungs and the chest wall?
    A. Point A
    B. Point B
    C. Point D
    D. Point E

43. At which point on the relaxation pressure curve in Figure 4–8 will the outward-directed elastic recoil force be maximal for both the lungs and the chest wall?
    A. Point D
    B. Point E
    C. The chest wall will not show an outward directed elastic recoil force at any point on the relaxation pressure curve.
    D. The lungs will not show an outward directed elastic recoil force at any point on the relaxation pressure curve.

44. Starting at point A on Figure 4–8, what muscular force will be required in order to produce exhalation?

    A. Contraction of exhalation muscles

    B. Contraction of the inhalation muscles

    C. Contraction of both the exhalation muscles and the diaphragm

    D. No muscle contraction will be needed, as the elastic recoil forces will be strong enough to produce exhalation.

45. Starting at point B on Figure 4–8, what muscular force will be required in order to produce exhalation?

    A. Contraction of exhalation muscles

    B. Contraction of the inhalation muscles

    C. Contraction of both the exhalation muscles and the diaphragm

    D. No muscle contraction will be needed, as the elastic recoil forces will be strong enough to produce exhalation.

46. Starting at point C on Figure 4–8, what muscular force will be required in order to produce exhalation?

    A. Contraction of exhalation muscles

    B. Contraction of the inhalation muscles

    C. Contraction of both the exhalation muscles and the diaphragm

    D. No muscle contraction will be needed, as the elastic recoil forces will be strong enough to produce exhalation.

47. Starting at point D on Figure 4–8, what muscular force will be required in order to produce exhalation?

    A. Contraction of exhalation muscles

    B. Contraction of the inhalation muscles

    C. Contraction of both the exhalation muscles and the diaphragm

    D. No muscle contraction will be needed, as the elastic recoil forces will be strong enough to produce exhalation.

48. Starting at point B on Figure 4–8, what muscular force will be required in order to produce inhalation?

    A. Contraction of exhalation muscles

    B. Contraction of the inhalation muscles

    C. Contraction of both the exhalation muscles and the diaphragm

    D. No muscle contraction will be needed, as the elastic recoil forces will be strong enough to produce exhalation.

49. Starting at point D on Figure 4–8, what muscular force will be required in order to produce inhalation?

    A. Contraction of exhalation muscles

    B. Contraction of the inhalation muscles

    C. Contraction of both the exhalation muscles and the diaphragm

    D. No muscle contraction will be needed, as the elastic recoil forces will be strong enough to produce exhalation.

50. Starting at point E on Figure 4–8, what muscular force will be required in order to produce inhalation?

    A. Contraction of exhalation muscles

    B. Contraction of the inhalation muscles

    C. Contraction of both the exhalation muscles and the diaphragm

    D. No muscle contraction will be needed, as the elastic recoil forces will be strong enough to produce inhalation.

51. What muscular force would be required to reach point A on Figure 4–8?

    A. Maximum contraction of inspiratory muscles

    B. Maximum contraction of expiratory muscles

    C. Equal contraction of both inspiratory and expiratory muscles

    D. No muscle contraction would be needed, as point A shows maximum elastic recoil force.

52. Considering Figure 4–8, at which point in the relaxation pressure curve would initiating speech be most efficient?

    A. Point A

    B. Point B

    C. Point D

    D. Point E

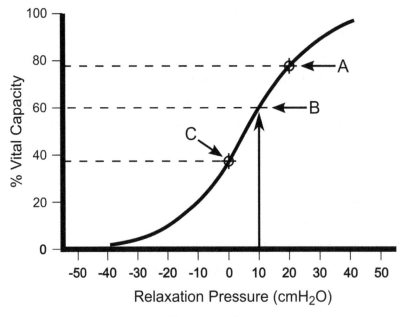

Figure 4–9

53. Using Figure 4–9, consider that you have taken a deep breath to approximately 78% of your vital capacity (point A), and you would like to sustain a vowel /a/ with the target lung pressure of 10 cmH₂O (vertical arrow). Starting at point A, you begin to exhale to produce the sustained /a/. What muscular force will you need at point A in order to produce the sustained vowel while maintaining the target lung pressure?

    A. You will need to contract exhalation muscles to generate outward airflow.

    B. You will need to contract inhalation muscles to counteract excessive elastic relaxation forces.

    C. You will need to contract both inhalation and exhalation muscles to balance their forces.

    D. No muscle contraction is required, as elastic relaxation forces will be sufficient to produce exhalation.

54. As you continue to produce the sustained /a/ in Figure 4–9, what will occur at point B, where the relaxation pressure curve meets the target lung pressure for your sustained vowel?

    A. You will need to contract exhalation muscles to supplement elastic relaxation forces in order to continue to generate outward airflow.

    B. You will need to contract inhalation muscles to counteract excessive elastic relaxation forces.

    C. You will need to contract both inhalation and exhalation muscles to balance their forces.

    D. No muscle contraction is required, as elastic relaxation forces will be sufficient to produce exhalation.

55. If you would continue to sustain your /a/ vowel in Figure 4–9 until you reached the resting lung volume, how much of your vital capacity would you have used?

    A. 22%

    B. 40%

    C. 78%

    D. 100%

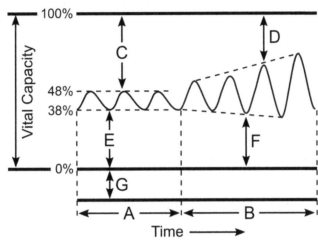

Figure 4–10

56. Figure 4–10 shows a spirometry plot of several cycles of respiration. What is likely occurring during time period A?

    A. Continuous speech

    B. Producing a sustained vowel

    C. Resting tidal breathing

    D. Holding a maximal inhalation breath

57. Figure 4–10 shows a spirometry plot of several cycles of respiration. What is likely occurring during time period B?

    A. Continuous speech

    B. Resting tidal breathing

    C. Beginning strenuous exercise

    D. Holding a maximal exhalation breath

58. In Figure 4–10, which of the following areas indicate inspiratory reserve volume?

    A. Areas indicated by C and E

    B. The area indicated by E

    C. Areas indicated by C and D

    D. Areas indicated by D and E

59. In Figure 4–10, what does area G represent?

    A. Resting lung volume

    B. Expiratory reserve volume

    C. Tidal volume

    D. Residual volume

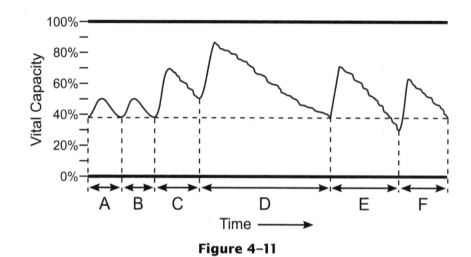

Figure 4–11

60. In Figure 4–11, which breath cycles represent speech breathing?

    A. A and B

    B. C and D

    C. D only

    D. C, D, E, F

61. In Figure 4–11, why is breathing cycle "D" longer in duration than the other cycles?

    A. The person is producing a long speech utterance on one breath.

    B. The person has fallen asleep.

    C. The person has taken as deep a breath as possible.

    D. The person is holding their breath for a period of time.

62. In Figure 4–11, which breathing cycle(s) will require the greatest amount of *expiratory* muscle contraction?

    A. B

    B. D

    C. E

    D. F

63. In Figure 4–11, which breathing cycles(s) will require the greatest amount of *inspiratory* muscle contraction?

    A. B

    B. C

    C. D

    D. E

64. An individual has a vital capacity of 5 liters of air. During a resting tidal breath, they inhale 1 liter of air. How much of their vital capacity (in percentages) did they use during that breath?

    A. 1%

    B. 5%

    C. 10%

    D. 20%

65. Starting at their resting lung volume, an individual rapidly inhales a breath that uses 30% of their vital capacity. At the height of their inhalation, what is the inspiratory reserve volume that they will have remaining?

    A. 0%

    B. 22%

    C. 30%

    D. 100%

66. True/False   If airway resistance doesn't change, the amount of airflow produced is proportional to the driving pressure of the air.

67. True/False   If you completely relax both your inspiratory and your expiratory musculature, your vital capacity will be at 0%.

68. True/False   In order to inhale to 100% of your vital capacity, you will need to produce maximum contraction force in your inspiratory muscles.

Clinical Application

4.9 Clinical Application: Disorder Related to Breathing

1. Paul has difficulty catching his breath sometime in the middle of the day. He has had numerous pulmonary tests that all show normal breathing function. His physician determined that his breathing difficulties may have a psychological component. His disorder can be classified as

   A. Chronic obstructive pulmonary disease

   B. Dysfunctional breathing disorder

   C. Restriction in the ability to expand the lungs

   D. Dysfunction in neuromuscular control

2. True/False   Dyspnea is a common symptom experienced by individuals with breathing disorders.

3. For people who have breathing disorders, taking a larger inhalation than is necessary for speaking and talking below resting expiratory level are common

   A. Maladaptive compensatory strategies

   B. Adaptive (beneficial) compensatory strategies

   C. Denial strategies

   D. Strategies that can cause a breathing disorder

4. Why is increased rate of speech not generally considered a helpful strategy to use for managing a speech-breathing problem?

Clinical Case 1: Breath-Holding Speech

1. What is inspiratory checking? What muscles was Seleena engaging to achieve inspiratory checking? Why would it become fatiguing to use checking action excessively?

2. Why would decreased airflow result in decreased intensity? What is the relationship between intensity and loudness?

3. Where would Seleena's speech fall on the relaxation curve?

4. Create a graph with percentage of vital capacity on the vertical y-axis and time on the horizontal x-axis. Can you draw several breathing cycles that might represent examples of the change in lung volume that would represent Seleena's characteristic lung volumes during speech? (Hint: Does Seleena exhale down to resting lung volume at the end of a phrase group?)

5. How does studying the physiology of breathing and speech breathing inform clinical practice in this case?

TRY IT!

1. Draw the pressure relaxation curve. Now inhale deeply and then hold your breath for a moment before you let the air out. Mark that point on the curve. Note how much pressure you feel against your chest during the breath holding. Now inhale less deeply and again hold your breath before exhaling. Mark that point on the curve. Repeat the gesture with an even shallower inhalation and mark that point on the curve. Note the decrease in pressure sensation against your chest during each breath-holding maneuver as you inhale less deeply. By charting the pressure at each of those points, you have drawn the curve above resting lung volume. Now explore the bottom part of the curve. Starting at resting expiratory level (the end of a cycle of quiet tidal breathing before you begin to inhale anew), mark that point, exhale just a bit more air, and then hold your breath and make a second mark. Note the sensation of pressure in your chest. Return to resting lung volume and exhale even more air, marking that point. Again, note the sensation of chest pressure. Charting the pressures at each of these moments of exhalation at different lung volumes provided the portion of the curve below resting lung volume.

2. Take a comfortably deep breath, begin to phonate any vowel, and then allow the lungs and chest wall to relax wholly. (Admittedly, allowing one's breathing system to completely relax is very difficult. But do the best you can.) If you were successful in relaxing your thoracic muscles, you very quickly ran out of air and the phonation was quite brief. Now once again take a comfortably deep breath, begin to phonate any vowel, but use braking action to resist the relaxation pressure. You should now be able to sustain phonation for at least 10 seconds. Braking action is essential to maintain the steady lung pressure essential for phonation.

3. Explore the relationship of speech breathing with length of breath group. Say a short sentence, like "I am happy." Now try to say the same sentence using two breath groups, that is, taking a short inhalation between "am" and "happy." How did the meaning of the sentence change with the brief pause to inhale? Now try a more complex sentence. Taking a moderately deep breath, and using only a single breath group, say, "I'm so happy when I can spend the day doing whatever I want, even if it means that I wake up late and don't get anything accomplished all day long!" This can be uttered as one phrase breath group. But to do so requires a substantially greater inhalation than was required for the first utterance. Repeat the utterance using two breath groups, then three, then four. How much effort (sensation of muscular contraction) was required

to say the utterance in one breath group compared to two? Why? (Think about muscle contraction and restorative forces!) At what point does it start to sound unnatural? Did you use the written punctuation to determine where to divide the breath groups?

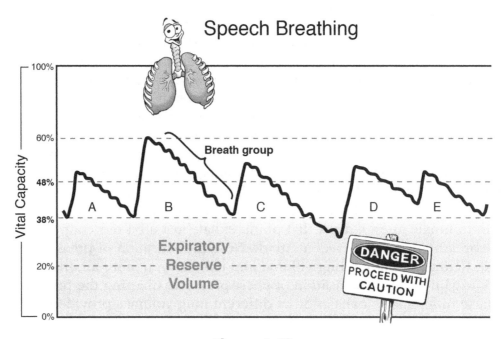

Figure 4–12

4. Select some reading material. Using Figure 4–12 as your guide, try to read aloud several sentences using the different styles of breathing. For example, using the style shown in B, read aloud using moderately deep inspirations and lengthy breath groups. Then, read aloud another group of sentences using the style depicted in cycles D and E. Finally, use the breathing styles shown in cycles A and C and read several more sentences. Which style is most characteristic of your own typical speech breathing? How does it feel when you use a style that is not characteristic of your usual speech breathing?

5. Shake up a can or bottle filled with a carbonated drink. This will release the carbon dioxide bubbles and will increase the pressure inside the container to greater than atmospheric pressure. Hold the can or bottle up to your cheek and open it. You've now experienced how pressure will determine the direction of air (and likely soda pop) flow!

6. Take as deep a breath as you can and produce a very quiet sustained vowel (of your choice!) for 5 to 10 seconds. As you begin to vocalize, can you feel the contraction of your diaphragm, your external intercostals, and other muscles of inspiration? This is the "inspiratory checking action" of the inspiratory muscles

working to counteract the elastic recoil forces of the lungs and the chest wall! Now, produce a sustained vowel for 5 to 10 seconds *without* first taking a breath. Do you feel contraction of abdominal expiratory muscles? In order to produce a vowel at low lung volumes (and especially lower than the resting lung volume of 38% of vital capacity), you need to contract the expiratory muscles to counteract the elastic recoil forces of (mainly) the chest wall to expand back toward its position at the resting lung volume.

7. Inhale a deep breath as quickly as you can using only your mouth (pinch your nose closed if that helps) and then compare to inhaling as quickly as possible using only your nose. Which takes less time? What would happen if you closed one of your nares with a finger and tried again? Considering the effort and time it takes to rapidly inhale air through your open mouth, your open nose, or your half-open nose, for which condition do you think there is the most airway resistance? By the way, unless you have a handkerchief handy, it's probably best to only try this exercise on inhalation.

5

Phonation I:
Basic Voice Science
Questions

Foundational Knowledge

5.1 Overview (p. 121)

1. The conversion of aerodynamic energy into acoustic energy is called (select one term) [phonation/oscillation].

2. True/False   Voice quality consists of pitch and loudness.

5.2 Anatomy of the Larynx (p. 122)

3. The larynx is located
   A. At the level of the cervical vertebrae
   B. Above the cervical vertebrae
   C. Posterior to the cervical vertebrae
   D. Parallel to the level of the shoulders

4. The space just above the larynx and below the pharynx is called the _____.

5. The unpaired laryngeal cartilages, in order from inferior to superior, are the
   A. Epiglottis, thyroid, and cricoid
   B. Cricoid, thyroid, and epiglottis
   C. Cricoid, thyroid, and hyoid
   D. Cricoid, epiglottis, and hyoid

6. True/False   The "Adam's apple" is the most prominent anterior point of the thyroid cartilage.

7. The paired arytenoid cartilages articulate with the cricoid cartilage by means of the _____ joint.

8. The hyoid bone
   A. Articulates directly with the mandible and the thyroid cartilage
   B. Starts out as a cartilage and ossifies to bone with age
   C. Attaches to the base of tongue via muscles and ligaments
   D. Is a paired bone

9. The ligaments that attach the larynx to the hyoid bone and the trachea are called (select one term) [intrinsic/extrinsic] ligaments.

10. The extrinsic ligaments and membranes consist of the
    A. Thyrohyoid membrane and the thyroepiglottic, hyoepiglottic, and cricotracheal ligaments
    B. Cricothyroid membrane and the thyroepiglottic, hyoepiglottic, and cricotracheal ligaments
    C. Thyrohyoid membrane, the cricothyroid membrane, and the thyroepiglottic, hyoepiglottic, and cricotracheal ligaments
    D. Approximately eight membranes and ligaments

11. The purpose of the intrinsic laryngeal ligaments is to
    A. Interconnect the laryngeal cartilages
    B. Connect the laryngeal cartilages to stabilize structures above the larynx
    C. Connect the laryngeal cartilages to stabilize structures below the larynx
    D. Allow the larynx to expand and contract during breathing and swallowing

12. For each of the ligament and membranes listed below, indicate whether they are intrinsic, extrinsic, or both.

    Quadrangular membranes   _____

    Thyrohyoid membrane   _____

    Aryepiglottic folds   _____

    Vocal ligament   _____

    Thyroepiglottic ligament   _____

    Cricotracheal ligament   _____

    Cricothyroid membrane   _____

    Conus elasticus   _____

    Hyoepiglottic ligament   _____

13. The quadrangular membrane forms the _____ folds superiorly and the _____ folds inferiorly.

14. True/False   The conus elasticus is a cone-shaped membrane that encircles the sides of the epiglottis and allows the cartilage to move forward and backward.

15. The laryngeal vestibule is also referred to as the (select one term) [supraglottic/ transglottic space].

16. The Valsalva maneuver
    A. Is the first stage of a cough
    B. Results in a decrease in intrapleural pressure if performed correctly
    C. Is the forceful expelling of air up through the vocal tract
    D. Is performed in cases of voice disorders

17. The group of muscles responsible for vocal fold movement and adjustments for regulation of vocal characteristics are the (select one term) [intrinsic/extrinsic] laryngeal muscles.

18. Abduction refers to the _____ movement of the vocal folds, and adduction refers to the _____ movement of the vocal folds.

19. The only muscle that abducts the vocal folds is the _____.

20. Match the muscle on the left with the function on the right. Functions may be used more than once or not at all.

Muscle	**Function**
Thyromuscularis	Tensor
Thyrovocalis	Relaxor
Cricothyroid	Adductor
Posterior cricoarytenoid	Adductor

21. Match the muscle with the movement upon contract. Movements may be used more than once or not at all.

Muscle	**Movement**
Lateral cricoarytenoids	Pulls thyroid cartilage downward
Thyromuscularis	Glides arytenoids together
Cricothyroid: pars recta	Draws thyroid cartilage upward
Posterior cricoarytenoid	Tenses vocal folds
Cricothyroid: pars oblique	Pulls arytenoids forward
Oblique interarytenoids	Draws thyroid cartilage forward
Thyrovocalis	Pulls apex of arytenoids medially
Transverse interarytenoids	Rotates vocal process of arytenoids laterally
	Rotate muscular process of arytenoids forward and inward
	Pulls epiglottis posteriorly
	Pulls hyoid bone inferiorly

22. The purpose of the extrinsic laryngeal muscles is to
    A. Manage swallowing
    B. Interconnect the cartilages of the larynx
    C. Connect the larynx to the trachea
    D. Adjust the overall position of the larynx and to stabilize the larynx

23. True/False   The extrinsic laryngeal muscles do not affect voice production.

24. For each extrinsic muscle, identify whether the muscle acts as a laryngeal depressor or elevator or both.

    Sternohyoid   _____

    Stylohyoid   _____

    Geniohyoid   _____

    Omohyoid   _____

    Thyrohyoid   _____

    Diagastric   _____

    Sternothyroid   _____

    Mylohyoid   _____

25. The thyrovocalis and thyromuscularis together comprise the _____ muscle.

26. True/False   The thryovocalis muscle is the medial portion of the thyroarytenoid and the thyrovocalis is the lateral portion of the thyroarytenoid.

27. Another term for the superficial layer of lamina propria is _____.

28. The layers of the vocal folds, from superficial to deep, become (choose one term) [more/less] stiff.

29. Match the histologic layer of the lamina propria of the vocal folds with the description of its composition.

Histologic layer	**Composition**
Superficial	Cellular matrix composed of lymphatics for drainage
Intermediate	Tightly packed collagen fibers
Deep	Disorganized and loosely arranged elastin fibers
	Densely distributed, organized elastin fibers
	Mixture of muscle and collagen fibers

30. True/False   The *mucoserous blanket* and the *epithelium* are synonymous terms to describe the covering of the vocal folds.

31. The epithelium is attached to the superficial layer of lamina propria by the _____.

32. In the body cover mechanical model of the vocal folds, the body consists of the
    A. Epithelium and the superficial and intermediate layers of the vocal folds
    B. Epithelium and the superficial layer of the vocal folds
    C. Superficial and intermediate layers of the vocal folds
    D. All of the layers except for the muscle

33. In the three-layer mechanical model of the vocal folds, the vocal ligament consists of the
    A. Superficial, intermedia, and deep layers of the lamina propria
    B. Intermedia and deep layers of the lamina propria
    C. The deep layer of the lamina propria
    D. The deep layer of the lamina propria and the muscle

34. The cricothyroid joint
    A. Allows the cricoid cartilage to rock forward and downward to achieve vocal fold elongation
    B. Allows the cricoid cartilage to rock forward and downward to achieve vocal fold shortening
    C. Allows the thyroid cartilage to rock forward and downward to achieve vocal fold elongation
    D. Allows the thyroid cartilage to rock forward and downward to achieve vocal fold shortening

35. The cricothyroid joint results in cartilage movement upon contraction of the _____ muscle.

36. The abduction and adduction of the vocal folds is achieved by movement of the
    A. Cricothyroid joints
    B. Cricoarytenoid joints
    C. Both the cricothyroid and the cricoarytenoid joints
    D. Thyroid cartilage forward and downward

37. The movement of the arytenoid cartilages is achieved through contraction of the muscles attached to the
    A. Muscular and vocal processes
    B. Vocal processes
    C. Muscular processes
    D. Apexes

38. The movement of the cricoarytenoid joints is
    A. Primarily rocking
    B. Primarily sliding
    C. Primarily rotation
    D. Primarily rotation and rocking

5.3 Neural Control of Phonation (p. 142)

39. Most of the neurological control to the larynx originates on the (select one term) [same/opposite] side of the brain.

40. All of the intrinsic laryngeal muscles receive innervation from cranial nerve
    A. XII vagus
    B. X vagus
    C. XII hypoglossal
    D. X hypoglossal

41. The cricothyroid muscle is innervated by the _____ branch of the _____ laryngeal nerve.

42. All intrinsic laryngeal muscles except for the cricothyroid muscle are innervated by the
    A. External branch of the superior laryngeal nerve
    B. Internal branch of the superior laryngeal nerve
    C. External branch of the recurrent laryngeal nerve
    D. Recurrent laryngeal nerve

43. The right thyroarytenoid muscle is innervated by the
    A. Right inferior laryngeal branch of the recurrent laryngeal nerve
    B. Left inferior laryngeal branch of the recurrent laryngeal nerve
    C. Right inferior laryngeal branch of the superior laryngeal nerve
    C. Left inferior laryngeal branch of the superior laryngeal nerve

44. All of the extrinsic laryngeal muscles are innervated by
    A. CN X
    B. CN XII
    C. A combination of CN V, CN VII, CN X, and CN XII
    D. A combination of CN V, CN VII, and CN XII

5.4 Theories of Voice Production (p. 145)

45. The Bernoulli effect tells us that
   A. The rate of airflow through the vocal tract will slow down through an area of constriction.
   B. The air pressure will decrease as the air flows through the vocal tract in an area of constriction.
   C. The air pressure will increase as the air flows through the vocal tract in an area of constriction.
   D. The flow of air through the vocal tract can be slow through some areas of the vocal tract and fast through other areas.

46. The neurochronaxic theory of voice production
   A. Is a competing theory of the myoelastic theory, which is still popular today
   B. Is physiologically possible but does not account for how we make our voice louder
   C. Specifies that each cycle of vocal fold vibration is achieved by a neural pulse
   D. Is consistent with the organization of the fibers of the vocal fold muscles

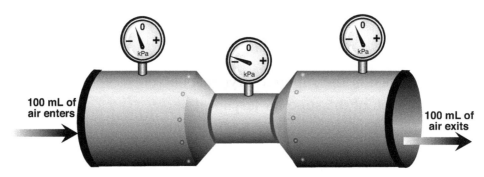

Figure 5–1

47. Figure 5–1 describes the [Bernoulli/Venturi] effect.

48. Vocal fold vibration during phonation is explained by what theory of voice production? _____.

49. The Bernoulli effect by itself [can/cannot] sustain vocal fold vibration.

50. The self-oscillation of the vocal folds during phonation is considered a [passive/active] event.

51. A larynx that has been removed from a human cadaver for purposes of research is called a/an _____ larynx.

52. True/False   The myoelastic-aerodynamic theory of voice production describes passive vibration of the vocal folds when adducted into the airstream.

53. True/False   The Bernoulli effect is the primary means by which the vocal folds are adducted into the airstream during phonation.

54. The Venturi effect is a critical aerodynamic phenomenon that contributes to vocal fold vibration.

5.5 Biomechanics of Vocal Fold Vibration (p. 150)

55. During vocal fold oscillation, the vocal folds are pushed apart by the
    A. Relaxation of the laryngeal muscles
    B. Buildup of lung pressure
    C. Inferior border of the vocal folds pushing the vocal folds apart
    D. Convergent shape of the glottis

56. During the opening phase of vocal fold oscillation, the upper border of the vocal folds
    A. Separates before the lower border
    B. Separates after the lower border
    C. Separates at the same time as the lower border
    D. Creates a convergent shape to the glottis

57. During vocal fold vibration, the air pressure below the vocal folds
    A. Must be greater than the air pressure above the vocal folds
    B. Must be lesser than the air pressure above the vocal folds
    C. Must be equal to the air pressure above the vocal folds
    D. Is not directly related to the air pressure above the vocal folds

58. During vocal fold vibration, the arytenoid cartilages
    A. Maintain adduction of the vocal folds
    B. Move continually to rotate the vocal folds open and closed for each cycle of vibration
    C. Maintain abduction of the vocal folds
    D. Do not have a direct role in vocal fold vibration

59. During vocal fold vibration, the restorative forces of the vocal fold tissues
    A. Help to return the vocal folds to their midline position
    B. Help to extend the vocal folds laterally away from midline
    C. Do not play an important role
    D. Are involved in bringing damaged vocal folds back to a healthy state

60. The term *vertical phasing* or *out-of-phase* movement describes
    A. Abnormal mucosal wave vibration
    B. The relationship of the supraglottal and subglottal vocal tract pressures
    C. The difference in the directional movement of the right and left vocal fold during oscillation
    D. The difference in directional movement of the upper and lower borders of the vocal folds during oscillation

61. The *mucosal wave* is the term used to refer to
    A. Vocal fold oscillation
    B. The upward and downward movement of the vocal folds
    C. An additional movement of the vocal fold tissues during oscillation
    D. Abnormal vocal fold oscillation

62. The anterior-posterior phase difference describes the
    A. Zipper-like opening and closing of the vocal folds
    B. Uniform opening and closing of the vocal folds as one unit
    C. Vertical phase difference of vocal fold vibration
    D. Opening and closing of the vocal folds from the midpoint outward anteriorly and posteriorly

63. Glottal volume velocity is best described as
    A. A graphical display of the air as it flows through the glottis during vocal fold opening and closing
    B. The amount of air that is low subglottally during glottal opening
    C. The volume of air flowing through the glottis as a function of time during vocal fold oscillation
    D. The type of glottal attack during phonation

64. Laryngeal airway resistance

    A. Is the same as glottal resistance

    B. Is a measure of the amount of resistance of the airflow to the vocal folds

    C. Is the ratio of the lung pressure to the supraglottal pressure

    D. Is measured in cm of H_2O.

65. Phonation threshold pressure

    A. Is a constant that does not vary within each individual

    B. Is measured in liters per second

    C. Is the lowest lung pressure required to sustain phonation

    D. Is the lower lung pressure required to initiate phonation

66. Which order of type of phonation onset corresponds to vocal fold adduction that is simultaneous with onset of airflow, after onset of airflow, and before onset of airflow?

    A. Glottal attack, breathy, gentle

    B. Glottal attack, gentle, breathy

    C. Gentle, breathy, glottal attack

    D. Breathy, gentle glottal attack

67. Match the name of the phonation onset on the left with the correct description on the right. Descriptions may be used more than once or not at all.

    _____ Gentle onset

    _____ Breathy onset

    _____ Hard onset

    1. Vocal folds are firmly approximated prior to initiation phonation.

    2. Vocal folds approximate at the same time as exhalation is initiated.

    3. Vocal folds do not approximate during exhalation.

    4. Vocal folds approximate after exhalation is initiated.

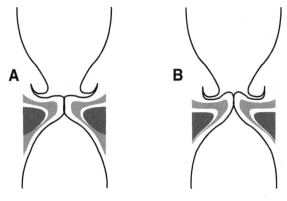

Figure 5–2

68. In the two images of the vocal folds in Figure 5–2, the opening phase is represented by letter _____.

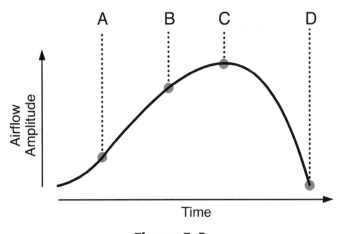

Figure 5–3

69. In the waveform in Figure 5–3, glottal closure is represented by the letter _____.

70. The beginning portion of the phonatory cycle in which the vocal folds approximate is called the _____ phase.

71. During vocal fold vibration, the arytenoid cartilages [do/do not] abduct and adduct the vocal folds.

72. The biomechanical force that contributes to the upward movement of the vocal fold tissue during mucosal wave movement is the [shear/collisional] force.

73. The force that helps the vocal folds move laterally away from midline during phonation is [momentum/elastic restorative force].

74. The mucosal wave describes the [vertical out-of-phase/anterior-posterior] movement of the vocal folds during vibration.

75. During phonation, glottal closure results in [rarefaction/compression] of the air molecules in the supraglottal vocal tract.

76. The glottal volume velocity is the volume of air flowing through the glottis as a function of [air pressure change/time].

77. The glottal resistance is the amount of resistance of the [vocal folds/glottis] to the airflow.

78. The lowest level of lung pressure necessary for phonation is called the _____.

79. True/False   A divergent-shaped glottis occurs as the vocal folds are closing during the vibratory cycle.

80. True/False   Viscoelasticity includes both properties of elasticity and stiffness.

81. The mucosal wave is the out-of-phase movement by which the upper margin of the vocal folds opens and closes before the lower margin.

82. A pressure difference between the sub- and supraglottis must be present in order for vocal fold vibration to occur.

83. True/False   Sound energy cannot travel downward into the trachea during vocal fold vibration because the airflow is moving from the trachea upward into the vocal tract.

84. True/False   Laryngeal airway resistance is an average of the resistance of the vocal folds to the airflow across multiple openings and closing of the vocal folds during phonation.

85. True/False   The amount of lung pressure required to initiation vocal fold vibration is generally the same as the amount of lung pressure required to sustain the vibration for 5 seconds.

86. True/False   Vocal rise time varies as a function of type of phonation onset.

5.6 Biomechanical Stress-Strain Properties of Vocal Fold Tissues (p. 160)

87. Biomechanical properties of the vocal folds include
    A. Stress, which is the force per unit area, and strain, which is the force acting on the tissue when it is stretched
    B. Stress, which is the force acting on the tissue when it is stretched, and strain, which is the force per unit area
    C. Stress, the pressure exerted parallel to the tissue, and strain, the force exerted perpendicular to the tissue
    D. Stress, strain, and linearity

88. The stress-strain curve describes
    A. The relationship of the biomechanical forces acting on the vocal folds as they actively stretch themselves beyond resting length
    B. The relationship of the biomechanical forces acting on the vocal folds as they are passively stretched beyond resting length
    C. The relationship of the biomechanical forces acting on the vocal folds as they vibrate
    D. The relationship of the biomechanical forces acting on the vocal folds as they abduct and adduct

89. Stress is a measure of force per _____.

90. Strain is the force acting upon the vocal folds when they are _____.

91. True/False   Change in vocal fold stress as a function of strain is constant across all levels of vocal fold stretch.

5.7 Physiology of Phonatory Control (p. 162)

92. Fundamental frequency is controlled by
    A. The mass per unit length and stiffness of the vocal folds
    B. The overall length of the vocal folds
    C. The cricothyroid muscle but not the thyroarytenoid muscle
    D. The thyroarytenoid muscle but not the cricothyroid muscle

93. Average fundamental frequency during reading aloud has been measured at approximately
    A. 215 Hz for women and 315 Hz for men
    B. 100 Hz for women and 50 Hz for men
    C. 215 Hz for women and 115 Hz for men
    D. 250 Hz for women and 50 Hz for men

94. Two factors that contribute to the increased fundamental frequency in soft- or high-pitched phonation are
    A. Decreased stiffness of the vocal fold cover and decreased mass per unit length
    B. Increased stiffness of the vocal fold cover and increased mass per unit length
    C. Decreased stiffness of the vocal fold cover and increased mass per unit length
    D. Increased stiffness of the vocal fold cover and decreased mass per unit length

95. Evidence from electromyographic research shows that control of fundamental frequency in conversational speech [does/does not] involve the extrinsic laryngeal muscles.

96. The major regulator of intensity is
    A. Increased vocal fold stiffness
    B. Increased rate of airflow
    C. Increased lung pressure
    D. Increased mass per unit length of the vocal folds

97. On average, sound pressure level (SPL) is proportional to
    A. The lung pressure
    B. The square of the lung pressure
    C. The airflow × the lung pressure
    D. The ratio of airflow to lung pressure

98. Average conversational-level moderate intensity is approximately
    A. 50 dB SPL
    B. 60 dB SPL
    C. 70 dB SPL
    D. 80 dB SPL

99. Three features of vocal fold closure that are important in the regulation of intensity are

   A. Duration, speed, and degree

   B. Duration, degree, and firmness

   C. Degree, contraction of the thyroarytenoid muscles bilaterally, and lung pressure

   D. Duration, degree, and lung pressure

100. The Lombard effect tells us that

   A. Greater lung pressure is required to achieve a given vocal intensity when speaking within noise compared to quiet.

   B. Lesser lung pressure is required to achieve a given vocal intensity when speaking within noise compared to quiet.

   C. People tend to decrease their vocal intensity when speaking within noise.

   D. People tend to increase their vocal intensity when speaking within noise.

101. Research suggests that auditory feedback

   A. Is an important component of overall sensory feedback that helps us control both fundamental frequency and intensity

   B. Is the only type of sensory feedback that helps us control both fundamental frequency and intensity

   C. Is not an important component of overall sensory feedback in the control of both fundamental frequency and intensity

   D. Is an important component of overall sensory feedback in the control of fundamental frequency but not intensity

102. Match the name of the mechanical stress on the left with the phonatory event described on the right.

   _____ Tensile

   _____ Contractile

   _____ Impact

   _____ Inertial

   _____ Aerodynamic

   _____ Shear

   1. Air pressure within the glottis during the open phase of phonation

   2. Collision of the vocal folds at midline

   3. Longitudinal force applied in an anterior-to-posterior direction

   4. Force applied parallel to the surface of the vocal folds

   5. Acceleration and deceleration of the vocal folds

   6. Active stress arising from activation of the thyroarytenoid muscles

103. The two major properties of the vocal folds that govern fundamental frequency are mass per unit length and _____.

104. Increased fundamental frequency is achieved by elongating the vocal folds, which [decreases/increases] their stiffness and [decreases/increases] their mass per unit length.

105. Increased lung pressure may [increase/decrease] fundamental frequency.

106. The major regulator of intensity is _____.

107. Increased vocal fold stiffness requires [increased/decreased] lung pressure for phonation.

108. Incomplete glottal closure during phonation can [increase/decrease] vocal intensity.

109. The duration of glottal closure is [increased/decreased] for greater intensity.

110. The tendency for a speaker to increase their vocal intensity when speaking in a noisy environment is referred to as the _____ effect.

111. True/False   The relationship between length and frequency is the same for vocal folds as it is for strings of musical instruments.

112. True/False   An adult with an average speaking fundamental frequency of 105 Hz would most likely be male.

113. True/False   Vocal fold stiffness is a critical variable in control of fundamental frequency.

114. True/False   Vocal fold stiffness is the major regulator of intensity of the voice.

115. True/False   In the lower frequencies typically used for conversational speech, a doubling of lung pressure will result in an increase in intensity of approximately 5 dB.

116. True/False   The physiologic range of vocal intensity for both men and women is approximately 50 to 100 dB SPL.

117. True/False   Duration of glottal closure is greater at higher intensities than at lower intensities.

118. True/False   Amplitude of mucosal wave vibration is greater at higher fundamental frequencies than at lower fundamental frequencies.

119. True/False   Shear stress and collision stress are both forces applied perpendicular to the vocal fold tissue during phonation.

5.8 Voice Quality (p. 174)

120. Which statement about voice quality is accurate?
    A. It is a perceptual phenomenon that can be fully described by the characteristics of the acoustic signal.
    B. It is a perceptual phenomenon that is only partially related to the acoustic signal.
    C. It is defined by four major descriptors.
    D. Is synonymous with mode of vibration.

121. Rough, harsh, breathy, and nasal are all descriptors of [voice quality/vocal acoustics].

122. True/False   Breathy vocal fold is associated with incomplete glottal closure during phonation.

Conceptual Integration

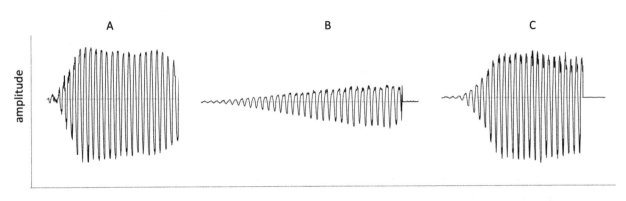

Figure 5–4

1. Three waveforms are shown in Figure 5–4. Each waveform is approximately 0.14 seconds in duration. Match the letter associated with each waveform with the type of vocal onset. Onsets may be used more than once or not at all.

Waveform letter	**Vocal onset type**
A	Breathy onset
B	Hard onset
C	Vibratory onset
	Soft onset
	Voiced onset

2. How does the valving action of the larynx differ among the three functions served by the larynx?

3. The myoeleastic aerodynamic theory of voice production tells us that
   A. Vocal fold vibration occurs passively due to the interaction of the aerodynamics and the biomechanical properties of the vocal fold tissues.
   B. Vocal fold vibration is an active process involving the interaction of the aerodynamics and the biomechanical properties of the vocal fold tissues and sequential contraction of muscles.
   C. The Bernoulli effect is the most important component of the aerodynamic contribution of vocal fold vibration.
   D. The Venturi effect is a fundamental principle governing voice production.

4. The prephonatory phase of vocal fold vibration
   A. Always involves a completely closed glottis
   B. Is when the vocal folds are approximated
   C. Allows for release of the airflow from the subglottis to the supraglottis
   D. Is an abductory movement

5. During vocal fold vibration, momentum
   A. Must be controlled with a muscular "braking action" in order to maintain stable oscillation
   B. Does not play an important role
   C. Helps the vocal folds stretch laterally away from the midline resting position
   D. Helps the vocal folds snap back toward midline after being stretched laterally

6. The transglottal pressure is often referred to as the driving pressure because
   A. The pressure within the glottis must be lower than the pressure below and above the vocal folds.
   B. Vocal fold vibration can only occur if the transglottal pressure is equal.
   C. It helps to push the vocal folds apart and open the glottis.
   D. There must be a transglottal pressure drop in order for vocal fold vibration to occur.

7. Which statement best describes the events of glottal closure during vocal fold vibration?
   A. The upward trajectory of the air mass above the vocal folds continues at the moment of vocal fold closure.
   B. The upward trajectory of the air mass above the vocal folds is halted at the moment of vocal fold closure and pulled backward toward the closed glottis.
   C. Acoustic excitation of the air molecules in the vocal tract occurs just before the vocal folds close.
   D. Acoustic excitation of the air molecules in the vocal tract occurs just after the vocal folds reopen.

8. Phonation threshold pressure varies [indirectly/directly] with vocal fold thickness, it varies [indirectly/directly] with vocal fold viscosity, and it varies [indirectly/directly] with fundamental frequency.

9. The driving pressure of vocal fold vibration refers to the [transglottal pressure/amount of lung pressure] necessary to sustain phonation.

10. Biomechanical properties of the vocal folds include
    A. Stress, which is the force per unit area, and strain, which is the force acting on the tissue when it is stretched
    B. Stress, which is the force acting on the tissue when it is stretched, and strain, which is the force per unit area
    C. Stress, the pressure exerted parallel to the tissue, and strain, the force exerted perpendicular to the tissue
    D. Stress, strain, and linearity

11. The stress-strain curve is nonlinear, in that

    A. The relationship between force and elongation is not predictable for either the vocal fold cover or the thyroarytenoid muscle.

    B. The relationship between force and elongation is predictable for the vocal fold cover and the thyroarytenoid muscle.

    C. The relationship between force and elongation is like a straight line for tissue stretch and relaxation, and for the vocal fold cover and the thyroarytenoid muscle.

    D. The relationship between force and elongation is different for tissue stretch and relaxation, and for the vocal fold cover and the thyroarytenoid muscle.

12. The reason that increased lung pressure can result in an increase in fundamental frequency is because

    A. Increased lung pressure results in greater dynamic elongation of the vocal folds away from midline, resulting in greater elastic recoil force, and therefore, faster movement of the vocal folds in returning to midline.

    B. Increased lung pressure results in faster airflow through the open glottis.

    C. High fundamental frequency requires greater lung pressure than low fundamental frequency.

    D. Increased lung pressure decreases the mass per unit length and stiffness of the vocal folds, resulting in increased fundamental frequency.

13. Why is the mean f_0 of men's voices, on average, significantly lower than the mean f_0 of women's voices?

14. Contraction of the cricothyroid muscle results in elongation of the vocal folds. If larger vocal folds generally predict lower f_0, why does contraction of the cricothyroid muscle result in increased f_0 for both men and women?

15. Describe the positioning of the arytenoid cartilages during the prephonatory and phonatory phases of voice production.

16. The vocal folds are a variable impediment to the airflow. Order the list of laryngeal maneuvers below from least to greatest laryngeal airway resistance as a function of glottal opening (1 = least and 4 = most resistance).

    Inhalation during quiet tidal breathing _____

    Lifting a heavy object _____

    Breathy phonation _____

    Loud speech _____

17. Which of the following statements is true about the relationship between vocal fold stiffness and mass per unit length?

    A. When the longitudinal tension of the vocal folds is increased, it results in a decrease in mass per unit length and an increase in stiffness.

    B. When the longitudinal tension of the vocal folds is increased, it results in a decrease in mass per unit length and decrease in stiffness.

    C. A person with longer vocal folds will have decreased mass per unit length and decreased stiffness compared to someone with shorter vocal folds.

    D. A person with longer vocal folds will have increased mass per unit length and increased stiffness compared to someone with shorter vocal folds.

18. The vertical phase difference during mucosal wave vibration

    A. Is caused by a difference in the rate of contraction of the thyrovocalis and thyromuscularis components that make up the thyroarytenoid muscle

    B. Is caused by the change from a convergent- to a divergent-shaped glottis during each cycle of vibration

    C. Is caused by the interaction of the aerodynamic forces and the biomechanical characteristics of the vocal folds

    D. Occurs during loud phonation but is largely absent during soft phonation

19. Why is a greater phonation threshold pressure necessary to initiate phonation than to maintain phonation? (Hint: consider momentum and inertia)

20. Why does increased stiffness of the vocal folds usually result in increased f_0?

21. Vocal fold vibration is often likened to vibration of the string of a musical instrument, in that a longer string will generally produce a lower rate of vibration, and a stiffer string will generally produce a higher rate of vibration. What are the major differences between vocal fold vibration and the vibration of the string of a musical instrument?

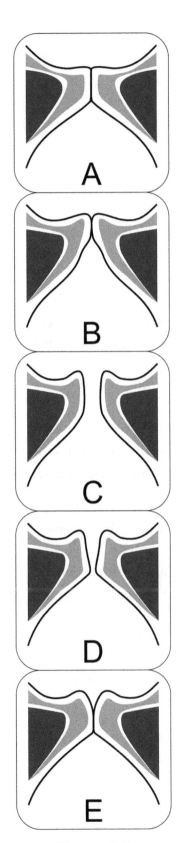

Figure 5-5

22. Figure 5–5 shows a cross section of the vocal folds from a frontal plane during one complete cycle of phonation. Which of the panels in the figure shows the initiation of the opening phase of phonation?

    A. Panel A

    B. Panel B

    C. Panel D

    D. Panel E

23. In Figure 5–5, which panel shows the initiation of the closing phase of phonation?

    A. Panel A

    B. Panel B

    C. Panel D

    D. Panel E

24. In Figure 5–5, what event is occurring in panel C?

    A. Subglottal air pressure is at a maximum.

    B. Rapid inhalation is occurring.

    C. A release of subglottal pressure results in outward airflow.

    D. Airflow has stopped due to the cessation of lateral movement of the vocal folds.

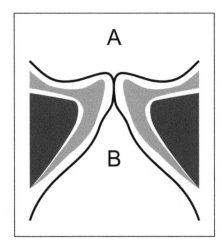

Figure 5–6

25. Figure 5–6 shows a cross section of the vocal folds from a frontal plane. If we say that the air pressure in area A is less than in area B, what conclusion can you make about what is occurring?

    A. The vocal folds are being blown open, beginning the opening phase of phonation.

    B. The vocal folds have closed at the end of the closing phase of phonation.

    C. The vocal folds are in the process of opening in order to allow for inhalation.

    D. The vocal folds are being pulled upward due to the Bernoulli effect occurring in area A.

26. How does Figure 5–6 show evidence of vertical phase difference (the mucosal wave) occurring?

    A. The vocal folds are closing from their superior to their inferior margins.

    B. The vocal folds are being pushed apart due to higher air pressure in area B as compared to area A.

    C. The vocal folds are moving laterally but also superiorly, as there is an upheaval of the vocal fold cover toward area A.

    D. The Bernoulli effect has produced high pressure in area B, which will cause the vocal folds to move inferiorly.

27. Considering what is shown occurring in Figure 5–6, what will occur next?

    A. The inferior margins of the vocal folds will close to complete the closed phase of phonation.

    B. The superior margins of the vocal folds will reverse and move inferiorly into area B.

    C. The superior margins of the vocal folds will begin to open, allowing air to flow through from area B to area A.

    D. The inferior margins of the vocal folds will open further but the superior margins will remain at the same position. This will result in positive air pressure in area A and negative air pressure in area B.

28. During the phase of phonation shown in Figure 5–6, what biomechanical force is being applied to the vocal folds?

    A. Impact stress

    B. Shear stress

    C. Tensile stress

    D. No biomechanical forces are being applied to the vocal folds in Figure 5–6.

29. Contracting the cricothyroid muscle during phonation will increase this biomechanical force

    A. Aerodynamic stress

    B. Shear stress

    C. Tensile stress

    D. Contraction of the cricothyroid muscle will not increase any biomechanical force.

Figure 5–7

30. Figure 5–7 shows a tube that represents the airway and a cross section of the vocal folds from a frontal plane. Consider that the airflow shown is in an exhalation direction through area A followed by areas B and C. What anatomical structure is represented by area A?

    A. The pharynx

    B. The glottis

    C. The trachea

    D. The lips

31. In Figure 5–7, the vocal folds are shown to be in a closing position. If area B represents the glottis, what area will have the lowest air pressure?

    A. Area A

    B. Area B

    C. Area C

    D. The pressure will be the same in all three areas.

32. In Figure 5–7, what can you say about the air pressure in each area of the tube?

    A. The air pressure in area B will be greater than in area C.

    B. The air pressure in area A will be lower than in area B.

    C. The air pressure in area A will be the same as in area C.

    D. There is no air pressure in area A or C, only airflow.

33. In Figure 5–7, which area will have the greatest velocity of air molecules?

    A. Area A

    B. Area B

    C. Area C

    D. The air velocity will be the same through all three areas.

34. Considering Figure 5–7, what can you conclude about airflow?

    A. The same amount of air molecules will pass through areas A, B, and C every second.

    B. A greater number of air molecules will pass through area A than areas B and C every second.

    C. A greater number of air molecules will pass through area B than areas A and C every second.

    D. Air molecules will flow through areas A and C while bypassing area B.

35. Considering Figure 5–7, what can you conclude about vocal fold movement?

    A. The air pressure in area B will exert an outward (pushing) force on the vocal folds causing them to move laterally.

    B. The air pressure in area B will exert an inward (pulling) force on the vocal folds, causing them to move medially.

    C. The air pressure in area A will exert an inward (pulling) force on the vocal folds, causing them to move medially.

    D. The air pressure in area C will exert an outward (pushing) force on the vocal folds, causing them to move downward.

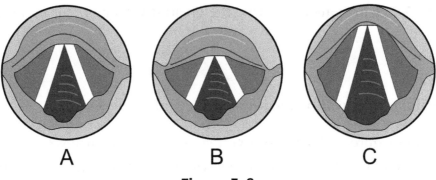

Figure 5–8

36. Figure 5–8 shows a superior view of larynges from three people: an adult male, an adult female, and a child. Which larynx is likely from the adult male?

    A. Larynx A

    B. Larynx B

    C. Larynx C

    D. There is no way to determine which larynx belongs to which person.

37. In Figure 5–8, what event is likely occurring for each of the larynges shown?

    A. Inspiration

    B. Phonation of an unvoiced consonant

    C. Phonation of a voiced consonant

    D. Coughing

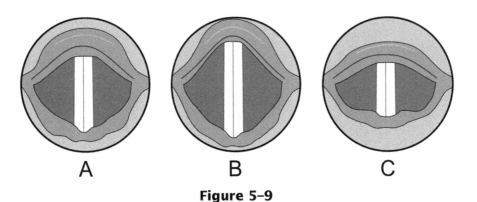

Figure 5–9

38. Figure 5–9 shows adjustments to the length of the vocal folds from a single person as they prepare to change their voice pitch. Which image shows the individual producing the highest fundamental frequency?

    A. Image A

    B. Image B

    C. Image C

    D. There's no way to tell what the relative fundamental frequency would be from these images.

39. Considering Figure 5–9 and the stress-strain (force-elongation) curve from the text, how can you explain the relationship between changing vocal fold length and the resulting change in voice fundamental frequency?

    A. Shortening the vocal folds will reduce the length of the vocal folds that vibrates, increasing the fundamental frequency.

    B. Shortening the vocal folds will reduce their total mass, lowering the frequency of vibration.

    C. Lengthening the vocal folds will increase the tension of the vocal folds, increasing the frequency of vibration.

    D. There is no relationship between vocal fold length changes and changes to vocal fundamental frequency.

40. In Figure 5–9, image B is associated with the greatest amount of what biomechanical force as compared to images A and C?

    A. Impact stress

    B. Shear stress

    C. Tensile stress

    D. Aerodynamic stress

41. Increasing your vocal fundamental frequency will

    A. Increase the longitudinal stress on the vocal folds

    B. Increase the amount of the body of the vocal folds in vibration

    C. Decrease the length of the vocal folds due to cricothyroid muscle contraction

    D. Require lower levels of subglottal pressure

42. In order to initiate phonation, what condition(s) must be present?

    A. The subglottal air pressure must be greater than supraglottal air pressure.

    B. The subglottal and supraglottal air pressures must be equal.

    C. The vocal folds must be in an abducted state in order to build subglottal pressure.

    D. The pressure in the glottis must be lower than supraglottal pressure.

43. If there were no Bernoulli effect, what aspect of phonation would be affected?
    A. The inferior margins of the vocal folds would not close as rapidly during each cycle of phonation.
    B. The superior margins of the vocal folds would not open during each cycle of phonation.
    C. The inferior margins of the vocal folds would not open during each cycle of phonation.
    D. The body of the vocal folds would not vibrate during phonation.

44. Why do we typically take a deeper breath when we plan on producing speech at an increased vocal intensity?
    A. A deeper breath will produce simultaneous (easy) vocal onset.
    B. A deeper breath will result in greater elastic recoil forces and greater relaxation pressure in the lungs.
    C. A deeper breath will result in lower impact stress on the vocal folds.
    D. A deeper breath will result in greater laryngeal airway resistance.

45. True/False   Producing a high vocal intensity will result in greater amount of translaryngeal airflow.

46. True/False   To produce a greater vocal intensity, we must generate greater subglottal air pressure.

47. Incomplete glottal closure during each cycle of phonation will be associated with
    A. Increased glottal resistance
    B. Glottal volume velocity that does not reach zero during the closed phase
    C. Low fundamental frequency
    D. High levels of impact stress

48. Which of the following conditions will require the greatest amount of subglottal air pressure to produce?
    A. Phonation at a high fundamental frequency and low vocal intensity
    B. Phonation at a high fundamental frequency and high vocal intensity
    C. Phonation at a low fundamental frequency and high vocal intensity
    D. Phonation at a low fundamental frequency and low vocal intensity

49. When speaking in a noisy environment, what is likely to occur?
    A. You will produce an increase in subglottal pressure.
    B. You will produce a decrease in vocal fold longitudinal tension.
    C. You will produce a decrease in airflow.
    D. You will produce a large increase in vocal fundamental frequency.

50. As you are phonating, you produce a sudden increase in subglottal pressure. What events will occur in relation to your increased subglottal pressure?

    A. Your vocal intensity will increase and your fundamental frequency will decrease.

    B. Your fundamental frequency will increase and your vocal folds will experience incomplete closure.

    C. Your vocal intensity will increase and your fundamental frequency will increase.

    D. Your vocal intensity will decrease and your vocal folds will experience incomplete closure.

51. A singer produces a crescendo: a smooth increase in vocal intensity. What will occur as their fundamental frequency rises?

    A. Less and less of the vocal fold body will vibrate.

    B. Subglottal pressure will decrease.

    C. The longitudinal tension of the vocal folds will decrease.

    D. The vocal folds will become shorter.

52. True/False   Lengthening the vocal folds will cause a linearly proportional increase in vocal fold stress.

53. To result in the lowest level of biomechanical force applied to the vocal folds during phonation, you would need to produce

    A. A low fundamental frequency at a high intensity

    B. A high fundamental frequency at a low intensity

    C. High intensity and breathy phonation onset

    D. Low intensity and easy phonation onset

54. What event is most responsible for producing the sound wave generated by vocal fold vibration?

    A. The impact of the vocal folds during collision (impact) stress

    B. Continual airflow through the glottis

    C. Rapid closure of the glottis, yielding rapid cessation of airflow during each vibratory cycle

    D. Laminar airflow through the oral cavity

55. True/False   The Bernoulli effect explains the outward movement of the inferior margins of the vocal folds.

56. Low fundamental frequencies of phonation are associated with

    A. Greater longitudinal tension of the vocal folds

    B. Increased activity of cricothyroid and thyroarytenoid muscles

    C. Greater subglottal pressure as compared to higher fundamental frequencies

    D. Vibration of the vocal fold cover and body

TRY IT!

1. Place your fingers gently across your larynx. (Use your Adam's apple to help you locate the thyroid cartilage. It's probably a bit higher in your neck than you think.) Sustain a vowel sound and feel the vibration. Compare that sensation with the lack of vibration when you sustain a nonvoiced whispered vowel. Now sustain the voiced vowel again and glide up in pitch. Do you feel your larynx elevate? Start at a high pitch and now glide downward to the lowest pitch you can achieve. Do you feel your larynx move downward in your neck?

2. Although the larynx is fixed atop the trachea, it is suspended from the hyoid bone by numerous muscles and ligaments. Place your thumb and forefinger lightly on either side of your larynx, and gently move your larynx side to side. The movement is essential for healthy voice production. If you hear some crackling sounds—that's called crepitus and it's completely normal as well!

3. Read aloud a paragraph. Toward the end of each sentence, try to allow your pitch to drop very low as you relax your throat muscles and decrease your loudness. Are you able to drop into glottal fry phonation? How does it feel and sound compared to modal phonation?

4. Say a short command, such as "Come here!" Repeat the phrase but say it loudly and urgently. Was your pitch elevated when you said the phrase more loudly? The increased lung pressure required for loud phonation is usually accompanied by increased vocal fold stiffness to withstand the greater aerodynamic force, which in turn raises the f_o. Our natural tendency is to elevate our pitch as we get louder. (Singers must practice maintaining a target pitch while they change loudness levels so that they don't sing off key!)

5. Hum a tune (or just a sustained hum will do) and pinch your nose shut as you continue to hum. Are you able to continue to hum? Closing your lips to hum and pinching your nose closed will immediately stop the airflow that was passing through your larynx, resulting in cessation of phonation (in other words, no hum). You've just proven that your larynx requires airflow to maintain phonation!

6. Your lips can substitute as models of the vocal folds. If you play a brass instrument such as a trumpet or a tuba, you know that you must "buzz your lips" in order to produce sound in the instrument. We "buzz" our vocal folds in a similar way to playing a trumpet or a tuba. Close your lips with a small amount of pressure. Blow some air through your closed lips. If your lips are not too tightly closed or too loosely closed, they will go into oscillation due to the air pressure in your mouth and the airflow between them, resulting in the "buzz" sound. This is very similar to how the vocal folds vibrate as explained by the myoelastic-aerodynamic theory!

7. We know that the myoelastic-aerodynamic theory of phonation posits that airflow is required to produce phonation. If you've tried the previous two TRY IT! activities, you've proven this by observing that stopping airflow will stop phonation. However, it's common for people to think that the neurochronaxic theory of phonation is valid, as it seems logical that laryngeal adductor and abductor muscles could produce phonation by, well, adducting and abducting the vocal folds. Once again, consider your lips as models of the vocal folds. Instead of blowing air through them to get them to buzz, though, just try to produce the same buzz sound by opening and closing your lips as fast as you can. It's likely that you will only achieve a frequency of oscillation of about 2 to 3 Hz, which is far too low for us to hear! Perhaps the neurochronaxic theory doesn't explain vocal fold vibration after all!

Clinical Application

Clinical Case 2: Running Out of Breath

1. What is the relationship between lung pressure and phrase breath groups? Revisit Figures 4–14 and 4–15 in the textbook and relate Christine's speech breathing habits to the relaxation pressure curve.

2. Why would Christine demonstrate vocal fry and decreased intensity at phrase endings? (Hint: What is the relationship between lung pressure and vocal fold stiffness and vocal fry?)

3. Compare Clinical Case 1 from Chapter 4 with this clinical case. How do the inefficient speech breathing patterns compare?

Clinical Application: Disorders Related to Voice Production

1. What might be the job of someone who has been diagnosed with a phonotraumatic voice disorder? Why?

2. Why might a patient with damage to the right recurrent laryngeal nerve have difficulty making his voice loud?

3. How are breathiness and inability to make the voice loud related aerodynamically?

4. What are communicative activities of daily living, and why are they important for a speech-language pathologist to know about in treating a patient with a voice problem?

6

Phonation II: Measurement and Instrumentation Questions

Foundational Knowledge

6.1 Measurement of f_o and Intensity (p. 187)

1. Three categories of measurement of f_o and intensity of the voice for clinical and research purposes that reflect how the voice is used are

   A. Family/home, work, recreational

   B. Daily voice use, singing and shouting, unusual behaviors

   C. Habitual use, singing and shouting, voice quality

   D. Habitual use, maximum performance, degree of regularity

2. True/False   Mean speaking f_o can be influenced by linguistic and emotional factors.

3. Tasks that might be used to assess mean speaking f_o and intensity include

   A. Reading, sustained vowel phonation, and spontaneous speech

   B. Reading and spontaneous speech

   C. Reading and sustained vowel phonation

   D. Sustained vowel phonation and spontaneous speech

4. Information about the physiologic capabilities of the voice in regard to f_o and intensity can be obtained from _____ tasks.

5. The span of frequencies from lowest to highest frequency at which a person can phonate is referred to as the _____.

6. Most adults tend to use a (select one term from within each bracket) [wide/narrow] range of frequencies toward the [lower/higher] end of their frequency range on a habitual basis.

7. The most common mean speaking f_o ranges for men and women are

   A. 70 and 100 Hz for men and 170 and 200 Hz for women

   B. 100 and 200 Hz for men and 200 and 300 Hz for women

   C. 80 and 150 Hz for men and 150 and 250 Hz for women

   D. 80 and 150 Hz for women and 150 and 250 Hz for men

8. Short-term (cycle-to-cycle) nonvolitional f_o irregularity is referred to as _____.

9. Jitter may be measured from the following speech tasks

   A. Reading, sustained vowel phonation, and spontaneous speech

   B. Reading and spontaneous speech

   C. Reading and sustained vowel phonation

   D. Sustained vowel phonation

10. True/False   At least a low level of jitter is expected in everyone's voice.

11. Match the jitter measurement method on the left with the term on the right.

(Average cycle-to-cycle variability: average period) × 100

Average cycle-to-cycle variability: average frequency

Average cycle-to-cycle variability: average period

Average difference in periods between each three adjacent cycles/average period

Average difference in periods between each five adjacent cycles/average period

Pitch perturbation quotient

Jitter ratio

Relative average perturbation

Jitter percent

Jitter factor

12. True/False   Short-term cycle-to-cycle variability in the amplitude of vocal fold vibration is called shimmer.

13. A common measure of shimmer—shimmer in dB—is measured as
    A. The ratio of the amplitudes of two adjacent cycles averaged over the length of the voice sample
    B. The ratio of the amplitudes of two adjacent cycles averaged over the length of the voice sample × 100 (expressed as a percentage)
    C. The mean difference in adjacent cycles averaged over the length of the voice sample and divided by the range of intensity (from lowest to highest)
    D. The ratio of the amplitudes of 11 adjacent cycles

14. The graphical display of the relationship between f_o plotted on the x-axis and intensity plotted on the y-axis across the range of frequencies at which the person can phonate is called a _____.

15. The task used to elicit a voice range profile is
    A. Sustained vowel phonation
    B. Reading
    C. Spontaneous speech
    D. Sustained vowel phonation, reading, or spontaneous speech can be used but the task must be consistent across all frequencies for the individual being tested.

16. In the VRP, the upper contour represents the highest (select one term) [frequency/intensity] at which the individual can phonate for a given f_o.

17. The wider the area enclosed by the upper and lower contours within the VRP,

    A. The greater the f_o range

    B. The greater the intensity range

    C. The stronger the voice

    D. The more likely the VRP characterizes a male voice

6.2 Measurement of Phonatory Aerodynamics (p. 193)

18. An electronic sensor that transduces the mean airflow is called a _____.

19. True/False   Intensity and f_o can influence the mean airflow measurement during speech production.

20. Clinically, lung pressure can be measured

    A. Directly

    B. Indirectly

    C. Both directly and indirectly

    D. Neither directly nor indirectly

21. The conversion of aerodynamic to acoustic power at the level of the glottis is called _____, while the conversion of aerodynamic to acoustic power as the acoustic signal is radiated from the lips is called _____.

22. The s/z ratio is used to assess

    A. Vocal efficiency

    B. Vital capacity

    C. Phonatory glottal closure

    D. Laryngeal airway resistance

23. The theory supporting the use of the s/z ratio is that greater laryngeal resistance is required for the phoneme _____ than for the phoneme _____.

24. In regard to the s/z ratio, the value for normal phonation and for phonation with incomplete glottal closure should be

    A. 1, > 1, respectively

    B. 1, < 1, respectively

    C. 1 for both conditions

    D. 0, 1, respectively

25. Eliciting the longest duration of a sustained vowel at comfortable pitch and loudness is a measure of _____.

26. Typical average values for maximum sustained phonation from men and women with healthy voices ranges from approximately

    A. 10 to 15 seconds

    B. 18 to 25 seconds

    C. 20 to 30 seconds

    D. A minimum of 30 seconds

27. Men, in general, produce greater maximum sustained phonation than do women because of

    A. Larger vocal folds

    B. Louder voices

    C. Lower pitch

    D. Greater lung volume

28. Maximum sustained phonation is used to assess _____.

29. Phonation quotient is calculated by

    A. Vital capacity divided by maximum phonation time of /s/

    B. Vital capacity divided by maximum phonation time of a vowel

    C. Maximum phonation time of /s/ divided by maximum phonation time of a vowel

    D. Maximum phonation time of a vowel divided by maximum phonation time of /s/

6.3 Instrumentation for Exploring the Dynamics of the Vocal Folds (p. 199)

30. Stroboscopy uses a pulsing light to

    A. Simulate vocal fold movement at a rate slower than the actual fundamental frequency

    B. Simulate vocal fold movement at a rate faster than the actual fundamental frequency

    C. Show vocal fold movement at the actual fundamental frequency

    D. Show vocal fold movement based upon higher harmonic frequencies

31. To show the mucosal wave, stroboscopy illuminates the vocal folds
    A. At the same point in each vibratory cycle
    B. At slightly different points of vibratory cycle
    C. At points alternating the open and closed phase of each vibratory cycle
    D. Only at the closed portion of each vibratory cycle

32. One disadvantage of stroboscopy is that the visual image
    A. Is not accompanied by the sound of the voice
    B. Is harder to use to visualize women's vocal folds than those of men
    C. Becomes jittery in cases of significant dysphonia
    D. Is very difficult to interpret

33. Videokymography
    A. Scans the entire length of the image of the vocal folds at a very rapid rate
    B. Scans only a single line of the images, typically at its widest point of vibratory amplitude
    C. Cannot show the true rate of vibration, because the vocal folds move too quickly
    D. Can stand on its own as a diagnostic instrument, without the need for other types of visualization of the vocal folds

34. Photoglottography
    A. Is a means of measuring airflow during phonation by taking sequential pictures of the glottis
    B. Is a popular clinical tool for assessing voice production because of the ready access to inexpensive instrumentation and packaged software for interpretation of the signal
    C. Is a noninvasive means of measuring sequential glottal opening during phonation
    D. Measures the amount of light passing through the glottis during each vibratory cycle

35. Electroglottography
    A. Produces a waveform that corresponds to the relative contact of the vocal folds during vibration
    B. Can be used to measure the degree to which the vocal folds close the glottis during each vibratory cycle
    C. Is noninvasive but does carry risk of exposure to a small amount of electric shock to the patient
    D. Can be used to diagnose the presence of benign (noncancerous) growths on the vocal folds, such as nodules

36. Match the name of the measure on the left with the appropriate ratio description of vocal fold movement on the right. Descriptions may be used more than once or not at all.

_____ Open quotient

_____ Speed quotient

_____ Contact quotient

1. Duration of opening phase/duration of closing phase

2. Duration of opening phase/duration of entire open phase

3. Duration of vocal fold contact/entire glottal cycle

4. Duration of open phase/entire duration of the glottal cycle

37. Match the phase of vibration on the left with the appropriate description on the right. Descriptions may be used more than once or not at all.

_____ Open

_____ Opening

_____ Closing

_____ Closed

1. Duration from peak opening until point of contact of inferior margin of vocal folds

2. Airflow through the glottis is gradually increasing

3. Air flows through the glottis

4. No air flows through the glottis

5. Duration from separation of upper margin of vocal folds until maximum glottal opening

38. The open, speed, and contact quotients, while helpful in an overall understanding of voice production, also have some disadvantages, one of which is

A. Knowledge of the phases of the vibratory cycle of a given individual is not relevant to clinical practice.

B. The same information can be gained from stroboscopy without the additional instrumentation necessary for calculation of these quotients.

C. The exact points on the waveform that correspond to vibratory events such as opening and closing are estimates only.

D. The ratios do not correspond to physiological phenomena of the vibrating vocal folds.

39. The analysis of vibratory movements of the vocal folds during phonation that provide waveforms corresponding to various aspects of vibratory behavior is called _____.

40. In stroboscopy, the flashing of the strobe light is synchronized to vocal fold vibration by means of a _____ or a _____.

41. The type of laryngeal imaging that allows for visualization of each cycle of vocal fold vibration is called _____.

42. Electroglottography is based upon the principle that tissue is a [good/poor] conductor of electrical current and air is a [good/poor] conductor of electrical current.

43. A sudden change from one state to another due to a continuously changing variable is called a _____ change.

44. True/False   Stroboscopy is based upon the continual illumination of the vocal folds during phonation.

45. True/False   In the case of moderate-to-severe dysphonia, jitter is present in the stroboscopic image.

46. True/False   Electroglottography is useful for analyzing the degree of glottal closure.

47. True/False   Open quotient, contact quotient, and speed quotient can be calculated from glottograms.

6.4 Vocal Registers (p. 210)

48. Match the name of the phase on the left with the approximate range of frequencies on the right. Descriptions may be used more than once or not at all.

    _____ Glottal fry   1. ~ 90–450 Hz in men, ~150–520 Hz in women

    _____ Modal   2. Below ~450 Hz in men and ~520 Hz in women

    _____ Falsetto   3. ~35–50 Hz in men and women

                              4. Above ~450 Hz in men and ~520 Hz in women

49. A voice register is a series of consecutive values of _____.

50. True/False   Pulse, model, and falsetto are vocal registers that can be used to analyze the voices of children and adults.

51. True/False   In vocal fry, the vocal folds are short and thick and have a prolonged closed phase.

52. True/False   Whisper is a type of vocal register.

Conceptual Integration

1. Why is measurement of jitter and shimmer from reading or spontaneous speech an invalid measure of cycle-to-cycle variability?

2. This measurement technique provides information about habitual use of the voice
   A. Measurement of the mean speaking fundamental frequency range
   B. Measurement of maximum phonation time
   C. The phonation quotient
   D. The maximum fundamental frequency range of phonation

3. This measurement technique provides information about the maximal performance of the voice
   A. Measurement of shimmer
   B. Measurement of jitter
   C. Voice range profile (VRP)
   D. Measurement of lung pressure for /p/

4. Which instrument is used to measure the contribution of the respiratory system to phonation?
   A. Microphone
   B. Stroboscopic equipment
   C. Electroglottograph
   D. Pneumotachograph

5. Which of the following vocal registers would likely show the most jitter?
   A. Vocal fry
   B. Modal register
   C. Falsetto register
   D. None of these vocal registers will have any jitter.

6. Which vocal register is likely to have the shortest closed quotient during phonation?
   A. Vocal fry
   B. Modal register
   C. Falsetto register
   D. The closed quotient will be the same for all of these vocal registers.

7. Which vocal register is produced with the lowest amount of longitudinal tension on the vocal folds?

   A. Vocal fry

   B. Modal register

   C. Falsetto register

   D. All of these vocal registers are produced with high levels of cricothyroid activity.

8. Which vocal register is associated with the lowest amount of lung (subglottal) pressure on average?

   A. Vocal fry

   B. Modal register

   C. Falsetto register

   D. Both vocal fry and modal register are typically produced with no lung (subglottal) pressure.

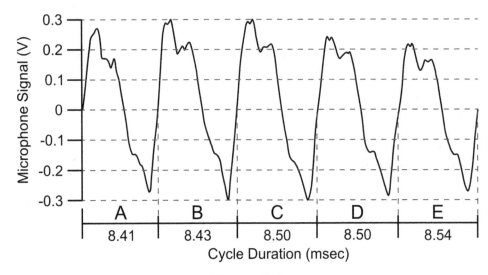

Figure 6–1

9. In Figure 6–1, which phonation cycles show no evidence of jitter?

   A. Cycles A and E

   B. Cycles B and C

   C. Cycles C and D

   D. Cycles D and E

10. In Figure 6–1, which phonation cycles show no evidence of shimmer?
    A. Cycles A and B
    B. Cycles B and C
    C. Cycles C and D
    D. Cycles D and E

11. What is the average fundamental frequency of the speaker shown by the waveform in Figure 6–1?
    A. Approximately 23.60 Hz
    B. Approximately 117.98 Hz
    C. Approximately 118.06 Hz
    D. The fundamental frequency cannot be calculated from the waveform shown.

12. What can you conclude about the speaker who produced the waveform in Figure 6–1?
    A. The speaker is likely a young child.
    B. The speaker is likely an adult female.
    C. The speaker is likely an adult male.
    D. Based on the waveform shown, no conclusions can be made regarding the speaker.

13. Considering how the waveform in Figure 6–1 changes over time, what can you conclude?
    A. On average, the speaker's voice is becoming lower-pitched and quieter.
    B. On average, the speaker's voice is becoming less regular in frequency over time.
    C. The speaker's voice is increasing in pitch but becoming quieter.
    D. The speaker's voice is increasing in pitch but becoming louder.

14. Why is the dynamic range of the VRP reduced at the upper and lower extremes and wider in the midfrequency range?

15. Both the upper and lower contours of the VRP tilt upward in the higher frequencies: That is, it is harder to phonate softly and easier to phonate loudly at the highest frequencies compared to the low- and midfrequency ranges. What is the explanation for this characteristic?

16. Why would one expect vocal efficiency to be reduced in a voice disorder such as an immobile vocal fold that results in a breathy voice?

17. True/False   The s/z ratio is a valid measure of vocal efficiency.

18. What are two major factors that contribute to the uncertain validity of the s/z ratio?

19. What factors can threaten the validity of the maximum phonation time measure?

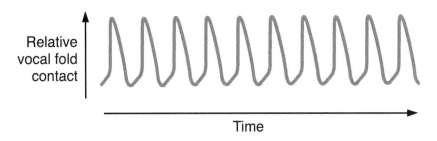

Figure 6–2

20. Figure 6–2 represents the glottographic signal of the relative contact of the vocal folds, with the lowest point of each cycle representing the least contact and the uppermost point of each cycle representing the most contact. Make a small mark on each cycle of vibration that could represent when the xenon strobe light flashes and then draw a dashed line (or use a colored pencil) to connect the flashes. What does your dashed line represent?

21. What is the relationship between periodicity of vocal fold vibration and validity of the stroboscopic image?

22. True/False   Fundamental frequency of phonation cannot be measured from the electroglottographic waveform.

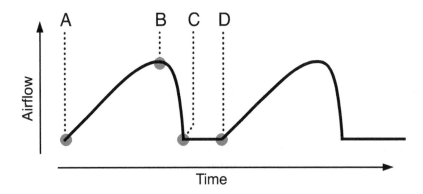

Figure 6–3

23. Figure 6–3 shows a waveform that represents airflow through the glottis during phonation. Calculate the estimates of open quotient, speed quotient, and contact quotient using the letters as reference points in the formula. For example, if you wanted to divide the time duration of one cycle in half, you could write (B-A)/2. Remember, your formulas represent rough estimates!

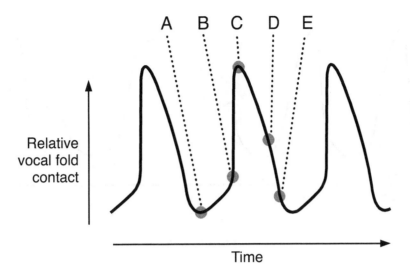

Figure 6–4

24. Figure 6–4 shows three cycles of the electroglottographic waveform during sustained vowel phonation. Match the letters on the waveform with the descriptions of vocal fold positions. Some positions may be used more than once or not at all.

Letter	Vocal Fold Position
A	Complete closure of the glottis
B	Separation of the lower margins of the vocal folds only
C	Maximum glottal opening
D	Contact of the upper margin of the vocal folds only
E	Initial complete separation of the upper and lower margins of the vocal folds

25. What is a limitation to using electroglottography?

   A. The waveform doesn't provide valid information about vocal fold closure.

   B. The waveform only shows amplitude, not frequency, of vocal fold vibration.

   C. Electroglottography can only be used when phonation is completely periodic and without perturbation.

   D. Electroglottography is highly invasive.

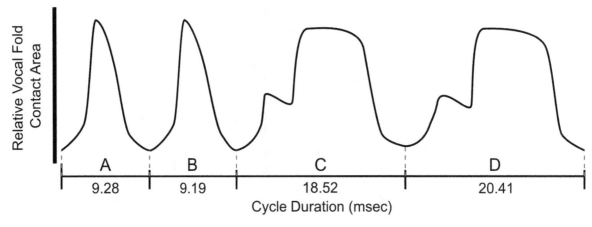

Figure 6–5

26. For the EGG waveform shown in Figure 6–5, what phonation register is shown in cycles A and B?

    A. Vocal fry

    B. Modal register

    C. Falsetto register

    D. Speech register

27. For the EGG waveform shown in Figure 6–5, what phonation register is shown in cycles C and D?

    A. Vocal fry

    B. Modal register

    C. Falsetto

    D. Speech register

28. In Figure 6–5, what can you conclude about the speaker?

    A. The speaker is likely a child.

    B. The speaker is likely an adult male.

    C. The speaker is likely an adult female.

    D. There is no way to determine characteristics of the speaker from this figure.

29. Considering phonation cycles A and B in Figure 6–5, what is the average fundamental frequency for the speaker?

    A. Approximately 54.14 Hz

    B. Approximately 107.76 Hz

    C. Approximately 108.28 Hz

    D. Fundamental frequency of phonation cannot be calculated from the waveform shown.

30. What do the small peaks at the beginning of cycles C and D in Figure 6–5 represent?

    A. The average vocal fold contact area

    B. Dichrotic vibration of the vocal folds

    C. The frequency of vocal fold contact

    D. No vocal fold contact

31. True/False   The change in the vibratory pattern from cycle B to cycle C in Figure 6–5 can be described as a quantal change.

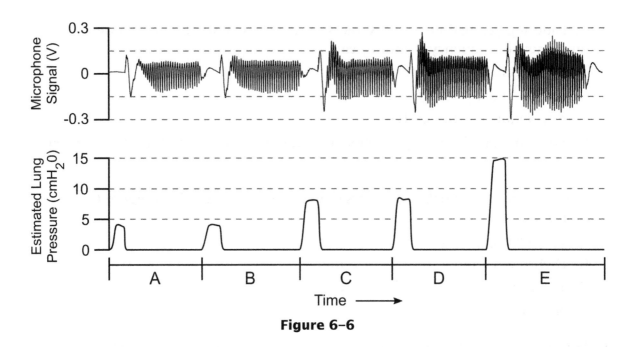

Figure 6–6

32. Figure 6–6 shows the audio (microphone) waveform and the intraoral pressure waveform recorded while a speaker repeated the syllable /pa/ five times. Which syllable was produced with the greatest amount of respiratory driving force?

    A. Syllable A

    B. Syllable C

    C. Syllable E

    D. No conclusions about respiratory activity can be made based on these waveforms.

33. How was the estimated lung pressure waveform shown in Figure 6–6 obtained?

34. For measurement of intraoral pressure used to estimate lung pressure for speech, why is the syllable /pa/ used as the speech utterance?

35. Which of the syllables in Figure 6–6 would be the quietest?

    A. Syllable B

    B. Syllable C

    C. Syllable E

    D. All of these syllables would be equally loud.

36. Considering the data in Figure 6–6, what can you conclude about syllables A and B?

    A. Syllables A and B were produced at approximately the phonatory threshold pressure.

    B. Syllables A and B were produced at a lung pressure that indicates a normal conversational speech level.

    C. Syllables A and B were produced at a lung pressure that indicates very loud speech.

    D. Syllables A and B were produced at lung pressures insufficient to produce and sustain phonation.

37. Considering the data in Figure 6–6, you can conclude that syllable C was produced

    A. At approximately the phonatory threshold pressure

    B. At a lung pressure that indicates a normal conversational speech level

    C. At a lung pressure that indicates very loud speech

    D. At lung pressures insufficient to produce and sustain phonation

38. Which of the following assessment techniques provides information on phonatory irregularity or variability?

    A. Intraoral pressure and s/z ratio

    B. Stroboscopy and maximum frequency range of phonation

    C. Voice range profile and phonation quotient

    D. Jitter factor and shimmer percent

39. What assessment technique(s) would you use if you were interested in learning about how a speaker uses their voice routinely?

    A. Relative active perturbation and phonation quotient

    B. Voice range profile and phonation quotient

    C. Electroglottography and mean speaking fundamental frequency

    D. Shimmer percent and maximum phonation time

40. Which of the following assessment techniques would NOT provide good information about the variability or irregularity of phonation cycles?

    A. Stroboscopy

    B. Relative average perturbation

    C. Videokymography

    D. Jitter factor

41. Which of the following assessment techniques does NOT provide a visual image of vocal fold vibration?

    A. Videokymography

    B. Photoglottography

    C. High-speed laryngeal imaging

    D. Stroboscopy

42. True/False   A voice disorder that produces incomplete glottal closure may result in an increase in airflow during phonation.

43. What assessment technique(s) provide information about the mucosal wave during phonation?

    A. Electroglottography and photoglottography

    B. Stroboscopy and videokymography

    C. Jitter percent and shimmer percent

    D. Voice range profile

44. To obtain a measure of aerodynamic power during phonation, we would need to measure

    A. Lung pressure and transglottal airflow

    B. Transglottal airflow and fundamental frequency

    C. Fundamental frequency and vocal intensity

    D. Closed quotient and maximum frequency range of phonation

45. Incomplete glottal closure during phonation may result in

    A. Decreased laryngeal resistance

    B. Increased fundamental frequency

    C. Increased glottal efficiency

    D. An s/z ratio of less than 1.0

46. Why should measures of vocal jitter be performed during a sustained vowel and not during conversational speech?

    A. During conversational speech, the vocal folds produce completely periodic vibration and, therefore, there is zero jitter.

    B. During conversational speech, a speaker's fundamental frequency will vary depending on prosodic considerations, thus increasing the value of jitter in relation.

    C. During sustained vowels, the measurement of jitter will be directly related to the measurement of shimmer.

    D. A sustained vowel is the vocal condition most similar to habitual use of the voice.

47. What advantages does high-speed laryngeal imaging have over laryngeal stroboscopy?

TRY IT!

1. Fill a clear, tall glass with water and grab a straw. Using a permanent marker, measure and mark 1-cm increments from the bottom of the straw. Make at least seven 1-cm markings, but even more (try 10 or more) is better if your glass is tall enough. Place the straw in the water so that the third marking (equaling 3 cm from the bottom of the straw) is at the level of the top of the water. Carefully blow into the straw so that a single bubble or a slow stream of bubbles is pushed out of the straw. Now, dunk your straw further into the water until you reach the seventh marking from the bottom (7 cm depth). Once again, blow carefully into the straw to produce a slow stream of bubbles. At the 3-cm depth, you were producing 3 cmH_2O of lung pressure, which is about the minimum amount of air pressure required to produce and sustain phonation. At the 7-cm depth, you produced 7 cmH_2O of lung pressure, or the amount of respiratory pressure required for conversational speech. Try producing a sustained vowel into the straw at different straw depths! This exercise was modified from the original idea by Hixon et al. (1982).

   Hixon, H. J., Hawley, J. L., & Wilson, K. J. (1982). An around-the-house device for the clinical determination of respiratory driving pressure: A note on making simple even simpler. *Journal of Speech and Hearing Disorders, 47*, 413–415. https://doi.org/10.1044/jshd.4704.413

2. Use a stopwatch app to measure how long you can phonate! Take a deep breath and phonate a vowel (your choice of vowel!) for as long as you can. Perform two more trials to see if your maximum phonation time improves with practice. What other factors do you think could influence maximum phonation time? Try a different vowel or a very low- or high-pitch vowel to see if these factors change your results. For a bonus activity, measure your maximum /s/ and /z/ durations to calculate your s/z ratio, and see how the s/z ratio may be altered by changes in voice pitch and intensity.

3. Elicit your own s/z ratio and your own maximum phonation time. How do your values compare to normative data? What is your impression of how you could have used a different phonatory strategy to yield different values for each task?

4. (Note: This exercise is a bit complicated. It requires you to download a free sound level meter app to measure your vocal intensity and to use a free piano keyboard app on the web to identify frequencies. However, it will be fun to try out and will provide you with an estimate of your personalized voice range profile and help you to explore your voice!)

Create a voice range profile of your own voice. The preparation: On a piece of paper (graph paper is ideal but not necessary), draw the x- and y-axes. Use Figure 6–3 from the textbook to mark the f_o and intensity values on each axis, respectively. Find a virtual piano keyboard on the web, such as https://www .imusic-school.com/en/tools/online-piano-keyboard/ or another application. Reference Appendix C (frequencies of the musical scale) in the textbook to identify the frequency of the piano keys. Now, download a free sound level meter application, such as Decibel X (available through iTunes or GooglePlay, for example) to your phone or other device.

Now you are ready to create your VRP: Make sure to position your virtual sound level meter at a consistent distance from your mouth for the entire VRP (about 11 inches away from your mouth should be the maximum distance you select). Select a note somewhere in your range at which you can phonate comfortably on the virtual keyboard. Use the vowel /a/ to match the pitch as well as you can. Phonate the vowel as softly as possible. Mark the intensity at the frequency you have selected on your paper plot. At the same pitch, phonate comfortably loudly and mark the intensity. (Note: Do not phonate as loudly as possible because it could be harmful to your vocal folds. Your VRP upper contour will thus represent the "comfortably loud" level at which you can phonate for each frequency.)

Continue in this fashion upward and downward from your comfortable pitch until you cannot maintain phonation. How does your VRP compare to the male and female examples in Figure 6–3 in the textbook?

Clinical Application

Clinical Case 3: Camp Voice

1. What factors might contribute to a child's dysphonia after participating in outdoor group activities on a daily basis over several weeks?

2. What characteristics of vocal fold vibration might be contributing to the vocal quality of hoarseness (breathiness combined with roughness)?

Clinical Case 4: Persistent Falsetto

1. Investigate the average values of mean speaking f_o in pre- and postpubescent boys. How do those average values compare to Alexei's pre- and posttherapy values?

2. Alexei's pretherapy videostroboscopy examination revealed vocal folds that were elongated and thinned. Would you expect these characteristics, given his f_o? Why or why not?

3. Why might speaking intensity be reduced in a person who maintains an unusually high mean speaking f_o?

7

The Production and Perception of Vowels Questions

Foundational Knowledge

7.1 Introduction (p. 226)

1. Within a language, the group of all variations in production of a given sound that do not cause a word to change meaning is called a _____.

2. True/False   Each letter in the alphabet of a given language represents a different phoneme.

3. Match the description of transcription with the name of the type of transcript. Types may be used more than once or not at all.

Transcription Definition	Type of Transcription
Includes the difference in pronunciation within a phonemic class	Phonemic/phonetic
	Phonemic
Represents the symbols that result in a difference in meaning	Narrowband
	Phonetic
Represents the actual pronunciation, more or less	International Phonetic
	Transcript System
Use of forward slashes (/ /)	
Use of brackets ([ ])	

4. A variation in individual pronunciation of a phoneme is called an _____ variation.

5. In English, vowels
   A. Form the nucleus of a syllable and are produced with a relatively open vocal tract
   B. Are both voiced and voiceless
   C. Are produced with a relatively open vocal tract except at the level of the vocal folds
   D. Form the nucleus of most but not all syllables

7.2 Acoustic Theory of Speech Production (p. 227)

6. The acoustic theory of speech production tells us that
   A. Not all sounds are influenced by the vocal tract.
   B. Acoustics is a theoretical description of speech sounds that cannot be quantified.
   C. Specific articulatory configurations of the vocal tract produce specific sounds.
   D. Sounds cannot be identified by a specific articulatory configuration because they vary too much among individuals.

7. True/False   The source filter theory of speech production is synonymous with the acoustic theory of speech production.

8. The acoustic theory of speech production describes the major components of the speech production system
   A. The power source from the respiratory system and the filter function from the vocal tract
   B. The respiratory, laryngeal, articulatory, and resonatory subsystems
   C. The acoustic pressure wave and the oral cavity articulators
   D. The sound source and the sound filter

9. When air inside a partially closed container is set into vibration, the container is set to be an _____ _____.

10. The vocal tract resonates sounds depending upon their (select one term) [intensity/frequency/ physical location in the vocal tract].

11. The spectral roll-off characteristics of the acoustic spectrum refers to the
    A. Decrease in amplitude of successive harmonics with decreasing frequency of the harmonics
    B. Decrease in amplitude of successive harmonics with increasing frequency of the harmonics
    C. Decrease in frequency of successive harmonics with increasing amplitude of the harmonics
    D. Decrease in frequency of successive harmonics with decreasing amplitude of the harmonics

12. The spectral roll-off (select one term) [is/is not] heavily influenced by the glottal closure during phonation.

13. In general, during phonation
    A. The faster and more complete the glottal closure, the greater the energy in the higher-frequency harmonics.
    B. The slower and more complete the glottal closure, the greater the energy in the higher-frequency harmonics.
    C. The faster and more open the glottal closure, the greater the energy in the higher-frequency harmonics.
    D. The slower and more open the glottal closure, the greater the energy in the higher-frequency harmonics.

14. The source spectrum of the human voice consists of the
    A. f_0
    B. f_0 and its harmonic multiples and its formants
    C. f_0 and its formants
    D. f_0 and its harmonic multiples

15. The way in which the harmonics are filtered depends upon the
    A. Resonant characteristics of the vocal tract
    B. Resonant characteristics of the source spectrum
    C. f_0
    D. Intensity of the acoustic spectrum

16. The resonance characteristics of the vocal tract are defined by the
    A. Length and number of angles
    B. Length and cross section
    C. Length and density of air molecules in the column of resonated air
    D. Length and frequency of the fundamental and harmonics of the source spectrum

17. True/False   The resonance characteristics of the vocal tract are also called the vocal tract transfer function.

18. Resonance frequencies of the vocal tract are located at
    A. Integer multiples of the f_o
    B. Integer multiples of the lowest formant frequency
    C. Odd multiples of the f_o
    D. Odd multiples of the lowest formant frequency

19. Shortening the vocal tract will (select one term) [raise/lower] formant frequencies.

20. For a vocal tract that is 18 cm in length, what are the frequencies of the first and second resonance of the vocal tract of uniform diameter? (Refer to the formula in the chapter to obtain the answer.)

21. True/False   The vocal tract, due to its length, contains only five resonance frequencies at most.

22. The relationships between the volume velocity and the particle vibration are as follows
    A. A node, located at the mouth opening, is a region of volume velocity maximum, and an antinode, located at the vocal folds, is a region of volume velocity minimum.
    B. A node, located at the mouth opening, is a region of volume velocity minimum, and an antinode, located at the vocal folds, is a region of volume velocity maximum.
    C. An antinode, located at the mouth opening, is a region of volume velocity maximum, and a node, located at the vocal folds, is a region of volume velocity minimum.
    D. An antinode, located at the mouth opening, is a region of volume velocity minimum, and an antinode, located at the vocal folds, is a region of volume velocity maximum.

23. True/False   Vocal tract formants are present in the vocal tract only when a sound source provides an acoustic pressure wave for filtering.

7.3 Vowels (p. 237)

24. A constriction at or near a node or antinode for a particular formant
    A. Dampens or intensifies the formant
    B. Changes the frequency of the formant
    C. Adds a formant
    D. Removes a formant

25. The location of a node or antinode is due to
    A. Volume velocity minima or maxima associated with a standing wave pattern
    B. Movement of the tongue or pharyngeal muscles or lips
    C. The formant frequency
    D. The spectral characteristics of the voice source (f_0 and harmonics)

26. True/False   Formants are located in order of their frequency from lowest to highest along the vocal tract.

27. In regard to constrictions at or near volume velocity minima or maxima of a standing wave,
    A. Constriction near a node increases the resonance (energy that is transmitteD. while constriction near an antinode dampens the resonance.
    B. Constriction near a node dampens the resonance (energy that is transmitteD. while constriction near an antinode increases the resonance.
    C. Constriction near a node raises the formant frequency and constriction near an antinode lowers the formant frequency.
    D. Constriction near a node lowers the formant frequency and constriction near an antinode raises the formant frequency.

28. The opening at the lips
    A. Always represents an antinode
    B. Always represents a node
    C. Represents a node or an antinode depending upon whether the lips are rounded (as in a pucker) or spread (as in a smile)
    D. May represent an antinode or a node, depending upon the resonance characteristics of the standing wave pattern

29. All formant frequencies are (select one term) [raised/lowered/variably affected] by constriction at the lips.

30. The relationship between mouth opening and formants is as follows
    A. A lowered mandible tends to lower formant frequencies.
    B. A lowered mandible tends to raise formant frequencies.
    C. A lowered mandible tends to damp formant energy.
    D. A raised mandible tends to increase formant energy.

31. Common notation for the first three formants is
    A. f1, f2, f3
    B. f_1, f_2, f_3
    C. F_1, F_2, F_3
    D. F1, F2, F3

32. Constriction at the following locations lowers the frequency of the first formant
    A. Constriction at the anterior oral cavity and in the pharynx
    B. Widening at the anterior oral cavity and in the pharynx
    C. Constriction at the anterior oral cavity and widening in the pharynx
    D. Widening at the anterior oral cavity and constriction in the pharynx

33. Constriction at the following locations lowers the frequency of the second formant
    A. Constriction at the anterior oral cavity and in the pharynx
    B. Widening at the anterior oral cavity and in the pharynx
    C. Constriction at the anterior oral cavity and in the posterior oropharynx
    D. Widening at the anterior oral cavity and in the posterior oropharynx

34. Constriction at the following locations lowers the frequency of the third formant
    A. Constriction at the anterior oral cavity and in the oropharynx
    B. Widening at the anterior oral cavity and in the oropharynx
    C. Widening at the anterior oral cavity and in the mid-oral cavity
    D. Constriction at the anterior oral cavity and in the mid-oral cavity

35. The four corner vowels in American English are
    A. /i/, /æ/, /u/, /ɑ/
    B. /i/, /ɪ/, /u/, /a/
    C. /i/, /æ/, /o/, /ɑ/
    D. /i/, /a/, /u/, /o/

36. The five front vowels in American English, moving from low to high, are
    A. /i/, /æ/, /e/, /ɛ/, /æ/
    B. /æ/, /ɛ/, /e/, /æ/, /i/
    C. /i/, /ɪ/, /e/, /æ/, /o/
    C. /o/, /æ/, /e/, /ɪ/, /i/

37. The five back vowels in American English, moving from high to low, are
    A. /e/, /ɑ/, /u/, /o/, /ɔ/
    B. /ɔ/, /u/, /o/, /ɑ/, /e/
    C. /ɑ/, /ɔ/, /o/, /ʊ/, /u/
    D. /u/, /ʊ/, /o/, /ɔ/, /ɑ/

38. Neutral vowels are those that are
    A. Most central
    B. Front and back vowels that are midway between high and low
    C. High and low vowels that are midway between front and back
    D. Indistinguishable from one another

39. The most common central vowel in American English is _____.

40. Vowel quality refers to
    A. The vocal clarity of the vowel
    B. The distinctness of the vowel compared to the other vowels in a given language
    C. The perception of the acoustic representation of the vowel
    D. The perception of how accurately it is produced

41. The perception of vowel "backness" is likely a function of
    A. F1
    B. F2
    C. F3
    D. The relationship between F1 and F2

42. True/False   F1 varies inversely with vowel height for both front and back vowels.

43. For the front vowels, the frequencies of F1 and F2 are generally spaced (select one phrase) [close together/far apart] and the frequencies of F2 and F3 are generally spaced [close together/far apart].

44. Compared to a large acoustic resonating space, the air inside a small resonating space will

    A. Vibrate at a lower frequency and thus the formant frequency would be lower

    B. Vibrate at a higher frequency and thus the formant frequency would be higher

    A. Vibrate at a lower frequency and thus the formant frequency would be higher

    B. Vibrate at a higher frequency and thus the formant frequency would be lower

45. True/False   Movement of the articulators creates resonating spaces of different sizes that create formants of different frequencies.

46. The F1–F2 plot of the seminal research of Peterson and Barney (1952) and later expanded by Hillenbrand et al. (1995) is a graphical display of

    A. F1 and F2 average frequencies for several American English vowels spoken by many speakers

    B. The ideal F1 and F2 frequencies for several American English vowels

    C. All of the possible range of F1 and F2 frequencies for several American English vowels

    D. F1 and F2 frequencies for several American English vowels generated by acoustic instrumentation to be used as a model for understanding vowels

47. The set of F1–F2 points that specify a vowel in an F1–F2 plot is called the _____.

48. Tense vowels are generally produced with (select on term) [less/greater] duration than lax vowels.

49. The inherent duration of a vowel refers to the

    A. Duration of the formant throughout the different vowels

    B. Difference in duration of vowels that appear in open and closed syllables

    C. Time it generally takes for the articulators to create an articulatory posture for a given vowel

    D. Vowel duration that a speaker most overcomes to produce a sound with a unique duration

50. Rhotacization is the process of

    A. Making a vowel more rounded

    B. Making a vowel more centralized

    C. Altering the perceptual quality of the vowel associated with /r/

    D. Altering the perceptual quality of the vowel associated with an adjacent vowel

51. A vowel that is produced with an unchanging vocal tract posture is called a
_____.

52. The major differentiation between a diphthong and a double vowel is that, in a
diphthong,
    A. The shift in the articulatory posture is not a smooth glide.
    B. The shift in the articulatory posture is a smooth glide.
    C. A double vowel typically has a short pause (silence) between each vowel.
    D. Diphthongs typically cross syllable boundaries.

53. Common diphthongs in American English are
    A. /eɪ/, /aɪ/, /ɔɪ/, /aʊ/, /oʊ/
    B. /e/, /aɪ/, /ɔɪ/, /aʊ/, /oʊ/
    C. /ie/, /ɪa/, /ɪɔ/, /ʊa/, /ʊo/
    D. /e/, /ɪa/, /ɪɔ/, /ʊa/, /ʊo/

54. The articulatory starting and ending points for a diphthong are called,
respectively, _____ and _____.

55. Diphthongs generally tend to move from
    A. Lax to tense and low to high tongue articulatory position
    B. Tense to lax and low to high tongue articulatory position
    C. Lax to tense and high to low tongue articulatory position
    D. Tense to lax and high to low tongue articulatory position

56. Vowel centralization is also commonly referred to as vowel _____.

57. The tongue is a muscular hydrostat, which means that
    A. It is composed of muscle groups that are oriented in different directions.
    B. The tongue muscles function like mechanical levers.
    C. For any given lingual movement, all of the tongue muscles act as either
    agonists or antagonists.
    D. All of the tongue muscles contain a larger percentage of water than do the
    other skeletal muscles.

58. The anatomical divisions of the tongue are the
    A. Anterior body, middle body, and posterior root
    B. Anterior body and posterior root
    C. Anterior body, middle body, posterior body, and root
    D. Tongue tip, tongue blade, tongue root

59. The intrinsic muscles of the tongue are the
    A. Longitudinal, superior transverse, inferior transverse, and vertical
    B. Longitudinal, transverse, vertical, and rotational
    C. Superior longitudinal, middle longitudinal, and inferior longitudinal
    D. Superior longitudinal, inferior longitudinal, transverse, and vertical

60. The major extrinsic lingual muscles are the
    A. Genioglossus, hyoglossus, styloglossus, linguaglossus
    B. Genioglossus, hyoglossus, styloglossus
    C. Inferior genioglossus, superior genioglossus, hyoglossus, styloglossus
    D. Genioglossus, styloglossus, linguaglossus

61. All motor innervation to the tongue muscles is supplied by cranial nerve (number and name) _____.

62. Analysis of tongue muscle movement is complex because
    A. The tongue is a large structure.
    B. The tongue has no bones or cartilage against which the muscles can act as levers.
    C. Tone muscle fibers differ in size and density and are often interwoven with one another.
    D. Instrumentation does not exist that can identify different muscles.

7.4 Language and Dialect Influences on Vowel Production (p. 259)

63. The "vowel inventory" of a given language is
    A. A listing of the allophonic variations of the vowels of a language
    B. The most commonly used vowels of a language
    C. A listing of how vowels have changed and evolved in the language throughout history
    D. The vowels that are native to a language

64. The vowel that is slowly losing its distinction with /ɑ/ in American English is _____.

65. Dialectical differences
    A. Are common in all languages
    B. Are common in some but not all languages
    C. Are generally identified only in less educated individuals
    D. Are the same as language differences

66. True/False   Dialectical differences tend to be highly stabilized with few changes over the decades.

67. American, British, and Indian Englishes are examples of different (select one term) [languages/dialects].

68. A nonnative accent is due to
    A. Random errors by the speaker
    B. Consistent differences produced by the speaker
    C. Speaking in a "broken" fashion
    D. A lack of knowledge of the language

7.5 The Vocal Tract as a Regulator of Intensity (p. 260)

69. Some portion of the acoustic energy of the voice is lost in the vocal tract
    A. Into the lungs through the open vocal folds
    B. In the walls of the vocal tact, through friction between the air molecules, and into the lungs through the open vocal folds
    C. In the walls of the vocal tact and through friction between the air molecules
    D. In the walls of the vocal tact, in the nasal passages, and through friction between the air molecules

70. A power spectrum will generally show a larger range of frequencies between the harmonics in a woman's voice compared to that of a man's voice because
    A. The fundamental frequency of a woman's voice is generally higher.
    B. The harmonics of a woman's voice generally have lesser energy.
    C. The woman's voice generally is more breathy.
    D. The woman's voice generally has fewer harmonics.

71. Formant tuning is the process of
    A. Singing with a wider mouth opening to achieve greater intensity
    B. Singing with greater lung pressure to adjust the frequencies of the formants of vowels
    C. Matching harmonic frequency with formant frequency through adjusting the shape of the vocal tract to maximize acoustic power
    D. Widening the range of frequencies between the first and second formants to maximize acoustic power

72. Except at the very highest frequencies, the vocal tract generally resonates acoustic power more efficiently as the fundamental frequency is [raised/lowered].

73. The increase in frequency achieved when the fundamental frequency or a harmonic coincides with a formant frequency is called _____.

74. The relationship between intensity and fundamental frequency, as displayed in a voice range profile, is influenced by the relationship of the formant frequencies and the _____ frequencies.

7.6 Acoustic Filters (p. 265)

75. Match the type of filter on the left with the filter characteristics on the right. Characteristics may be used more than once or not at all.

    _____ low-pass

    _____ high-pass

    _____ band-pass

    1. Allows only a specified range of frequencies to be passed through

    2. Allows only the low-frequency components to be passed through

    3. Allows only a specified range of lower frequencies and higher frequencies to be passed through

    4. Allows only the high-frequency components to be passed through

76. The characteristic of a sharply or broadly tuned acoustic filter refers to

    A. Whether a filter is high- or low-pass

    B. A band-pass filter

    C. Whether or not a filter has cutoff boundaries

    D. The steepness of the slope of the cutoff boundaries

77. Formants can be described as a

    A. Resonance curve of a bandpass filter

    B. Resonance curve of a low-pass filter

    C. Resonance curve of a high-pass filter

    D. Center frequency without a resonance curve

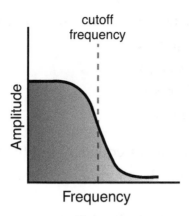

Figure 7–1

78. Figure 7–1 shows a [high-pass/low-pass/band-pass] filter.

79. Attenuation is the [increase/decrease] in [frequency/amplitude] of a harmonic through filtering.

80. The frequency at the midpoint, or peak of a filter, is called the _____ frequency.

81. The width in Hz of an acoustic filter containing half the acoustic energy is called the [bandwidth/half-power point].

82. The cutoff frequency of a filter at which the amplitude of the frequency component is decreased by 3 dB is called the _____.

83. A formant acts as a [low-pass/high-pass/bandpass] filter.

7.7 Instrumentation for Measuring Vocal Tract Acoustics (p. 268)

84. A spectrogram is
    A. The graphic representation of the frequencies and intensities of an acoustic wave as a function of time
    B. A "snapshot" of the frequencies and intensities of an acoustic pressure wave at a given moment in time
    C. A graphic representation of the airflow and air pressure characteristics of an acoustic wave as a function of time
    D. A means of displaying the vocal tract, similar to an x-ray

85. In a spectrogram, the *x*-axis, *y*-axis, and *z*-axis represent, respectively
    A. Time, energy, and frequency
    B. Frequency, time, and energy
    C. Time, frequency, and energy
    D. Frequency, energy, and time

86. The relationship between time, frequency, and filter bandwidth is such that
    A. A narrow bandwidth resolves frequency information well but has poor time resolution.
    B. A narrow bandwidth resolves time information well but has poor frequency resolution.
    C. A narrow bandwidth resolves intensity information well but has poor frequency resolution.
    D. In order to resolve both time and frequency information well, a band-pass filter must be used.

87. When setting the filter of a spectrogram using digital sampling points,
    A. The higher number of points equates to a wideband filter.
    B. The lower number of points equates to a wideband filter.
    C. The higher number of points equates to good frequency resolution.
    D. The lower number of points equates to good time resolution.

88. In a narrowband spectrogram of a healthy voice
    A. The formants appear as parallel black lines and vertical striations represent the glottal pulses.
    B. The harmonics appear as parallel black lines and vertical striations represent the glottal pulses.
    C. The formants appear as parallel black lines.
    D. The harmonics appear as parallel black lines.

89. In a narrowband spectrogram of a healthy voice
    A. The harmonics whose frequencies are far from a formant frequency are poorly visible.
    B. The harmonics whose frequencies are far from a formant frequency are strongly visible.
    C. The harmonics whose frequencies are far from a formant frequency appear wavier than harmonics whose frequencies are close to a formant frequency.
    D. Formants are not visible at all.

90. The vertical striations visible in a wideband spectrogram represent
    A. Harmonics
    B. Formants
    C. Cycles of glottal opening and closing
    D. Spectral peaks

91. In an acoustic pressure wave that represents a sustained vowel glide from low to high pitch, the narrowband spectrogram would show
    A. Harmonic bands changing in darkness as the harmonics move closer to and farther from the formant frequencies
    B. Formant spectral peaks changing in darkness as the formants move closer to and farther from the harmonic frequencies
    C. Increased waviness of the harmonic bands
    D. Increased waviness of the formant spectral peak bands

92. A significant disadvantage of voice metrics such as jitter, shimmer, and harmonics to noise ratio is that
    A. In cases of significant irregularity in vocal fold vibration, the measures are often not reliable.
    B. No normative data are available for comparison of healthy and abnormal voice production.
    C. Voices that are severely abnormal often have normal-appearing vocal metrics.
    D. All voices, including healthy ones, have some level of abnormality.

93. An advantageof cepstral analysis of acoustic signals is that
    A. It can be reliably calculated from highly irregular voices, but only for sustained vowel phonation, not connected speech.
    B. It is not dependent upon identification of individual glottal cycles, so that it is reliably calculated from highly irregular voices in connected speech.
    C. It is not sensitive to the phonemic content of the utterance being analyzed.
    D. It can be calculated in high levels of ambient background noise.

94. A shorter window length of a digital filter, compared to a longer window length, corresponds to a [narrowband/wideband] filter.

95. In a high fundamental frequency, the vertical striations of a wideband spectrogram would be spaced [closer together/farther apart] than in a low fundamental frequency.

96. Spectrograms [can/cannot] be used to definitively identify a particular speaker.

97. Spectral peaks are broad bands of energy (represented as dark gray) associated with [harmonics/formants].

98. The averaging of the spectral energy over a window of specified duration of sustained vowel phonation is called the _____.

99. The ratio of the energy of the fundamental and harmonics to the energy in the noise of the acoustic signal is called the _____.

100. A spectral-based method of quantifying the relative energy of the fundamental frequency and harmonics compared to the noise energy in both sustained vowel and connected speech is called _____.

101. True/False   The three dimensions of a spectrogram are time, frequency, and intensity.

102. True/False   A narrowband spectrogram provides better frequency information and a wideband spectrogram provides better time resolution.

103. True/False   To clearly visualize the spectral peaks associated with vocal tract formants, a narrowband spectrogram is best.

104. True/False   A spectrogram of a series of different vowels produced at the same pitch and loudness would likely show changes in the frequencies of the harmonics.

105. True/False   A wideband spectrogram of a single vowel produced on a pitch glide would likely show minimal changes in the spectral peaks associated with the vocal tract formants.

106. True/False   Forensic phonetics uses spectrograms to assist in identification of individuals for the legal system.

107. True/False   The long-term average spectrum is particularly useful in assessing features of the voice spectrum that are momentary phenomena.

108. True/False   In general, a harmonic to noise ratio of a healthy adult speaker will have a value between 0 and 25 dB.

109. True/False   Both harmonics to noise ratio and cepstral peak prominence can be validly calculated from continuous speech and sustained vowel phonation.

7.8 Vocal Tract Imaging: Current Research and Future Trends (p. 279)

110. Which of the following statements about x-ray, computed tomography, magnetic resonance imaging, and ultrasound technologies is accurate?

    A. They are all currently used in clinical research.

    B. They all provide data about vocal tract movements.

    C. They all have both advantages and disadvantages to their use.

    D. None of the technologies are currently used in clinical research.

111. True/False   Ultrasound imaging of the vocal tract remains experimental and beyond the scope of clinical practice.

Conceptual Integration

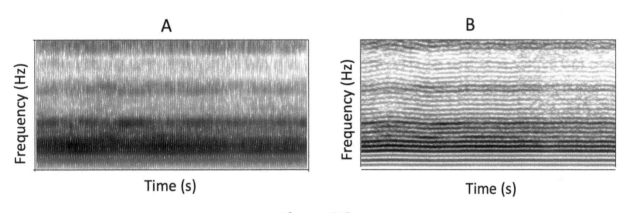

Figure 7–2

1. Figure 7–2 shows two spectrograms. Identify by letter the wideband and the narrowband spectrogram. What evidence did you use to make your choice?

2. In the wideband spectrogram shown in Figure 7–2, indicate the approximate locations of the formants.

3. In the narrowband spectrogram shown in Figure 7–2, label the f_0 and the sixth harmonic above the f_0.

4. In the narrowband spectrogram shown in Figure 7–2, what evidence allows you to identify the approximate locations of the formants?

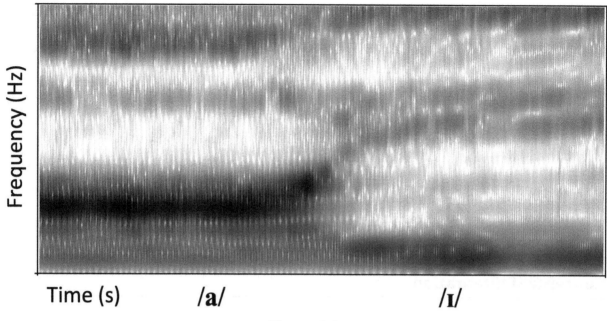

Time (s)   /a/   /ɪ/

Figure 7–3

5. Figure 7–3 shows two vowels produced sequentially, /a/ and /ɪ/. Label the steady-state portion and the offglide of the /a/ vowel and the onglide of the /ɪ/ vowel.

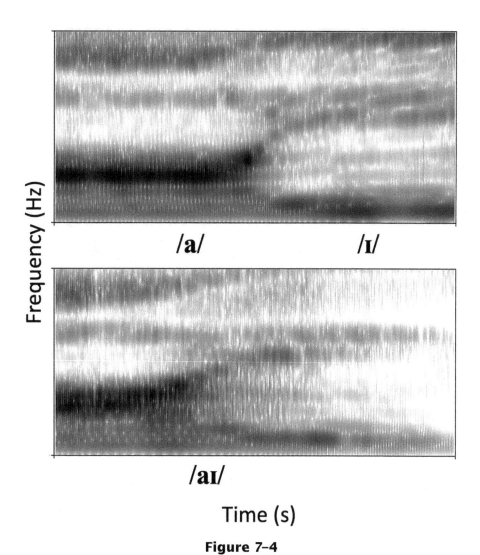

/a/   **/ɪ/**

/aɪ/

Time (s)

Figure 7–4

6. Figure 7–4 shows spectrograms of the vowels /a/ and /ɪ produced sequentially (top) and the diphthong /aɪ/ (bottom). Both spectrograms show approximately 1 second of the acoustic signal. What is the major difference between the two spectrograms?

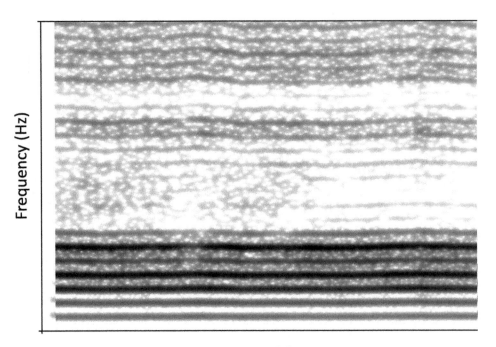

Time (s)

Figure 7–5

7. Figure 7–5 is a narrowband spectrogram representing
   A. Speech
   B. A sustained vowel at a constant pitch and loudness
   C. A sustained vowel at a constant pitch and increasing loudness
   D. A sustained vowel at an increasing pitch and constant loudness

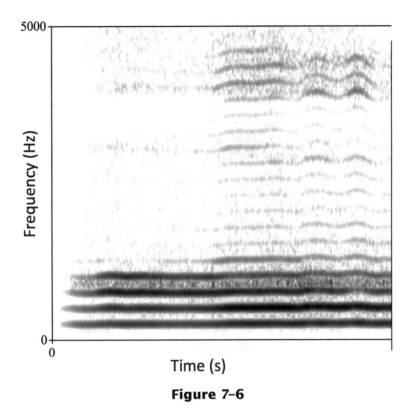

Figure 7–6

8. Figure 7–6 is a narrowband spectrogram representing
   A. Connected speech
   B. A sustained vowel at an increasing pitch and increasing loudness
   C. A sustained vowel at a constant pitch and increasing loudness
   D. A sustained vowel at an increasing pitch and constant loudness

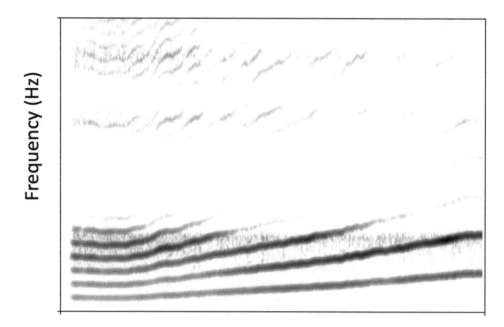

Figure 7–7

9. Figure 7–7 shows a narrowband spectrogram representing

    A. Speech

    B. A sustained vowel at a constant pitch and loudness

    C. A sustained vowel at a constant pitch and increasing loudness

    D. A sustained vowel at an increasing pitch and constant loudness

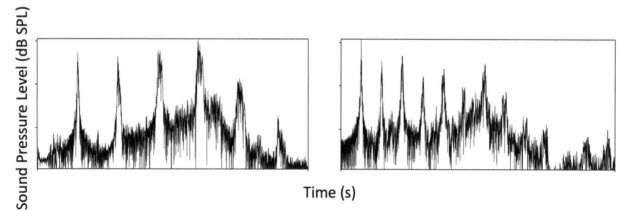

Figure 7–8

10. Figure 7–8 shows two power spectra. Identify by the letter which spectrum is likely from a woman's voice, and which spectrum is from a man's voice.

11. Note that in Figure 7–8, noise is present between the harmonics. Why?

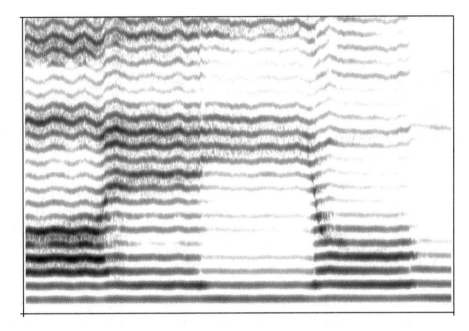

Time (s)

Figure 7–9

12. Figure 7–9 is a narrowband spectrogram from the acoustic signal of a person phonating a series of different vowels at a constant pitch and intensity. The harmonics become lighter and darker, sometimes appearing and disappearing, throughout the phonation. Explain what is occurring to cause the change in intensity of the harmonics over time. (Hint: Think about how formants are produced for each vowel!)

13. Note that in Figure 7–9, the higher harmonic frequencies show greater jitter (waviness) than do the lower harmonic frequencies because

    A. The percentage of jitter increases with frequency.

    B. The percentage of jitter remains the same across the harmonic frequencies but the absolute value of the jitter in Hz increases because the frequency of the harmonics increases.

    C. Although the percentage of jitter remains constant, the percentage of shimmer increases.

    D. The instrumentation has greater difficulty resolving higher-frequency harmonics than lower-frequency harmonics.

14. The rate at which the column of air in the vocal tract is set into vibration is determined by the (select one term) [larynx/vocal tract] and the frequencies at which the column of air resonates is determined by the (select one term) [larynx/ vocal tract].

15. Explain the difference between harmonics and formants and whether they are characteristics of the voice source spectrum or vocal tract filter function.

16. Why does lip rounding lower formant frequencies?

17. Why do the higher-frequency harmonics resonate with greater energy than do the lower- frequency harmonics as the acoustic pressure wave exits the oral cavity?

18. Explain the following statement: "Vocal tract constrictions define vowel quality."

19. Considering the relationship of the tongue and the mandible, and the incompressible nature of the tongue, explain why describing vowels in terms of tongue height and tongue advancement is problematic.

20. Draw the vowel quadrilateral without referring to the figures of the quadrilateral. Include arrows that indicate the change in F1 and F2 from low to high frequency.

21. Why is *vowel height* a more accurate term than *tongue height* when describing the arrangement of vowels in the vowel quadrilateral?

22. Describe how a Helmholtz resonator works. Include reference to the elasticity, restorative forces, and momentum of the air molecules.

23. In an acoustic pressure wave that represents a sustained vowel glide from low to high pitch, the narrowband spectrogram would show
    A. Formant spectral peaks moving from low to high frequency
    B. Harmonic bands moving from low to high frequency
    C. Formant spectral peaks appearing progressively closer in frequency to one another
    D. Harmonic bands appearing progressively closer in frequency to one another

24. In an acoustic pressure wave that represents a series of different vowels produced all at the same frequency and intensity, the wideband spectrogram would show
    A. Movement of the harmonic bands across different frequencies in time
    B. Movement of the formant spectral peaks across different frequencies in time
    C. Vertical striations that change in width across time
    D. A variable fundamental frequency across time

25. What does it mean that the vocal tract is a variable acoustic resonator?

26. The source-filter theory of speech production identifies a source and a filter function. Give an example of how the source can be independent of the filter. (Hint: What type of sounds could you make to demonstrate this example?)

27. A speaker phonates the American English vowel /i/, which has a low F1 and high F2. If the speaker wanted to change the vowel to represent a vowel from another language that has a low F1 but also a low F2, what articulatory adjustment would she have to make?

28. Using a voiceless whisper, shape your vocal tract into each of the four corner vowels. You can hear the four vowels distinctly, despite the lack of voicing. How is that possible, given that no f_o and harmonic energy is being supplied to the vocal tract?

29. Why is the vocal tract NOT accurately modeled by a tube that is uniform in diameter along its length and is closed at one end?

30. What vowel is produced when the vocal tract is in the shape most like a tube that is uniform in diameter along its length?
    A. /ɑ/
    B. /i/
    C. /ə/
    D. /u/

31. When producing a very high vocal pitch that is associated with elevation of the larynx in the neck, what will result?
    A. The frequencies of the harmonics of the voice will be decreased.
    B. The formant frequencies will be decreased.
    C. The formant frequencies will be increased.
    D. The amplitude of the harmonics of the voice will be decreased.

32. You see two children talking. Although they are the same age, one child is much taller than the other. How might the speech of the children differ considering the source-filter theory of speech production?
    A. The taller child will likely have lower formant frequencies due to a longer vocal tract.
    B. The shorter child will likely have a lower vocal fundamental frequency due to a shorter vocal tract.
    C. The taller child will likely have formants that are lower in amplitude due to a shorter vocal tract.
    D. All children will have the same formant frequencies.

33. Protruding the lips for a /u/ vowel will result in
    A. Raising the formant frequencies
    B. Lowering the formant frequencies
    C. Changing the roll-off of the power spectrum of glottal volume velocity waveform
    D. Decreasing the first formant but increasing the second formant frequency

34. A singer produces a note at 800 Hz. What is the effect on the production of vowels?
    A. The radiated spectrum will not show the first formant for any vowel.
    B. Only one harmonic will be produced.
    C. The radiated spectrum will not show the second formant for any vowel.
    D. A second harmonic will be produced at 1,000 Hz.

35. Opening the mouth while producing the /i/ vowel will result in
    A. Decreasing the amount of lip radiation of sound
    B. Raising the vocal fundamental frequency
    C. Raising the first formant frequency
    D. Raising the second formant frequency

36. Why do (on average) adults have lower formant frequencies than children?
    A. Adults typically have longer vocal folds than children.
    B. Adults typically speak with a wider mouth posture than children.
    C. Adults typically have longer vocal tracts than children.
    D. Adults typically have larger tongues than children.

37. Why can the vocal tract be described as a variable resonator?

38. An articulatory posture with a relatively wide-open mouth would be expected to produce
    A. A relatively low first formant frequency
    B. A relatively high first formant frequency
    C. A relatively low second formant frequency
    D. A relatively high second formant frequency

39. Producing an /u/ vowel and then advancing the tongue anteriorly would be expected to

    A. Raise the first formant frequency

    B. Lower the first formant frequency

    C. Raise the second formant frequency

    D. Lower the second formant frequency

40. This vowel may be characterized by a relatively high intrinsic pitch and a relatively long duration

    A. /a/

    B. /I/

    C. /ɔ/

    D. /i/

41. Using a uniform-diameter tube as a simplistic model of the vocal tract, what would the first formant (resonant) frequency be for a tube (vocal tract) that is 12 cm in length?

    A. Approximately 0.01 Hz

    B. Approximately 708 Hz

    B. Approximately 1,416 Hz

    C. Approximately 2,833 Hz

42. An individual produces a first formant frequency of approximately 515.2 Hz for a neutral /ə/ vowel. Considering a uniform diameter tube as a simplistic model, what is their approximate length of their vocal tract?

    A. 16.6 cm

    B. 33.2 cm

    C. 66.4 cm

    C. 515.2 cm

43. Using a tube model of the vocal tract, as the tube resonates, the sound wave will produce

    A. An area of maximum air pressure at the "lips"

    B. An area of maximum air particle velocity at the "vocal folds"

    C. An area of minimum air pressure at the "lips"

    D. An area of minimum air particle velocity at the "lips"

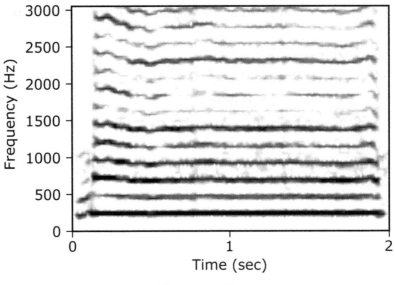

Figure 7–10

44. Figure 7–10 shows the spectrogram for a sustained vowel. What type of spectrogram is shown?

    A. Narrowband spectrogram

    B. Wideband spectrogram

    C. The type of spectrogram cannot be determined from this figure.

45. For Figure 7–10, what do the horizontal lines represent?

    A. Vowel formants

    B. Harmonics of phonation

    C. Resonant frequencies of the vocal tract

    D. Lip radiation of sound

46. Using Figure 7–10, what can you determine about the speaker who produced this vowel?

    A. It is most likely a child due to the value of the formants.

    B. It is most likely an adult female due to the value of the formants.

    C. It is most likely an adult male due to the fundamental frequency.

    D. It is most likely a child due to the fundamental frequency.

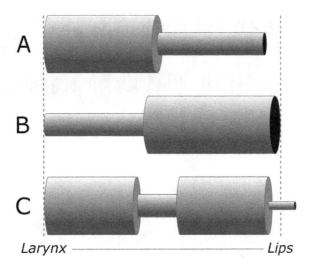

Figure 7–11

47. Figure 7–11 shows simplistic models of the vocal tract in articulatory postures for three vowels showing locations of widening and narrowing of cross-sectional area. Note that the "larynx" end of the vocal tracts is to the left and the "lips" end is to the right. Given the relative vocal tract shapes, what vowel is shown by model A?

    A. /a/

    B. /u/

    C. /i/

48. Using Figure 7–11, what vowel is shown by vocal tract model B?

    A. /a/

    B. /u/

    C. /i/

49. Considering Figure 7–11, which vocal tract vowel configuration likely has the lowest first and second formant frequencies?

    A. Model A

    B. Model B

    C. Model C

50. Considering Figure 7–11, which model vocal tract configuration likely has the greatest difference between the first and second formant frequencies?

    A. Model A

    B. Model B

    C. Model C

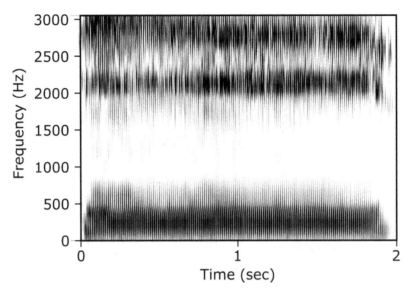

Figure 7–12

51. Figure 7–12 shows the spectrogram for a sustained vowel. What type of spectrogram is shown?

    A. Narrowband spectrogram

    B. Wideband spectrogram

    C. The type of spectrogram cannot be determined from this figure.

52. For Figure 7–12, what do the horizontal lines represent?

    A. Vowel formants

    B. Harmonics of phonation

    C. Vowel duration

    D. Lip radiation of sound

53. Using Figure 7–12, what vowel is being produced?

    A. /a/

    B. /u/

    C. /ae/

    D. /i/

54. Considering Figure 7–12, what can we conclude about the articulatory posture that created this vowel?

    A. The mandible was likely in a depressed position, producing a large volume of the oral cavity.

    B. The tongue was likely in a retracted position, creating a narrow pharynx.

    C. The lips were likely rounded.

    D. The tongue was likely in a raised position, creating a small volume of the oral cavity.

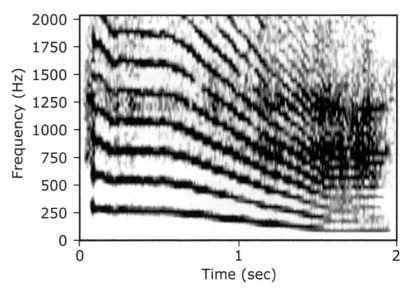

Figure 7–13

55. Figure 7–13 shows the narrowband spectrogram of a vowel. What can you conclude from this spectrogram plot?

    A. The vowel shown is a diphthong.

    B. The vowel shown has a first formant of approximately 280 Hz and a second formant of approximately 560 Hz.

    C. The fundamental frequency of this vowel begins at approximately 280 Hz and then decreases to approximately 100 Hz.

    D. The seven formants of this vowel decrease in frequency throughout the duration of the vowel.

56. Why do the horizontal lines in Figure 7–13 converge and have less space between them by the end of the vowel production?

    A. The formants are dropping in frequency throughout the duration of the vowel due to lowering of the mandible.

    B. The fundamental frequency is dropping throughout the duration of the vowel, which will lower the frequencies of the harmonics proportionally.

    C. The amplitude of the formants is dropping throughout the duration of the vowel.

    D. The reduced space between the horizontal lines near the end of the vowel production suggests increased lip rounding.

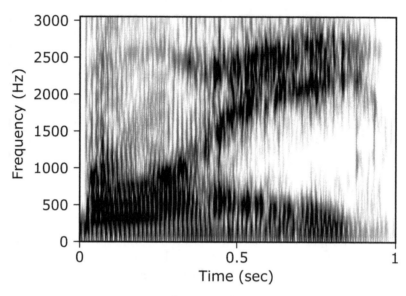

Figure 7–14

57. Figure 7–14 shows the spectrogram of an utterance. What can you conclude about this utterance?

    A. This is an /o/ vowel with a rising pitch.

    B. This is the diphthong /æ/.

    C. This is an /i/ vowel with a falling pitch.

    D. This is an /u/ vowel with a rising pitch.

58. Considering Figure 7–14, what can you conclude about the speaker?

    A. This utterance was likely produced by an adult male speaker.

    B. This utterance was likely produced by an adult female speaker.

    C. This utterance was likely produced by a child.

59. Comparing the beginning versus the end of the utterance shown in Figure 7–14, what can you conclude about the articulatory positioning?

    A. The individual's mandible was lowering from the beginning to the end of the utterance.

    B. The individual's mandible was elevating from the beginning to the end of the utterance.

    C. The individual's tongue was moving posteriorly into the pharynx from the beginning to the end of the utterance.

    D. The individual was changing from a lip-retracted to a lip-rounded position from the beginning to the end of the utterance.

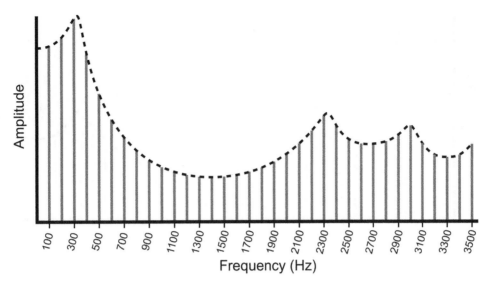

Figure 7–15

60. Figure 7–15 shows an idealized spectrum of a vowel showing source harmonics and LPC envelope (dashed line) displaying formant frequencies. What can you conclude about the speaker of this vowel?

   A. This speaker is likely an adult male based on the fundamental frequency of the vowel.

   B. This speaker is likely an adult female based on the fundamental frequency of the vowel.

   C. This speaker is likely a child based on the fundamental frequency of the vowel.

61. Considering Figure 7–15, what vowel is being produced?

   A. /a/

   B. /u/

   C. /o/

   D. /i/

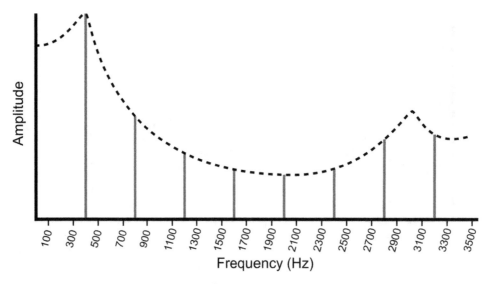

Figure 7–16

62. Figure 7–16 shows an idealized spectrum of the vowel /i/ showing source harmonics and LPC envelope (dashed line) displaying formant frequencies. What can you conclude about the speaker of this vowel?

A. The speaker is likely an adult male based on the formant frequencies.

B. The speaker is likely a child based on the formant frequencies and the source harmonics.

C. The speaker is likely an adult female based on the formant frequencies.

D. The speaker is likely an adult female based on the fundamental frequency.

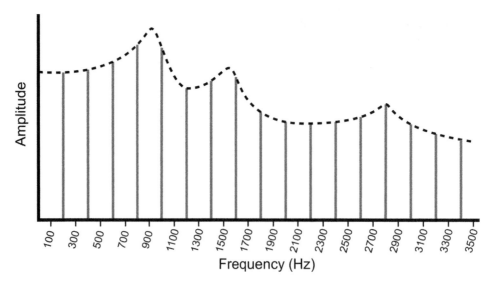

Figure 7–17

63. Figure 7–17 shows an idealized spectrum of a vowel showing source harmonics and LPC envelope (dashed line) displaying formant frequencies. What can you conclude about the speaker of this vowel?

    A. The speaker is likely an adult male based on the formant frequencies.

    B. The speaker is likely a child based on the formant frequencies.

    C. The speaker is likely an adult female based on the formant frequencies.

    D. The speaker is likely a child based on the fundamental frequency.

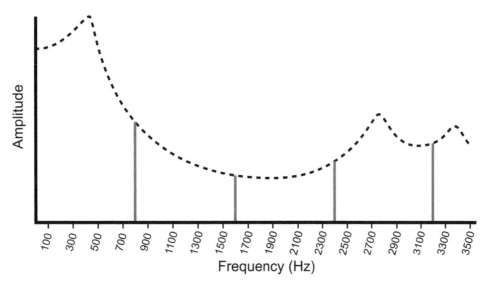

Figure 7–18

64. Figure 7–18 shows an idealized spectrum of the vowel /i/ showing source harmonics and LPC envelope (dashed line) displaying formant frequencies. What can you conclude about the individual who produced this vowel?

    A. The speaker is likely an adult male based on the formant frequencies. This individual is likely singing a low musical note based on the fundamental frequency.

    B. The speaker is likely an adult female based on the formant frequencies. This individual is likely singing a high musical note based on the fundamental frequency.

    C. The speaker is likely a young child with a vocal tract 10.5 cm long based on the formant frequencies and the fundamental frequency.

65. Considering Figure 7–18, how well would a listener be able to identify this vowel?

    A. A listener will have no difficulty in identifying this vowel based on the fundamental frequency.

    B. A listener will have no difficulty in identifying this vowel based on the formant frequencies.

    C. A listener will have difficulty in identifying this vowel as the source harmonics do not closely approximate the formant frequencies, in particular the first formant frequency.

    D. A listener will have difficulty in identifying this vowel due to the low amplitude of the harmonics.

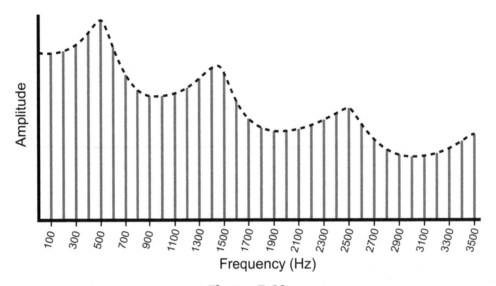

Figure 7–19

66. Figure 7–19 shows an idealized spectrum of source harmonics and LPC envelope (dashed line) displaying formant frequencies derived from a uniform tube model. Considering the formant frequencies, what can you conclude about the modeled vocal tract?

    A. The modeled vocal tract is approximately 10 cm in length.

    B. The modeled vocal tract is approximately 14 cm in length.

    C. The modeled vocal tract is approximately 17 cm in length.

    D. The modeled vocal tract is approximately 23 cm in length.

67. For the spectrum plot shown in Figure 7–19, what real vowel would be most closely approximated by this modeled vocal tract?

    A. A child producing an /a/ vowel

    B. An adult female producing an /ɝ/ vowel

    C. An adult female producing an /o/ vowel

    D. An adult male producing an /ɝ/ vowel

TRY IT!

1. Open a bottle of your favorite beverage and blow across the open top. Can you create a whistling tone? You've just made a Helmholtz resonator! Take another sip and play another note. The pitch of the note will have lowered somewhat as you have increased the volume of air inside the resonator bottle. As you continue to enjoy your refreshing beverage, the note you can play with your air chamber bottle will continue to drop commensurate with a decrease in liquid volume and an increase in air volume. For more fun, find more bottles that you can use, and "tune" them by adjusting the amount of fluid inside. With a bit of patience, you will be able to produce a series of bottles that will make up a musical scale! Maybe it's best to keep an additional bottle to the side for quenching your thirst instead of drinking from your new Helmholtz resonator bottle instrument.

2. Did you know that you can produce speech without vibrating your vocal folds? Don't shout it from the rooftops; instead, just whisper! Whispered speech is produced by generating turbulent air at the level of the larynx but without vibrating the vocal folds. This turbulent air noise is the source of sound for whispered speech, and it can be used to set the air in the vocal tract into resonance, generating phonemes without phonation.

3. Each vowel has an inherent or intrinsic pitch. Say each set of vowels by prolonging the vowel slightly. Then repeat each set in a voiceless whisper. First set: high front to low front /i, ɪ, ɛ, æ/ as in the words *heed, hid, head,* and *had*. Second set: low back to high back /ɑ, ɔ, ʊ, u/ as in the words *hod, hawed, hood,* and *who'd*. In both the voiced and voiceless productions, you will likely hear that the pitch descends as you proceed from high front to low front, then to low back and up to high back.

4. You can modulate or change the parameters of the sound source for speech and the filter for speech independently. Produce a monotone sustained /a/ vowel for a few seconds, then change it to an /i/ vowel without changing your voice pitch. You have modulated the parameters of the vocal tract as a filter by changing the shape of the vocal tract without changing your voice source of phonation. Try doing the opposite: Produce a sustained /a/ vowel but alter your voice pitch a bit, perhaps raising and lowering it. You've now modulated the parameters of the voice source without changing the vocal tract as a filter!

Clinical Application

Clinical Case 5: Accent Management

1. What are the major acoustic cues that predict vowel identity in English? How might you expect these cues to differ in Spanish?

2. How do articulatory movements correspond to spectral cues of vowels?

3. The SLP used spectrographic analysis to help her identify differences between vowel targets and Jaime's actual vowel production. What filter setting would be most appropriate for the SLP to use, and how might the spectrograms show such differences?

4. Once you have studied Chapter 8 (Consonants), return to this clinical case and discuss how nasal coarticulation occurs and how the SLP might help Jaime distinguish between nasalized vowels and production of the nasal consonant.

5. Once you have studied Chapter 9 (Prosody), return to this clinical case and discuss how the SLP might use both duration and spectral cues to help Jaime produce a greater distinction between unstressed and stressed syllables.

6. How is the acoustic theory of speech production relevant to Jaime's case?

Clinical Case 6: Ataxic Dysarthria

1. During the initial evaluation, the SLP asked Paul to sustain the vowel /a/ and /i/. During both tasks, Paul was unable to maintain consistent vowels. The vowel changed continually during each task. Given that Friedreich's ataxia produces uncontrolled movements, explain why the vowels changed. Include reference to resonance characteristics of the vowel tract and formant frequencies.

2. Consider the acoustic theory of vowel production: How has Paul's disease affected the biomechanics of sound source production? How has it affected resonance? Could you characterize Paul's communication disorder as a voice disorder? A speech disorder? Explain.

3. After your study of Chapter 9 (Prosody), return to this case study and explain why rate, f_0 contour, and syllabic stress would be impaired.

8

The Production and Perception of Consonants Questions

Foundational Knowledge

8.1 Introduction (p. 295)

1. Consonants can be produced with (type of airflow) _____ generated by the vibrating vocal folds and (type of airflow) generated by supraglottal vocal tract constriction.

2. A vocal tract constriction that is closer to the vocal folds is said to be (select one term) [downstream/upstream].

3. American English consonants are produced with
   A. Ingressive airflow
   B. Egressive airflow
   C. Both ingressive and egressive airflow
   D. Either ingressive or egressive airflow

4. The upper and lower boundaries of the pharynx, respectively, are the
   A. Cranium, esophagus and hypopharynx
   B. Cranium, base of tongue
   C. Nasal cavity, hyoid bone
   D. Nasal cavity, esophagus and hypopharynx

5. The inferior, middle, and superior constrictor muscles are, together, referred to as the _____.

6. A synonym for the soft palate is the _____.

7. Which of the following muscles is NOT a muscle of the soft palate?
   A. Levator veli palatini
   B. Palatopharyngeal
   C. Palatoglossus
   D. Hyoglossus

8. Closure of the velopharyngeal port is achieved primarily by contraction of the
   A. Levator veli palatini and musculi uvulae
   B. Levator veli palatini and tensor veli palatini
   C. Palatoglossus and palatopharyngeal
   D. Palatoglossus and tensor veli palatini

9. Opening of the velum is achieved primarily by contraction of the
   A. Levator veli palatini and musculi uvulae
   B. Levator veli palatini and tensor veli palatini
   C. Palatoglossus and palatopharyngeal
   D. Palatoglossus and tensor veli palatini

10. Communication of the oral and nasal cavities for production of nasal phonemes is achieved by (select one term) [raising/lowering] the velopharyngeal port.

11. True/False   The term *anatomic restructuring* refers to the growth in the overall length of the vocal tract from infancy to adulthood.

8.2 Three Sources of Speech Sounds (p. 298)

12. For each phoneme, indicate the type(s) of airflow that provides the source(s) of that sound.

    A = nearly periodic   B = turbulence   C = transient

    /s/ _____

    /z/ _____

    /b/ _____

    /r/ _____

    /m/ _____

    /p/ _____

13. Retentive coarticulation is also called _____ coarticulation.

14. Nasalization of the vowel in the word *mat* is an example of what type of coarticulation?
    A. Anticipatory
    B. Retentive
    C. Both anticipatory and retentive
    D. Both forward and backward

15. A formant transition in the VC context is the
    A. Frequency change in the vowel formants as articulation moves from the vowel to the consonant
    B. Cessation of the vowel formants as articulation moves from the vowel to the consonant
    C. Onglide of the vowel formants as articulation moves from the vowel to the consonant
    D. Decrease in intensity of the vowel formants as articulation moves from the vowel to the consonant

8.3 Phonetic Description of Consonants (p. 299)

16. The three features that traditionally describe articulation of consonants are
    A. Voicing, place of constriction, and airflow type
    B. Voicing, place of constriction, and manner
    C. Degree of constriction, airflow type, and place of articulation
    D. Voicing, place of articulation, and degree of constriction

17. True/False   All consonants in American English include lingual manipulation of the airstream.

Table 8–1. The Consonants of American English, Organized by Manner and Place of Articulation and Presence (+V) or Absence (–V) of Voicing

	Labial		Labiodental		Dental		Alveolar		Palatal		Velar		Pharyngeal or Glottal	
	–V	+V	–V	+V	–V	+V	–V	+V	–V	+V	–V	+V	–V	+V
Stops														
Fricatives														
Affricates														
Nasals														
Liquids lateral														
Liquid retroflex														
Glides (semi-vowels)														

18. Complete Table 8–1 for the consonants of American English.

19. The category of consonant continuants in American English consists of
    A. Glides, liquids, nasals, voiced fricatives
    B. All voiced consonants
    C. Fricatives glides, liquids
    D. Fricatives, glides, liquids, nasals

20. Manner of articulation refers to
    A. The degree of vocal tract constriction
    B. The presence or absence of voicing
    C. Whether or not the tongue is used for constriction
    D. Complete or partial obstruction of the airflow

8.4 Acoustic Representation of Consonants (p. 301)

21. Stop consonants are also called _____.

22. In production of a stop consonant,
    A. Complete or nearly complete occlusion of the airway occurs.
    B. Complete obstruction of the airway occurs.
    C. Release of the occlusion may be gradual or sudden.
    D. Low-amplitude voicing is always present during a stop consonant.

23. The presence of low-amplitude voicing during the closed portion of a plosive is referred to as a _____ on the spectrogram.

24. True/False   The closed portion of the vocal tract during production of a stop is called the stop gap.

25. Match the description of the energy of the spectral content of the release burst of a plosive and the phoneme. Descriptions may be used more than once or not at all.

    Bilabial   A. Energy concentrated in the higher harmonics

    Alveolar   B. Energy concentrated in the lower harmonics or across
    all harmonics
    Velar

                    C. Energy broadly distributed across all harmonics

                    D. Energy concentrated in the midfrequency harmonics

                    E. Spectral content energy is highly variable, depending upon phonetic context

26. True/False   When comparing the duration of the release burst for voiced and voiceless stop cognates, the duration is usually (select one) [shorter/longer] for voiceless stops.

27. The release of voiceless turbulent noise after the release of a voiceless stop is called _____.

28. The spectrum of aspiration noise upon release of a voiceless stop is similar to the spectrum of which fricative?
    A. /s/
    B. /f/
    C. /h/
    D. /z/

29. In American English, aspiration upon release of a stop generally may occur with

    A. Voiced stops

    B. Voiceless stops

    C. Both voiced and voiceless stops

    D. Voiceless stops in clusters

30. VOT stands for _____.

31. Voice onset time is a critical acoustic cue for perception of

    A. Stop versus fricative

    B. Manner of articulation of a plosive

    C. Voiced versus voiceless stop

    D. Rate of speech

32. Voice onset time is measured as the duration from the

    A. Stop closure to the onset of voicing

    B. Release of stop closure to the onset of voicing

    C. End of the voice bar in voiced stops to the onset of voicing

    D. Duration from the aspiration noise to the onset of voicing

33. The onset of voicing in a plosive prior to release of the closure is termed _____.

34. Positive VOT refers to

    A. Short-lag onset time of voicing after oral release

    B. Long-lag onset time of voicing after oral release

    C. Both short- and long-lag onset time of voicing after oral release

    D. Onset of voicing greater than 100 ms

35. Identify the perception of voiced or voiceless or both for each of the following VOTs

    −75 to −25 ms   _____

    40 to 100 ms   _____

    0 to 25 ms   _____

36. True/False   Duration of the closure in stops is a secondary cue for perception of voiced/voiles cognates, with longer closure duration perceived as voiced.

37. Vowels preceding voiced stops tend to be (select one) [shorter/longer] than vowels preceding voiceless stops.

38. Which of the following statements about developmental aspects of VOT is accurate?

    A. Young children produce VOTs for voiced and voiceless stops that fall within the adult range of voiceless stops.

    B. Young children produce VOTs for voiced and voiceless stops that fall within the adult range of voiced stops.

    C. By 30 months of age, all normally developing children have attained the ability to produce voiced and voiceless VOTs distinctly.

    D. Adults demonstrate greater variability than do young children in production of VOTs.

39. In the CV context, where C is a plosive, the onglide of F1 rises upward because

    A. The cross section of the vocal tract in the oral cavity is enlarging.

    B. The cross section of the vocal tract in the oral cavity is narrowing.

    C. Formant onglides are always rising and offglides are always falling.

    D. The acoustic pressure wave has greater intensity as the oral cavity opens.

40. A velar pinch describes

    A. A constriction that is produced at the velopharyngeal port

    B. A constriction that is produced in the posterior oral-pharyngeal cavity

    C. Movement of F2 and F3 toward each other in production of velar stops

    D. Movement of F1 and F2 toward each other in production of velar stops

41. True/False   Some consonants have almost no distinguishing acoustic features by themselves: The listener perceives the consonant only by formant transitions of the adjacent vowels.

42. A glottal stop is

    A. A voiced stop in which the voicing stops simultaneously with the closure of the oral cavity

    B. The sudden cessation of voicing through closure of the supraglottal vocal tract, which results in equalizing of the sub- and supraglottal pressures

    C. The sudden cessation of voicing through closure of the vocal folds

    D. A plosive produced at the level of the larynx, which, although not present in American English, is present in some other languages

43. Fricatives

    A. All have the same amount of constriction, resulting turbulent airflow

    B. Have differing degrees of constriction, all resulting in turbulent airflow

    C. Have differing degrees of constriction, some of which result in turbulent airflow

    D. In American English all have voiceless/voiced cognates

44. In regard to fricatives,

    A. The narrower the constriction, the higher the frequency range of the frication noise.

    B. The narrower the constriction, the lower the frequency range of the frication noise.

    C. The location and not the degree of constriction is the primary determining factor of the frequency range of the frication noise.

    D. Frication noise does not have specific frequencies because it is noise.

45. In American English, the /h/

    A. Is always voiceless

    B. Is produced with glottal constriction

    C. Has little energy relative to the other fricatives because, in part, the degree of constriction is quite broad

    D. Has a significant amount of higher-frequency energy

46. In regard to duration of sibilants, in general

    A. Utterance final position has minimal effect upon the duration of the sibilants.

    B. Both voiced and voiceless cognates are lengthened when occurring in utterance-final position, likely due to anticipation of cessation of voicing.

    C. The voiced cognates are longer than the voiceless cognates when occurring in utterance-final position, likely due to anticipation of cessation of voicing.

    D. The voiceless cognates are longer than the voiced cognates when occurring in utterance-final position, likely due to anticipation of cessation of voicing.

47. Fricatives reveal effects of anticipatory coarticulation in a

    A. Shift in the frequency of the frication noise and the frequency of the formants

    B. Narrowing of the frequency range of the frication noise

    C. Widening of the frequency range of the frication noise

    D. Change in the energy of the frication noise

48. Approximants are

    A. Glides and liquids

    B. Glides, liquids, and fricatives

    C. Any phoneme in which the lips or the tongue narrows the airway but does not completely occlude it

    D. Semivowels

49. The acoustic evidence for place of articulation for the approximants is
    A. A discontinuity in the waveform
    B. The formant transition of the adjacent vowel
    C. A significant reduction in the energy of the acoustic signal
    D. A stop gap

50. Tongue movement
    A. Can be independent of mandibular movement
    B. Has three degrees of freedom of movement, similar to that of the mandible
    C. Is like a hydrostat for vowel production but not for consonants
    D. Is like a hydrostat for both vowel and consonant production

51. The acoustic evidence for manner of articulation for all rhotic sounds is
    A. Low frequencies for the first three formants
    B. Low frequency for F3
    C. High frequencies for the first three formants
    D. High frequency for F3

52. In regard to the light and dark allophonic variations of /r/,
    A. The dark /r/ has a more advanced tongue than the light /r/.
    B. The dark /r/ has a more superiorly placed tongue than the light /r/.
    C. The dark /r/ occurs in the VC context and the light /r/ occurs in the CV context.
    D. The dark /r/ occurs in the CV context and the light /r/ occurs in the VC context.

53. Antiformants
    A. Are present when airflow is divided, such as in the /l/ and /m/
    B. Are present only in nasals
    C. Dampen harmonic energy
    D. Are similar to formants, in that they allow harmonic energy to pass well

54. Nasal phonemes are not considered vowels because they
    A. Are continuants, similar to certain consonants
    B. Do not completely occlude the vocal tract
    C. They completely occlude the vocal tract
    D. Are produced with a large degree of constriction of the vocal tract

55. The acoustic evidence for manner of articulation for a nasal is
    A. A low F1 frequency and a low level of energy throughout the consonant
    B. Low frequencies of the first three formants and a low level of energy throughout the consonant
    C. A high F1 frequency and a low level of energy throughout the consonant
    D. High frequencies of the first three formants and a low level of energy throughout the consonant

56. Nasals are sometimes referred to as nasal plosives because
    A. The nasal cavity is completely occluded for production of nasals, similar to production of plosives.
    B. The oral cavity is completely occluded for production of nasals, similar to production of plosives.
    C. Perceptually, nasals and plosives sound alike.
    D. Airflow is stopped momentarily for nasals and plosives.

57. Antiresonances
    A. Occur during the production of a nasal consonant but once the oral cavity is opened, the adjacent vowel is unaffected by the antiresonances
    B. Occur during the production of both oral and nasal plosives
    C. Increase the energy of the harmonics that are near the same frequency as the antiresonance
    D. Reduce the energy of harmonics that are near the same frequency as the antiresonance

58. An affricate is produced when
    A. A stop followed immediately by a homorganic fricative
    B. Any stop is followed by a fricative
    C. A stop followed immediately by a homorganic fricative or a fricative is followed by a homorganic stop
    D. A voiceless stop is followed by a voiceless fricative

59. The acoustic evidence for place of articulation of fricatives is _____.

60. The vocal tract resonates the frication noise of fricatives [upstream/downstream] from the point of constriction.

61. The alveolar and palatal voiceless fricatives "s" and "sh" (/s, ʃ/) are often referred to as _____ because of their high-frequency frication noise.

62. The location of the constriction for production of /h/ is far [upstream/downstream].

63. Stops and fricatives together are referred to as _____.

64. Approximants [are/are not] produced with turbulent airflow.

65. Glides are also called _____.

66. Two allophonic variations of the /r/ in American English are the _____ and the _____ /r/.

67. Another term for the low frequency of F1 in a nasal phoneme is _____.

68. The movement toward each other of F2 and F3 is referred to as the _____.

69. In general, spectrography is [very helpful/not very helpful] for identification of degree of nasalization.

70. The place of articulation for each stop-nasal pair is similar: that is, the place of articulation for each pair is _____.

71. True/False   The aerodynamic phenomenon that describes the generation of frication noise is the Venturi effect.

72. True/False   Frication noise is not acoustic evidence for place of articulation for fricatives because all fricatives are produced with frication noise.

73. True/False   Some voiceless fricatives are referred to as sibilants because of the high-frequency frication noise.

74. True/False   The labiodental fricatives are produced too anteriorly to allow for any vocal tract filtering.

75. True/False   Approximants, like fricatives, are distinctive in appearance from neighboring vowels in an acoustic waveform.

76. True/False   A glide produced immediately after a vowel is produced as a diphthong.

77. True/False   The formant transition from glide to vowel is more rapid than is the formant transition from vowel to vowel within a diphthong.

78. True/False   Both oral and nasal plosives have an energy burst upon release of the oral occlusion.

8.5 Clinical Application: Speech Sound Disorders (See Clinical Application Questions Section)

8.6 Language and Dialect Influences on Consonant Production (p. 342)

79. The inventory of consonants for a given language is

    A. The set of consonants that are native to that language

    B. All of the variations in the way consonants are produced within a given language

    C. The consonants that a specific speaker of a language is able to produce accurately

    D. All of the dialectical differences in pronunciation of the consonants of a given language

80. American English has a total of _____ consonants in its inventory.

81. True/False   Shared consonants are those that are common to two or more languages, but they are not necessarily pronounced exactly the same in the different languages.

82. A nonnative accent is due to

    A. Speaking an incorrect version of a language

    B. Not being a citizen of a country in which the language is spoken

    C. Differences in phonemic inventory and phonological rules between a native language and another language learned after childhood

    D. Difficulty being understood

8.7 Instrumentation and Measurement of Vocal Tract Aerodynamics (p. 344)

83. High-pressure consonants consist of

    A. Stops only

    B. Stops and fricatives

    C. Stops and nasals

    D. Stops, fricatives, and nasals

84. Intraoral pressure and breathing effort are generally greater for

    A. Fricatives than for plosives

    B. Plosives than for fricatives

    C. Nasals than for fricatives

    D. Voiceless consonants compared to voiced consonants

85. Nasalance is defined as the

    A. Ratio of nasal airflow to oral airflow

    B. Ratio of nasal energy to oral energy

    C. Ratio of nasal energy to the overall combined nasal and oral energy as measured from the acoustic pressure waveform

    D. Ratio of nasal airflow to the overall combined nasal and oral airflow

86. Nasalance scores for a speaker with normal velopharyngeal port function should be

    A. Close to zero using a reading passage that contains no nasal phonemes

    B. Approximately 25% using a reading passage that contains no nasal phonemes

    C. Approximately 25% using a reading passage that contains many nasal phonemes

    D. Approximately 59% using a reading passage that contains many nasal phonemes

87. Intraoral pressure is the pressure that builds up [anterior/posterior] to a constriction within the oral cavity.

88. Generally, children use [higher/lower] intraoral pressures than do adults.

89. True/False   Intraoral air pressures for voiced and voiceless plosives are generally approximately 100 and 75 mL of air, respectively.

90. True/False   Nasalance normative data are dependent upon the number of nasal phonemes within the tested utterance.

91. True/False   Nasalance is measured from the airstream flowing through the nose and mouth during speech.

8.8 Instrumentation for Measuring Articulation (p. 347)

92. Optoelectronic tracking systems used light-emitting diodes in three-dimensional space to track articulator movement

    A. Of the lips and mandible

    B. Of the tongue

    C. Of the lips, mandible, and tongue

    D. Of any articulator or point in the vocal tract

93. Electropalatography uses an array of touch-sensitive electrodes to record
    A. Location and timing of the contact between the tongue and the palate and between the tongue and the lips
    B. Location, timing, and pressure of the contact between the tongue and the palate and the tongue and the lips
    C. Location and timing of the contact between the tongue and the palate
    D. Location, timing, and pressure of the contact between the tongue and the palate

94. The research instrumentation that uses narrow-beam x-rays to track the movement of tiny gold pellets affixed to the articulators is called _____.

95. The instrumentation used to measure electromagnetically induced currents in receiver coils placed about the head to track midline articulator movement is called _____.

96. In electropalotography, the plate that is fit into the mouth and is used to insert the electrodes is called a _____.

97. True/False   Instrumentation for measuring articulation often uses point-tracking methodology on articulator locations both within and outside of the oral cavity.

98. True/False   Electropalatography can record either the location of articulator contact or the activity of contact across time, but not both location and timing.

Conceptual Integration

1. CV and VC refer to, respectively,
   A. Monosyllabic words containing one or more consonants and vowels
   B. Syllables of the structure consonant-vowel and vowel-consonant, respectively
   C. Consonant-vowel and vowel-consonant structures, respectively, that may or may not comprise a full syllable
   D. Consonant-vowel and vowel-consonant structures that represent heavily coarticulated phonemes

2. What is meant by the statement that obstruents are consonants that have a phonemic voicing distinction? Explain and also give an example.

3. What is meant by the statement that, in American English, consonants carry a heavier functional load for phonemic distinctions than do vowels?

4. Explain coarticulation.

5. What are vowel formant transitions and how do they provide acoustic cues for the identification of consonants in the VC environment?

6. Given that both the /b/ and the /m/ are produced with complete occlusion of the vocal tract, why is it that voicing cannot be maintained during the closed portion of the /b/ for as long as a nasal such as /m/?

7. Explain the meaning of the statement "The duration of voice onset time is on a continuum and other factors contribute to perception of plosive voicing."

8. Explain how hypernasal speech can reduce overall intelligibility.

9. You are interested in measuring the VOT for a series of plosives. How might the waveform that was obtained from the microphone signal assist in your measurements?

10. The frication noise for /f/ and /θ/ has a broader spectrum and lower energy compared to other fricatives because
    A. The resonating cavity anterior to the place of articulation is small and the constriction is not as narrow.
    B. The resonating cavity posterior to the place of articulation is quite large and the constriction is not as narrow.
    C. The constriction is much narrower.
    D. These phonemes are voiceless.

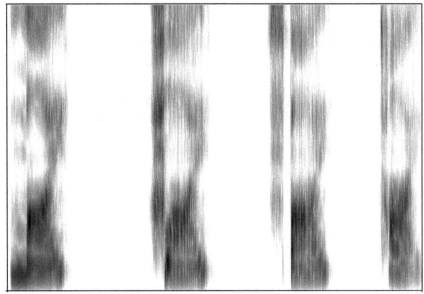

Time (s)

Figure 8–1

11. The four words /spaɪ/, /taɪ/, /maɪ/, and /flaɪ/ (but not necessarily in that order) are shown in the spectrogram in Figure 8–1. Identify the correct order of the words by labeling the spectrogram with each word. Then, label the major acoustic evidence that supports your decision.

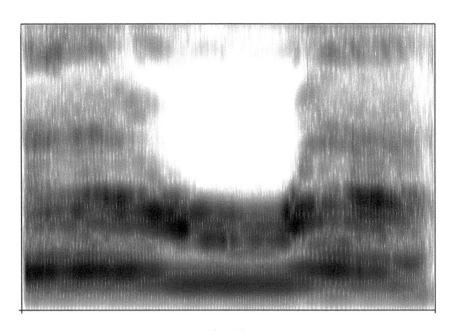

Time (s)

Figure 8–2

12. The spectrogram shown in Figure 8–2 represents a VCV syllable. What evidence do you see in the vowel formant offglides and onglides that suggests movement of the articulators as the consonant is produced? What manner(s) of consonant do you think was produced?

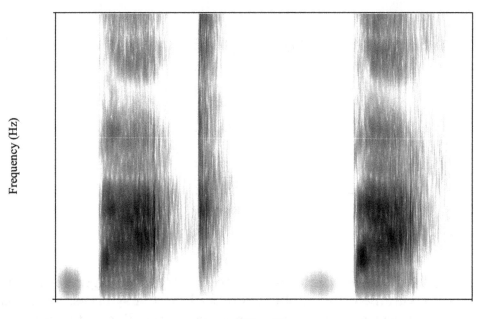

Time (s)

Figure 8–3

13. Figure 8–3 shows a spectrogram of two productions of the word *back*. In one production, the /k/ was released, and in the other production provide, the /k/ remained unreleased. Label the released and unreleased /k/ and the evidence to support your decision.

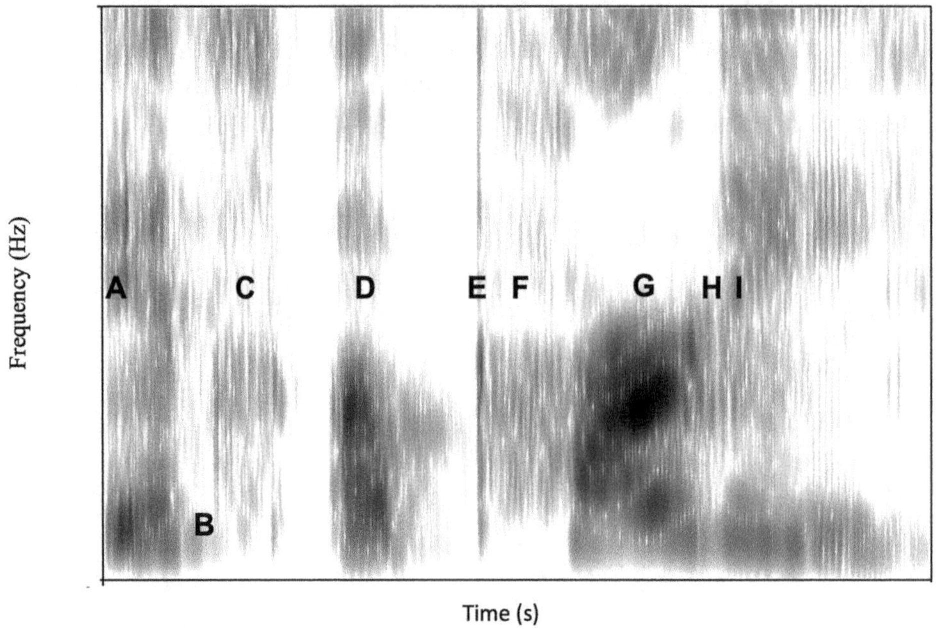

Figure 8–4

14. A spectrogram of the utterance "It's a party!" is shown in Figure 8–4. Label the spectrogram with the orthographic words and the IPA symbols. Then, match the letters in the spectrogram with the number corresponding to the appropriate description of events.

A = _____   1. Frication noise of /s/ of "it's"

B = _____   2. Formant movement of /ɑr/ of "party"

C = _____   3. /ɪ/ of "it's"

D = _____   4. Release burst of /p/ of "party"

E = _____   5. Final vowel /i/ of "party"

F = _____   6. Voice bar of closed portion of /d/ in the affricate
                       /ds/ affricate of the word *it's* (the /t/ is voiced due to
G = _____   carryover articulation of the preceding vowel)

H = _____   7. /ʌ/ vowel (centralized vowel in unstressed position) of
                       the word *a*
I = _____
                    8. Aspiration noise of released /p/ of *party*

                    9. Closed portion of /d/ (/t/ is voiced due to carryover
                       and anticipatory coarticulation and rapid production
                       obscures clear release burst)

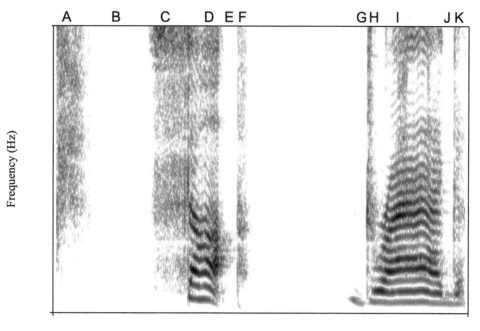

Frequency (Hz)

A B C D E F G H I J K

Time (s)

Figure 8–5

15. Figure 8–5 shows a narrowband spectrogram of the words *stop* and *drag* (although not necessarily in that order). Use the presence or absence of harmonic energy to identify the words and explain the events identified in each letter.

16. Producing a vowel and then moving the articulators to completely block all airflow will result in what type of consonant?

    A. Fricative

    B. Stop or affricate

    C. Nasal

    D. Glide

17. Producing a vowel and then moving the articulators to completely block airflow through the oral cavity while maintaining transglottal airflow will result in the production of this type of consonant

    A. Nasal

    B. Fricative

    C. Liquid

    D. Stop

18. What is the source of sound for the /v/ phoneme?
    A. Frication noise
    B. Transient noise
    C. Both frication noise and phonation
    D. Phonation

19. Which of the following phonemes is produced with the lowest resistance to transglottal airflow?
    A. /r/
    B. /b/
    C. /s/
    D. /k/

20. How can a phoneme have more than one source of sound?

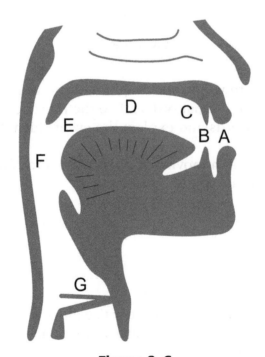

Figure 8–6

21. Figure 8–6 shows a midsagittal view of the vocal tract. What phoneme(s) can be produced if the lips (location "A") are completely closed?

22. Considering Figure 8–6, the tongue is positioned to produce a tight constriction made at location "C" and then at location "E." How will blowing air through the constriction at each of those locations result in a different sound quality?

23. If an individual would begin to vocalize with the articulatory posture shown in Figure 8–6, what would be the result?

    A. A voiced fricative would be produced.

    B. An unvoiced stop would be produced.

    C. A nasalized vowel would be produced.

    D. A glide would be produced.

24. Using Figure 8–6, consider closing the velopharyngeal port and producing frication noise at location "G" (the vocal folds). What characteristics of the resulting phoneme will occur?

25. Considering Figure 8–6, completely stopping the airflow through the oral cavity at location "E" but maintaining an open velopharyngeal port will result in what phoneme(s)?

    A. /k/ or /g/

    B. /ŋ/

    C. /r/

    D. No phonemes are produced this way, as all phonemes require airflow through the oral cavity.

26. Considering Figure 8–6, what phoneme(s) will be produced if the velopharyngeal port is closed and oral airflow is blocked at position "C"?

    A. /n/

    B. /l/ or /r/

    C. /t/ or /d/

    D. /w/ or /j/

27. Considering Figure 8–6, why do dental fricatives and labiodental fricatives sound very similar?

28. Using Figure 8–6, consider that the distance from location "C" to the lips is 4 cm. What will the lowest resonant frequency be for the tube defined by a constriction formed at location "C"?

29. How does the acoustic (or source-filter) theory of speech production account for production of consonant phonemes?

30. How will formants and antiformants affect the harmonics produced by phonation?

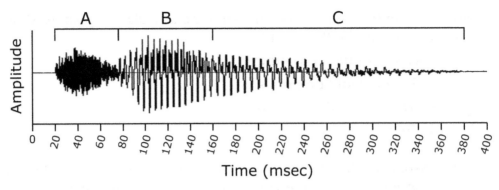

Figure 8–7

31. Figure 8–7 shows a syllable consisting of a consonant and a vowel. Which section(s) show(s) a vowel?

    A. Section A, as this section shows a relatively low amplitude, and vowels are typically low amplitude

    B. Section B, as the duration of this section is typical for a vowel

    C. Sections B and C, as both show a periodic waveform indicative of phonation as the sound source

32. For Figure 8–7, consider that the vowel is a stop. Measure the voice onset time to determine if it is a voiced or voiceless stop consonant.

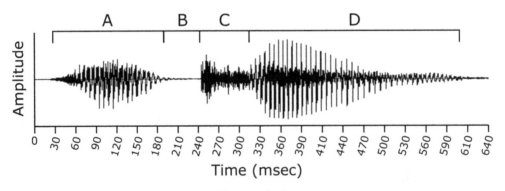

Figure 8–8

33. Figure 8–8 shows a VCV syllable. Sections A and D show the two vowels. What does section B represent?

    A. Antiformants and a nasal phoneme

    B. Stop gap for a stop consonant

    C. Frication noise

    D. A very low-amplitude vowel segment

34. In Figure 8–8, what is shown in section C?

    A. Aspiration noise

    B. A nasal phoneme

    C. A voiced fricative

    D. A glide

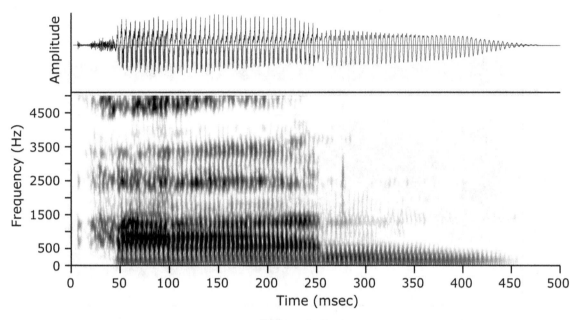

Figure 8–9

35. Figure 8–9 shows the waveform and spectrogram plots for a word containing a vowel and a consonant. At approximately what time does the vowel begin?

    A. 0 ms

    B. 50 ms

    C. 100 ms

    D. 250 ms

36. In Figure 8–9, consider that the consonant shown is a nasal. At approximately what time does the nasal consonant begin?

    A. 0 ms

    B. 50 ms

    C. 100 ms

    D. 250 ms

37. In Figure 8–9, why does the amplitude of the sound become reduced at approximately 250 ms?

    A. 250 ms indicates the onset of a voiced fricative.

    B. 250 ms indicates the onset of an unvoiced fricative.

    C. 250 ms indicates the onset of a nasal murmur and the effect of antiformants.

    D. 250 ms indicates the onset of a low-amplitude vowel.

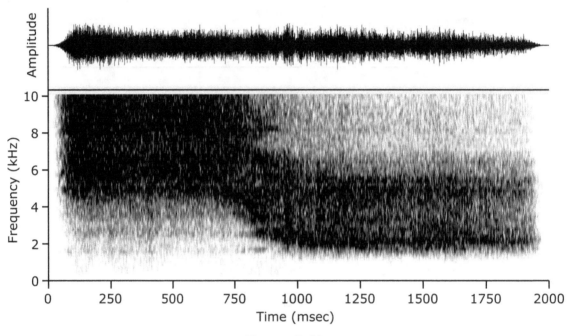

Figure 8–10

38. Figure 8–10 shows fricative production, with the fricative noise changing between 750 and 1,000 ms. What can you conclude about the position of the area of constriction that is producing the frication noise?

    A. A constriction near the front of the oral cavity is being moved backward.

    B. A constriction near the back of the oral cavity is being moved forward.

    C. The constriction is at the vocal folds and shows the effect of vocal tract vowel resonance.

    D. A nasal murmur is beginning at around 750 ms.

39. Considering Figure 8–10, what can you conclude about articulatory positioning?

    A. It is likely that the lips are opening, beginning at 750 ms and ending at around 1,000 ms.

    B. It is likely that the velopharyngeal port is opening, beginning at 750 ms.

    C. It is likely that the vocal folds are beginning to vibrate at approximately 750 ms.

    D. It is likely that the tongue is sliding backward along the hard palate beginning at around 750 ms.

40. Using Figure 8–10, what phoneme(s) do you suspect is/are being produced?

    A. An /f/ followed by a vowel

    B. An /s/ followed by a nasal

    C. An /s/ followed by an /ʃ/

    D. An /f/ followed by a /z/

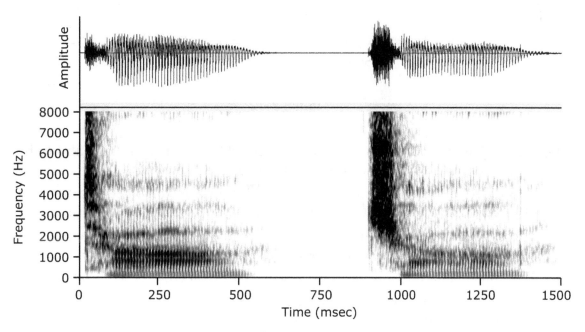

Figure 8–11

41. Figure 8–11 shows two CV syllables. What conclusion can you make about the manner of production for the consonants in each syllable?

    A. The consonants for both of these syllables appear to be a nasal.

    B. The consonants for both of these syllables appear to be a glide.

    C. The consonants for both of these syllables appear to have frication noise.

    D. The consonant for the first syllable appears to be a nasal, while the consonant for the second syllable appears to be a voiced fricative.

42. Considering both the waveform and the spectrogram shown in Figure 8–11, what consonant phonemes do you suspect are being produced?

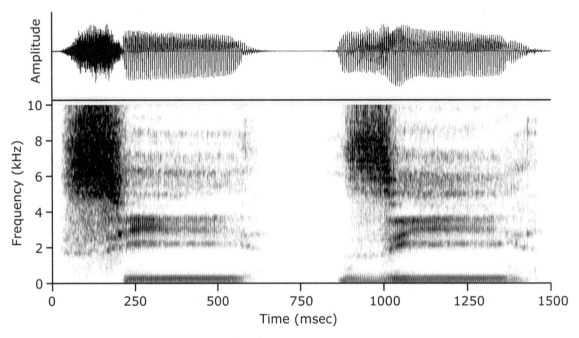

Figure 8–12

43. Figure 8–12 shows two CV syllables. What conclusion can you make about the manner of production for the consonants in each syllable?

   A. The consonants for the first syllable appear to be an unvoiced fricative, and the consonant for the second syllable appears to be a nasal.

   B. The consonants for the first syllable appear to be a stop, and the consonant for the second syllable appears to be a liquid.

   C. The consonants for both of these syllables are voiced.

   D. The consonant for the first syllable appears to be unvoiced, while the consonant for the second syllable appears to be voiced.

44. In Figure 8–12, what can you conclude about the place of production for each consonant?

   A. Based on the spectral energy of the consonants and the formant transitions of the following vowel, both consonants appear to be produced in the same articulatory location.

   B. Based on the duration of the spectral energy for the consonants, both consonants appear to be glottal in terms of place of articulation.

   C. Based on the formant transitions of the following vowel, the first and second consonants appear to be produced in different articulatory locations.

45. Considering both the waveform and the spectrogram shown in Figure 8–12, what consonant phonemes do you suspect are being produced?

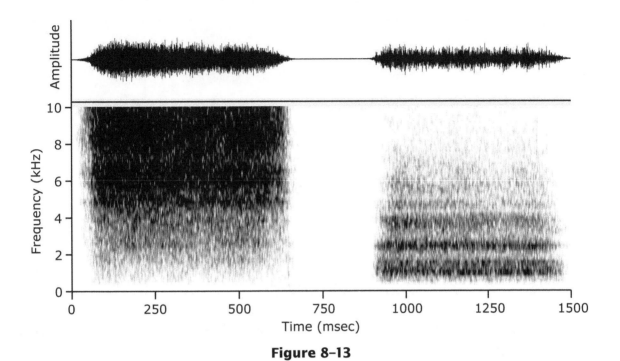

Figure 8–13

46. Figure 8–13 shows two fricative phonemes. Which phoneme is produced with the location of turbulent airflow generation closer to the lips?

47. For the right-side phoneme in Figure 8–13, why does the phoneme show a series of horizontal bars on the spectrogram plot?

    A. The right-side phoneme is likely an /h/ that is causing the entire vocal tract to resonate and therefore revealing the vocal tract formants.

    B. The right-side phoneme is likely a /z/ and the horizontal bars show the fundamental frequency and the harmonics of phonation.

    C. The right-side phoneme is likely a /f/ or /θ/, and the horizontal bars reflect the low resonant frequencies associated with those phonemes.

    D. The right-side phoneme is likely a /tʃ/, and the horizontal bars show the voice onset time.

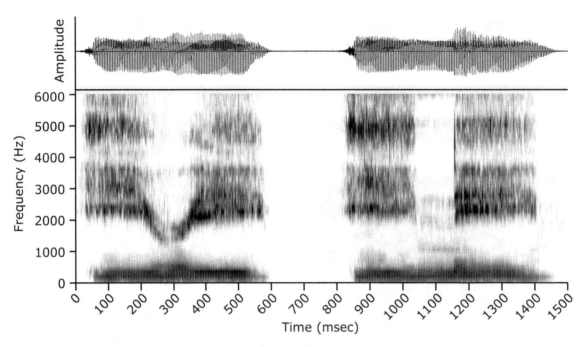

Figure 8–14

48. Figure 8–14 shows two VCV syllables. Which syllable shows evidence of an open velopharyngeal port?

A. The left syllable shows a "velar pinch" as the velopharyngeal port opens at about 300 ms.

B. The left syllable shows a nasal murmur that starts at approximately 200 ms and ends at approximately 350 ms.

C. The right syllable shows a nasal murmur and evidence of antiformants from about 1,050 to 1,150 ms.

D. The right syllable shows an increased amplitude and presence of a nasal murmur starting at approximately 1,150 ms, both of which indicate an open velopharyngeal port.

49. In Figure 8–14, what articulatory movement is causing the drop in formants 2 and 3 in the left (first) syllable from approximately 200 to 400 ms?

A. The velopharyngeal port is opening.

B. The lips are opening.

C. The lips are rounding and extending.

D. The tongue is moving to a retroflex position.

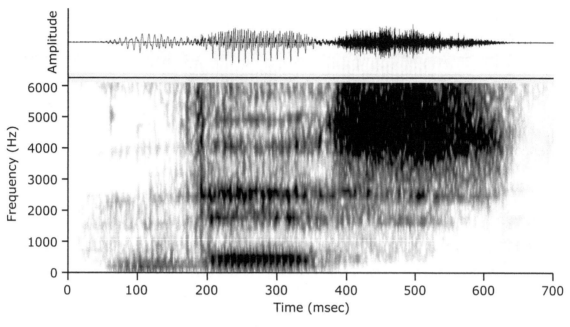

Figure 8–15

50. In Figure 8–15, how many phonemes are shown?

    A. Two phonemes: one vowel that begins at approximately 50 ms and one consonant that begins at approximately 400 ms

    B. Two phonemes: one consonant that begins at approximately 50 ms and one vowel that begins at approximately 400 ms

    C. Three phonemes: a weak voiced fricative that begins at approximately 50 ms, a vowel that begins at approximately 200 ms, and a strong unvoiced fricative that begins at approximately 400 ms

    D. Three phonemes: a nasal that begins at approximately 50 ms, a vowel that begins at approximately 200 ms, and a voiced fricative that begins at approximately 400 ms

51. Considering Figure 8–15, what characteristics of the initial phoneme provide clues as to its features of production?

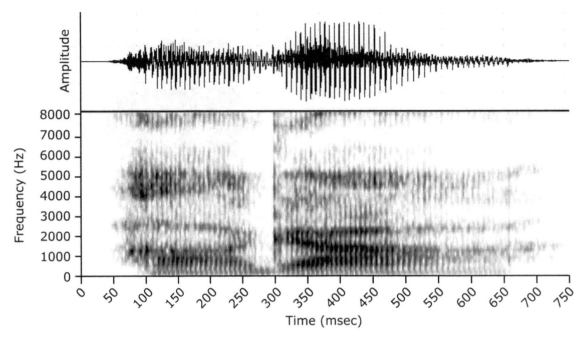

Figure 8–16

52. Figure 8–16 shows a syllable with a stop consonant. What characteristics indicate whether or not this is a voiced stop?

53. Why do the formants for the vowels change immediately prior to and immediately after the stop consonant in Figure 8–16?

54. Why does production of the nasal consonants and the liquid /l/ result in the generation of antiformants?

55. Why is relatively high air pressure necessary for the production of stops, affricates, and fricatives as compared to vowels, nasals, liquids, and glides?

TRY IT!

1. Pucker your lips and blow some air through them. If you keep them in an "o" shape (and don't blow too hard), the sound you're hearing is due to laminar airflow. With laminar airflow, the air molecules are moving in the same direction (i.e., parallel to each other) and at the same speed. In other words, they are moving with the same velocity. While some sound is produced, you can dramatically increase the sound generated by putting a finger in the airstream near your lips. When the airstream hits the obstacle (your finger), the air molecules begin to move in various directions and speeds, causing turbulent

airflow characterized by continual fluctuations in airflow and pressure. The turbulent airflow is the sound that you hear. Try blowing air through nearly closed lips or through the small gap produced when you bring your upper incisors into light contact with your lower lip. Yep, frication noise is indicative of turbulent airflow!

2. Now that you know how to make frication noise by having an airstream hit an obstacle or by forcing air through a tight constriction, produce some frication noise into an acoustic filter. Make a very loose fist with one hand to produce a shape like a tube or an air chamber. Make some frication noise with an airstream and direct it into your handheld acoustic filter. How does the sound change when it resonates in the filter? If you have a cardboard paper-towel roll or another tube, try that as a resonator as well. Consider the production of /f/ versus /s/ versus /ʃ/ phonemes in regard to your newfound knowledge of the effects of an acoustic resonator on frication noise.

3. Which phonemes use phonation as a sound source? While you can memorize the list of voiced and unvoiced phonemes, it's more fun to figure it out yourself! Place your fingers on the side of your larynx and say the phrase "where were you a year ago" in a low-pitched voice. In this phrase, all of the phonemes are voiced—you should feel constant or nearly constant vibration in your fingers as you say it. This vibration you feel is actually the vibration of the vocal folds. Now say the phrase "I see some sheep often," again using a low-pitched voice. Here, you'll feel the vibration start and stop depending on whether a voiced or voiceless phoneme is being produced. Try feeling your vocal fold vibration for other phrases, too, as most will have a combination of voiced and voiceless phonemes. Why bother memorizing lists of voiced and voiceless phonemes when you can just as easily figure it out for yourself!

4. Say the word *map* and then try to reproduce the /a/ sound in isolation just as you produced it within the word *map*. Most likely, you will hear nasalization of the vowel, due to carryover coarticulation from the nasal /m/. Now say the word *tap* and again, try to reproduce the /a/ sound in isolation just as you produced it within the word *tap*. Most likely, you will not hear any vowel nasalization. Finally, can you produce the nasalized /a/ and then the orally resonated /a/ and alternate between them? You should feel your velopharyngeal port open and close as you alternate between the two vowels.

5. Sustain the voiceless fricatives /s/, /f/, and /θ/. Listen for the difference in pitch among the three phonemes. Review the reasons as discussed in your textbook for the spectral characteristics of these fricatives. (Hint: Degree and location of constriction.) Can you alter your manner of articulation slightly to change the pitch of each phoneme? (Hint: Make the constriction a bit narrower or broader and shift the placement a bit more anteriorly or posteriorly.)

6. Say the words *laugh* and *all*. The /l/ in "laugh" is the light allophone. Feel how the light /l/ is produced forward in the oral cavity. The /l/ in "all" is the dark allophone. Feel how the dark /l/ is produced with a different tongue shape and positioned more posteriorly in the oral cavity. Try to say the word *laugh* with the dark /l/ and say the word *all* with the light /l/. Do the words sound and feel different? Is it more awkward to switch the two allophones? What role might coarticulation play in the production of these allophones?

Clinical Application

Clinical Case 7: Facial Nerve Trauma

1. What consonants would you expect Sean to have the most difficulty producing? Think carefully—he can't contract the orbicularis oris. In addition to bilabials, could he also have difficulty producing labiodental sounds?

2. Consider the primary acoustic cues for the consonants that Sean cannot produce correctly. How might you expect those cues to be altered? What effect might those changes have upon speech perception (that is, understanding the phonemes)?

3. Consider the acoustic cues for bilabial plosives. How would exaggerated movement of the mandible and rapid release (lowering) of the mandible simulate those acoustic cues?

4. What vowels would you expect Sean to have difficulty producing accurately? Identify those.

5. How are the formant frequencies of the vowels changed by lack of labial movement? Review Table 7–1 and Figure 7–14 to help you answer the question.

6. The listener cannot rely on the usual visual cues obtained from lip movement. How might the lack of visual cues affect listener understanding of Sean's speech? (See Chapter 11 for discussion of visual information and speech perception.)

7. Consider this case again after reading Clinical Case 12 in Chapter 10. Make the case for or against using nonspeech oral motor exercises to strengthen Sean's articulation and prosody.

Clinical Case 8: Articulation Errors

1. What are the major acoustic cues of /s/ and /ʃ/?

2. Explain why a difference in pitch is perceived between /s/ and /ʃ/. That is, what is responsible for the differences in pitch? What are the articulatory postures responsible for these differences in pitch?

3. How would you explain the acoustics of fricative production to the child's parents?

Speech Sound Disorders

1. Speech sound disorders can be divided broadly into two categories of causes
   A. Congenital and acquired
   B. Organic and nonorganic
   C. Physical and psychological
   D. Conscious (purposeful) and unconscious (automatic)

2. Childhood apraxia of speech is a type of speech sound disorder that
   A. Does not involve muscle weakness
   B. Usually involves muscle weakness
   C. Frequently involves only one phoneme
   D. Is usually identified as a simple type of disorder

3. The major difference between articulation and phonological problems relates to
   A. The time of onset of the disorder
   B. Whether the disorder is organic or nonorganic in origin
   C. Whether or not the child is a second-language speaker
   D. The involvement of linguistic rules

4. True/False Usually, an evaluation of speech sound disorders involves an oral motor examination only in the case of suspicion of an organic cause.

5. Why is the normal age of acquisition of phonemes important to consider when evaluating a child for a potential speech sound disorder?

6. A speech sound error that is an unavoidable consequence of a structural problem is called a(n) _____ error.

9

Prosody Questions

Foundational Knowledge

9.1 Introduction to Prosody (p. 363)

1. Prosody is
   A. The suprasegmental features of an utterance that are defined relative to each other
   B. One component of the suprasegmental level of speech
   C. Features of vowels, but not consonants, that add emotional intent
   D. Independent of speech intelligibility

2. Another term for prosody is the _____ level of speech.

3. A prosodic feature [can/cannot] be measured independent of other values of the same prosodic feature.

4. True/False   Suprasegmental refers to phenomena that do not involve vowels and consonants, while prosody refers to pitch and loudness changes independent of phonemes.

9.2 Basic Building Blocks of Prosody (p. 363)

5. The three basic acoustic features of prosody are
   A. Fundamental frequency contour, syllabic stress, and rhythm
   B. Fundamental frequency contour, intensity contour, and duration and juncture
   C. Pitch, loudness, and timing
   D. Fundamental frequency contour, intensity contour, and syllabic stress

6. Match the acoustic characteristics of prosody on the left with the corresponding perceptual features on the right. Perceptual features may be used more than once or not at all.

   _____ Fundamental frequency contour   1. Timing

   _____ Intensity contour   2. Stress

   _____ Duration and loudness   3. Intonation

   4. Loudness changes

7. Fundamental frequency declination
   A. Is due solely to the decrease in lung pressure over time as the utterance progresses
   B. Becomes steeper as the overall length of the utterance increases
   C. Is due to a combination of factors, relaxation of intrinsic laryngeal muscles, and possible linguistic factors associated with anticipation of the end of a phrase
   D. Is present in speakers with breathing disorders but not in healthy speakers

8. Juncture
   A. Occurs at the end of phrases but not between syllables themselves
   B. Is a synonym for the prosodic feature of duration
   C. Is always greater in emotional speech
   D. Is the pause time or separation between syllables

9. Duration is
   A. An inherent feature of vowels and consonants and cannot be manipulated at the prosody level without distorting words
   B. Both an inherent feature of vowels and consonants and a feature of prosody that can be manipulated to convey meaning
   C. How long a speaker holds vowels, on average
   D. Can be used to signal the end of a semantic unit, such as a phrase, by decreasing the duration of one or more syllables

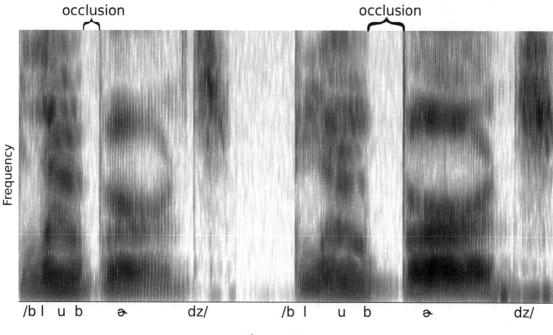

occlusion   occlusion

Frequency

/b l u b ə dz/   /b l u b ə dz/

Figure 9–1

10. In Figure 9–1, the spectrogram shows two productions of the same utterance with a difference in the occlusion of a voiced plosive. This difference is an example of a contrast in

   A. Fundamental frequency

   B. Intensity

   C. Duration

   D. Juncture

11. The utterance-level pitch contour is referred to, perceptually, as _____.

12. The tendency for fundamental frequency to decrease gradually over the course of an utterance is called _____.

13. The perceptual feature of timing is composed of the acoustic features of _____ and _____.

14. The loudness level of a sound relative to other sounds of similar length, pitch, and stress, is called _____.

15. At the prosodic level, the intensity and fundamental frequency contours often [do/do not] covary.

16. True/False   Intonation contour may vary from one syllable to the next within a statement, but often it will also slowly decline across the entire statement.

17. True/False   Juncture is the pause time or separation between one utterance (sentence) and the next one.

18. True/False   Preboundary lengthening is the use of increased duration of one or more syllables in utterance-final position.

19. True/False   Sonority refers to the change in intensity of syllables within an utterance that a speaker uses to create meaning or emotional context.

9.3 Syllabic Stress and Prominence (p. 370)

20. Syllabic stress
    A. Is accomplished by change in intensity across a phrase
    B. Is achieved through intonation changes
    C. Involves the use of changes in all three of the basic prosodic elements within a word
    D. Is defined by the communicative intent of the speaker

21. A stressed syllable is often
    A. Higher in pitch, softer, and shorter in duration
    B. Higher in pitch, louder, and shorter in duration
    C. Lower in pitch, softer, and longer in duration
    D. Lower in pitch, louder, and longer in duration

22. Phrase prominence
    A. Is specified by the communicative intent of the speaker
    B. Is language defined
    C. Is a synonym for stress
    D. Is identified by a single acoustic cue

23. True/False   Syllabic stress can involve the use of changes in frequency, intensity, and duration or just the change in one of the three components of prosody.

24. True/False   Syllabic stress can be heightened or lessened, depending upon the speaker's communicative intent, but the stress cannot be changed to a different syllable.

25. True/False   Only one syllable or word in an utterance can receive phrase prominence.

9.4 Speech Rhythm (p. 374)

26. Speech rhythm
    A. Is a poorly defined concept despite the fact that people readily perceive a rhythm to speech
    B. Is defined by periodicity of the phrase prominence pattern
    C. Is defined by the isochronicity of syllables within a given language
    D. Is generally consistent across all languages

27. Traditionally, the predominant rhythm of a given language was categorized as
    A. Characterized by syllabic stress or phrase stress
    B. Having either fluent or nonfluent characteristics
    C. Based upon the vowel, the consonant, or the syllable
    D. Syllable timed, stress timed, and mora timed

28. Temporal measures of speech rhythm identify ratios of the relative durations of
    A. Vocalic and consonantal segments
    B. Vowels and consonants
    C. Stressed and unstressed syllables
    D. Stress-timed and syllable-timed phrases

29. The temporal rhythm metric that compares the duration of sequential pairs of vocalic or consonantal intervals is called the _____.

30. ΔV is the _____ of the vocal interval durations.

31. True/False   Speech rhythm relates to temporal patterns: Rhythm is independent of spectral patterns.

32. True/False   A language that is on the syllable-timed end of the continuum tends to have syllables of equal duration.

33. True/False   A language that is on the stress-timed end of the continuum tends to contain syllables of variable duration and the stressed units occur at equal intervals, like "Morse code."

9.5 Accentedness and Prosody (p. 376)

34. Accentedness

   A. Refers mainly to the use of nonnative vowels and consonants—the use of different stress and prominence patterns is only a minor factor

   B. Refers to pronunciation differences between native and nonnative speakers of a language—not to differences between different dialects of the same language

   C. Reflects a perceptual difference in pronunciation that includes all features of prosody

   D. Reflects differences between some languages but not others

35. True/False   Not all languages use pitch, duration, and loudness to mark syllabic stress and phrase prominence.

9.6 In Summary of Prosody (p. 376)

36. A broad definition of prosody includes

   A. Interaction of fundamental frequency and intensity contours and duration

   B. Linguistic, paralinguistic, and nonlinguistic information that is not directly inferable from the written counterpart

   C. Segmental and suprasegmental features

   D. Speaker- and language-based features

Conceptual Integration

1. Prosodic changes, although considered "suprasegmental," occur at the segmental level. What does that mean?

2. Syllabic stress is language defined, while phrase prominence is speaker defined. What does that mean?

Prosody

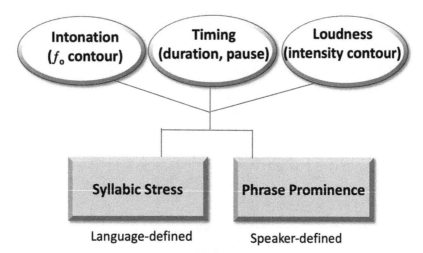

Figure 9–2

3. Figure 9–2 is a graphical representation of prosody. Explain the figure, making sure to identify the differences in perceptual and acoustic components and the contribution of language-based rules and speaker-defined choices to the components.

4. The current phonological approach to description of language-based rhythm emphasizes

   A. That all languages have the same basic rhythm: It is the individual speakers that demonstrate variety of rhythmic features

   B. Vowel reduction and the variety of available syllable structures, in addition to basic prosodic features

   C. All three basic prosodic features

   D. Speaker individuality

5. In syllabic stress and phrase prominence

   A. Fundamental frequency contour is the most important prosodic feature.

   B. Intensity contour is the most important prosodic feature.

   C. No single, defining prosodic feature has been proven.

   D. Fundamental frequency contour is most important for prominence while intensity contour and duration are most important for stress.

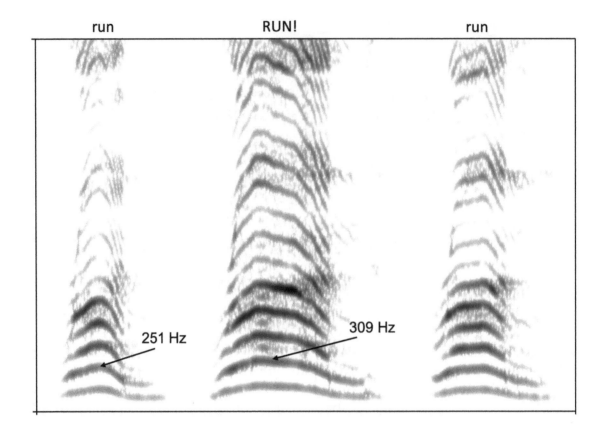

Time (s)

Figure 9–3

6. The spectrogram in Figure 9–3 represents three utterances of the word *run*. The first and third utterances were said in citation form, but the second utterance was said as a command, as though giving a person an urgent order to run. How might you describe the prosody of the command utterance compared to the citation utterances, and what acoustic evidence do you see to support your description?

7. Draw an f_o contour, similar to the ones shown in Chapter 9, for the phrase "I know" spoken as a factual statement, and then spoken in exasperation (as if to say "You've told me a hundred times already!"). Compare the two curves and identify the major differences between them.

8. See Question 1 in TRY IT! Think of a pair of words that differ only in syllabic stress. Draw an intensity contour, similar to the ones shown in Chapter 9, that might represent the words.

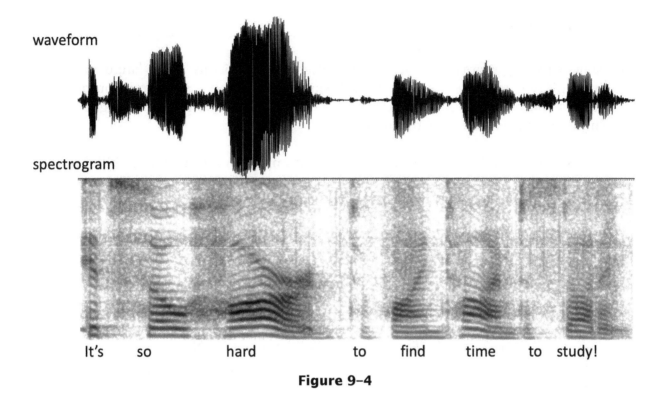

waveform

spectrogram

It's   so   hard   to   find   time   to study!

Figure 9–4

9. The waveform and spectrogram in Figure 9–4 represent the utterance, "It's so hard to find time to study!" On what syllables has the phrase prominence been placed, and what acoustic evidence do you see to support your answer?

TRY IT!

1. Some words change meaning with a change in syllabic stress, such as deSERT and DESert. Can you think of other examples?

2. Think of a simple sentence. With a conversational partner, say the sentence aloud and alter the prosody to convey a different emotion or meaning. Have your partner guess the intent. Then, discuss what attributes of prosody you manipulated to convey each emotion.

3. Two examples in which changes in juncture alter the meaning of an utterance are *white shoes* and *why choose*; *I'm making* and *I'm aching*. Can you think of another example in which change in duration played a significant role in change of meaning?

Clinical Application

1. Children with pragmatic disorders may often have difficulty using language appropriately to make their needs and wants known and may have incomplete understanding of the communicative rules of social interaction. Why might such a child also have a prosodic disorder?

2. Apraxia is a neurological-based disorder that impairs an individual's ability to coordinate and sequence the rapid movements required for speech. Why might an individual with apraxia have impaired prosody?

Clinical Case 9: Parkinson's Disease

1. What key features of prosody did the SLP address with Cheung in Mandarin and English? Which prosodic features were not addressed?

2. Explain the differences in the prosody approach used by the SLP for Mandarin and English. (Be aware of the difference between f_o contour, word stress, and phrase prominence.)

3. What is the relationship between intensity, increased depth of inhalation, and increased mouth opening (see Chapters 5 and 7)?

4. How is the acoustic theory of speech production relevant to Cheung's speech-voice deficit?

Clinical Case 10: Gender-Diverse Speech and Voice

1. What are the major acoustic characteristics that help define gender?

2. How does prosody help define gender?

10

Theories and Models of Speech Production Questions

Foundational Knowledge

10.1 Introduction (p. 386)

1. Theories of speech motor control seek to explain how we organize the movement of our articulators in three-dimensional space, called _____ organization, and also how we coordinate the timing of separate movements, called _____ organization.

10.2 Theories and Models (p. 388)

2. The relationship between hypotheses and theories can be described as

   A. Multiple hypotheses collectively support a theory.

   B. Multiple theories collectively support a hypothesis.

   C. A hypothesis is generally broad statements of prediction.

   D. A theory is synonymous with a model, which explains complex systems.

3. True/False   A hypothesis is not based upon observed phenomenon.

4. True/False   Models of speech production are always simple.

5. The principle of parsimony, which advises scientists to avoid excessive complexity in theories and models, is also called _____.

10.3 Theoretical Issues for Consideration (p. 390)

6. All of the potential ways in which the articulators can move to produce a sound is referred to as their [potential/effective] degrees of freedom.

7. True/False   The number of muscles that connect to a structure, such as the mandible, represents the degrees of freedom of that structure.

8. Models that propose acoustic output as the primary target of our speech production system are supported by
   A. Data from individuals with hearing loss and the concept of effective degrees of freedom of the articulators
   B. Data from individuals with hearing loss and from individuals with oral cavity sensory deficits
   C. Data from individuals with hearing loss and the concept of motor equivalence
   D. Data from artificial speech systems

9. Models that propose that the configuration of the articulators and the vocal tract are the primary goal in speech production are said to have the _____ as the primary output target.

10. Two levels of the motor system are proposed that comprise a motor program
    A. The central and peripheral nervous system levels
    B. The executive and effector levels
    C. The intentional and the feedback levels
    D. The executive and the error correction levels

11. True/False   Motor program theory does not explain very well the acquisition of novel articulatory gestures.

12. Problems with the motor program theory include
    A. The slowness of feedback systems for production of rapid speech movements
    B. The need for preprogrammed articulatory gestures in variable contexts
    C. The omission of the role of sensory feedback
    D. Insufficient room in the brain for storing the number of motor programs required for speech production

13. Feedback for regulation and error correction of output targets is achieved through sensory input from the
    A. Auditory sensors
    B. Auditory and tactile sensors
    C. Auditory, visual, and tactile sensors
    D. Auditory, tactile, pressure, and muscle spindle sensors

14. True/False   The phrase "muscle memory" refers to changes in neural networks associated with repetition of complex sequential movements.

15. The spatiotemporal organization of the articulators refers to the
    A. Relative position of the mobile and immobile articulators within the oral cavity
    B. The path of an articular in three-dimensional space and the trajectory or time within which it travels that path
    C. Relative distance between the articulators as a sound is produced
    D. The velocity of the movement of the articulators as a sound is produced

16. Movements of the mandible
    A. Are basically the same in speech and chewing, although the range of motion differs between the two activities
    B. Are achieved through distinct patterns of muscle activation for the two activities
    C. Occur in two dimensions: upward (closing) and downward (opening)
    D. Are generally not considered important in speech therapy

17. Coarticulation
    A. Involves mainly the temporal adaptation of articulator movement to produce more than one speech sound simultaneously
    B. Involves mainly the spatial adaptation of articulator movement to produce more than one speech sound simultaneously
    C. Involves both the temporal and spatial adaptation of articulator movement to produce more than one speech sound simultaneously
    D. Is a linguistic function that is largely independent from biomechanical constraints

18. Research on the development of speech motor control in children demonstrates that

    A. The smaller articulatory space of the child is not a factor in movement control because the relative distances between the articulators are similar to those of an adult.

    B. Maturation of temporal and spatial accuracy of articulatory gestures is complete by approximately 10 years of age.

    C. Incompletely developed perceptual skills are a greater factor in maturation of speech motor control than are development of biomechanical skills.

    D. The smaller articulatory space of a child, together with incomplete maturation of biomechanical and perceptual skills, are all likely factors that guide development.

19. The basic unit of analysis for examination of speech motor control is generally defined as

    A. The phoneme

    B. The syllable

    C. The articulatory gesture

    D. A variety of units, including the phoneme, syllable, phrase, and gesture

20. A prestructured set of commands that function to achieve a movement is called a _____.

21. The transfer of a portion of the speech production system's output back to the input for regulation and error correction is called _____.

22. A feedback system in which the controlling action is dependent upon the output is called a/an [open/closed] feedback loop.

23. The mandible has six dimensions of movement, of which three are _____ and three are _____.

24. The adjustment of articulator movement to target more than one speech sound simultaneously is called _____.

10.4 Models of Speech Production (p. 404)

25. The acronym DIVA to identify a model of speech production stands for

    A. Detailed interaction of variable articulators

    B. Diagrammed interchange of vectored articulators

    C. Directions into velocities of articulators

    D. Detailed view of interactions of articulators

26. The DIVA model is

    A. Computational and neuroanatomic

    B. Physical

    C. Animal based

    D. Chemical-neurologic

27. True/False   The DIVA model has been applied to simple speech disorders such as articulation errors but has not yet been used to explain complex disorders such as stuttering or hearing impairment.

28. Which of the following concepts does the DIVA model NOT address?

    A. Motor equivalence

    B. Coarticulation

    C. Prosody

    D. Speaking rate

29. The DIVA model proposes that, as infants are learning to produce speech sounds, infants (select one) [can/cannot] perceive a distinction between speech sounds prior to being able to produce the sounds.

30. The concept of a coordinative structure of muscles that work together synergistically to achieve production of a speech sound is part of the theory of _____.

31. A description of the path and trajectory of the articulators relative to some frame of reference is called the _____ organization of the articulators.

32. A numerical index of the consistency of movement across multiple repetitions of an utterance is called the _____.

33. The spatiotemporal index provides a quantitative assessment of the

    A. Amount of temporal and spatial variability of an articulator over multiple repetitions of an utterance

    B. Amount of temporal or spatial variability, depending upon how the index is measured, of an articulator over multiple repetitions of an utterance

    C. Total variability of all articulators, taken together, over multiple repetitions of an utterance

    D. The ideal path and trajectory of an articulator for a given movement, compared to the actual path and trajectory

10.5 Investigational Considerations (p. 408)

34. The speaking task used to investigate speech motor control in research
    A. Can include mono- or multisyllabic words produced in isolation, words produced within a carrier phrase, short phrases, or nonsense words
    B. Never includes nonsense words, because sensorimotor control of nonlinguistically meaningful movements is different than that of linguistically meaningful movements
    C. Is almost always running speech, because identification of temporal and spatial features of articulator movement requires multiple repetitions
    D. Is usually designed to remove almost all possible speaker variability, so that analysis of spatial and temporal features of articulator movement can be identified reliably

35. Research studies that use perturbation methodology
    A. Create cognitive distractions to the speaker
    B. Seek to examine the adaptive response of the speaker
    C. Always involve unanticipated sudden changes to the articulatory system of the speaker
    D. Always involve alterations of the range of motion of the articulators

36. The research methodology used to cause a sudden disturbance to the speaker's vocal tract is called _____.

10.6 Motor Learning Principles (p. 413)

37. The practice and feedback conditions that we use to facilitate learning and retention of new or revised speech sounds are called _____ principles.

38. True/False   Variable practice is generally more effective than constant practice in learning a new motor behavior.

39. Identify the preferred type of practice, according to motor learning theory, for learning new motor behaviors.

    Large amount/Small amount

    Massed/Distributed

    Constant/Variable

    Random/Blocking

    External target/Internal target

    Simple targets/Complex targets

40. Identify the preferred type of feedback, according to motor learning theory, for learning new motor behaviors.

    Knowledge of performance/Knowledge of results

    Lesser frequency/Greater frequency

    Immediate/Delayed

10.7 Language and Speech (p. 415)

41. Two theories to explain how increased motor and cognitive demands of speech are managed are
    A. Limitation of resources and serial processing
    B. Limited number of degrees of freedom of the articulators and limited cognitive resources
    C. Limited range of motion of the articulators and speech errors
    D. Slot-and-filler model and frame-and-content theory

42. The theory that describes an utterance as composed of smaller units of dynamic gestural postures is called _____.

Conceptual Integration

1. Speech events such as voice onset time or onset of lip rounding are examples of (select one term) [spatial/temporal] organization.

2. Current models of speech production
    A. Are designed to manipulate variables to predict outcome
    B. Cannot include data from animal experiments because animals do not have the capacity for speech production
    C. Must remain theoretical or based upon computer simulations, rather than physical, because of the complexity of speech production
    D. Are based upon research data that can only be interpreted in a way that supports the model

3. Theories of control of the degrees of freedom of the articulators during speech production

   A. Focus mainly upon the target output of the speech production system, that is, the sound

   B. All focus upon the hierarchical organization of the speech production system from the highest neurological levels to the peripheral sensory system

   C. Focus mainly upon how the articulatory movements can be grouped into smaller units of movement

   D. All seek to explain how all of the potential movements of the articulators are organized into a smaller set of actual movements

4. Models that propose aerodynamic variables, including stable air pressure and resistance to airflow, as a critical target of our speech production system are supported by data from individuals

   A. Who have impaired function of the velopharyngeal port or who have cleft palate

   B. With hearing loss

   C. With respiratory disease

   D. With no structural or health deficits

5. In an open feedback loop,

   A. The control is independent of the action.

   B. The control is dependent upon the action.

   C. The control is a central part of the activity itself and also an outside agent.

   D. Speech would not be possible.

6. Much of the research on speech motor control has explored articulator movement in one or two dimensions because

   A. Three-dimensional movement analysis does not contribute significant additional information to speech motor production.

   B. The frame of reference of movement for each articulator is the same, so three-dimensional analysis is not essential.

   C. Most instrumentation used for speech motor analysis has limited capabilities to analyze three-dimensional space.

   D. Articulatory movement occurs in two dimensions.

7. Briefly explain the DIVA model.

8. Review Figure 10–14 in the textbook, which provides a diagram of the early babbling phase of learning on the left and the imitation learning phase on the right according to the DIVA model. Briefly describe the major differences between the two speech acquisition phases, as proposed by this model.

9. What is the difference between learning and performance, according to motor learning theory?

10. Theories of motor learning are heavily based upon learning and retention of nonspeech motor activities. What difficulties might this present for application of motor learning theory to speech production?

11. The influence of changes in rate of speech are not consistent in the research literature because
    A. Articulatory strategies to adapt to changes in rate of speech are similar across all speakers.
    B. Articulatory strategies to adapt to increased rate are the same as those for decreased rate.
    C. Speaker variability may increase with change in rate of speech.
    D. Many research subjects cannot change their rate of speech.

12. What is the difference between a scientific hypothesis, a theory, and a model?

13. The "motor program" theory would be advantageous for speech production in situations where
    A. The individual is learning a new language
    B. The individual is carefully sounding out a novel word
    C. The individual is producing a commonly used word or phrase
    D. The individual is listening for errors in their phoneme production

14. In isolation, the motor program theory reflects what type of control process?
    A. Feedback control
    B. Feedforward (or open-loop) control

15. True/False   Perturbation studies have provided evidence to support feedback control of speech.

16. True/False   Information about the biomechanical properties of the articulators can help to inform theories of speech production.

17. Misarticulating a phoneme and then immediately correcting it is an example of
    A. Feedback control
    B. Feedforward control
    C. Coarticulation
    D. A motor program

18. The ability to produce rapid speech (i.e., a fast speech rate) provides some evidence in support of

    A. The motor program theory

    B. Feedback control

    C. Motor equivalence

    D. Degrees of freedom

19. How do experiments of altered sensory feedback support both feedback and feedforward aspects of sensorimotor control theory?

20. Why is the phoneme not considered to be the basic unit of speech that is coordinated and controlled by the speech motor system?

21. The phenomenon of coarticulation is likely due to

    A. Biomechanical constraints such as muscle mechanics as well as neural control of articulators

    B. Feedback control

    C. Motor programming

    D. Muscle memory

22. True/False   Acoustic characteristics that demarcate individual phonemes as seen on a spectrogram directly correspond to clear demarcations in data of movements of the articulators.

23. The use of a bite block can result in

    A. Reduction of the degrees of freedom of the jaw and an increase in jaw stability

    B. An increase in coarticulation effects

    C. An elimination of all sensory feedback

    D. A greater variability of jaw movement

24. The concept of motor equivalence means that

    A. If you produce multiple repetitions of the same utterance, your articulatory movements will be the same every time.

    B. Two people saying the same word will produce different articulatory movements.

    C. Words that sound the same acoustically are produced with the same articulatory movements.

    D. We will produce the same articulatory movements for the same word produced across the age span.

25. Why is motor equivalence evident during speech production?

26. Grouping of synergistic muscles into functional units may be a way to
    A. Eliminate motor equivalence
    B. Generate motor programs
    C. Reduce the degrees of freedom of an articulator
    D. Reduce sensory feedback

27. Why does reduction in auditory system function typically result in a deterioration of speech production?
    A. The sensory feedback loop using auditory information will be disrupted.
    B. The motor program for speech will not be carried out.
    C. The degrees of freedom of the articulators will be reduced.
    D. Feedforward control would no longer be able to use auditory information to correct errors as they happen.

28. Why is it unlikely that feedback control is the predominant control strategy for producing speech in adult speakers?
    A. With feedback control, no motor equivalence can be present.
    B. Feedback control produces an increase, not a decrease, of the degrees of freedom of the articulators.
    C. Error correction based on sensory feedback is too slow as compared to the rate of running speech.
    D. In adult speakers, elimination of all sensory feedback has no effect on the production of speech.

29. Why is it so difficult to come to a conclusion on whether or not the acoustic output, articulator positioning, or aerodynamic monitoring is the primary output target of our speech production mechanism?

30. Selecting the wrong set of prestructured central commands so that you would say "frog" when you meant to say "dog" suggests an error with
    A. Enacting a motor program at the cognitive level
    B. Feedback control of the articulators
    C. Motor equivalence
    D. Degrees of freedom of the articulators (specifically the tongue for this example)

31. How can the DIVA model of speech account for motor equivalence?

32. Why are experimental paradigms that strongly control the speech task limited in what they can explain about speech production?

33. What is meant by stating that articulatory movements are "combined into gestures"?

34. Why can't we conclude that a change to the rate of speech will have a corresponding change to the articulatory kinematics?

    A. Some studies have found an increased rate of speech to be associated with decreased amplitude of articulatory movement, while other studies have found the opposite.

    B. Articulatory kinematics are only related to production of the individual phoneme irrespective of speech rate.

    C. Speech rate increases will always yield a decrease in articulatory movement.

    D. While we can produce speech at different rates, the articulatory kinematics never changes; otherwise, we would affect the production of the phoneme.

TRY IT!

1. Let's explore the concept of "degrees of freedom." While observing yourself in the mirror, gently move your mandible around in every direction that you can. (Be gentle!) Next, while still observing yourself in the mirror, recite a nursery rhyme or speak a few lines of a song. Compare the movements of your mandible during the gentle movement and the speaking. Did you notice the same movements for the two tasks? Most likely, you noticed fewer directions of movements and smaller range of motion of the mandible during the speaking tasks. Speech constrains the many potential degrees of freedom of the mandible to a few effective degrees!

2. Let's explore rate of speech. In general, do you consider yourself to be a fast talker? Slow talker? Average talker? Try to increase your rate of speech. Grab some simple reading material—any of the reading passages at the end of the textbook in Appendix B would be good to try. Read aloud the paragraph at your typical speaking rate. Next, reread the paragraph approximately 50% faster. Read it one more time aloud, increasing your rate to twice as fast as your typical rate. How did the changes in rate influence the range of motion of your articulators and the extent of coarticulation? Most likely, you found that the range of motion was decreased and the coarticulation was increased, perhaps to the extent that your speech was not clear.

   Now explore a slower rate. Read the same passage at approximately a 50% slower rate, and then again twice as slow as your typical rate. Was it easier or more difficult to slow down? How did the slower rate affect the range of motion of your articulators and coarticulation? Was the clarity of your speech affected? Discuss with your fellow students why rate and coarticulation appear to be connected, in light of your reading on theories of speech production.

3. Take a (clean) pen or pencil and bite on it with your molars on one side of your mouth. Now say the phrase "Wherever you go, there you are" with your pencil bite block. Can you still produce each phoneme clearly or at least clearly enough to be understood? Try saying some other phrases and also try with an even larger bite block (perhaps a thicker pen), and pay attention to the compensatory movements your lips and tongue make to this alteration in your jaw position and movement. Your other articulators will compensate immediately! How amazing that you can immediately change how the articulators are controlled in order to compensate for such a disruption!

4. Say the word *smootinzate*. You've probably never said that word before, have you? But you likely didn't have any difficulty in saying this novel word. Why not? This novel word does follow phonotactic rules for sequencing phonemes in English, and perhaps you have motor programs in your speech motor system that correspond with those phonotactic rules. Or perhaps you have used feedforward control successfully to coordinate the movements of your articulators. Finally, you may have used feedback control to correct for errors during the production. If you repeat this novel word multiple times, it's likely that you will rely less and less on feedback control, allowing you to increase the rate of production of this word! Isn't it fun learning new (nonsensical) words?

5. Say the phrase "The sixth sheik's sixth sheep's sick." Now say it again, but with an increased speech rate. It's tough, isn't it? Tongue-twisters require us to produce articulatory gestures with challenging transitions. Consider the final /θ/ on "sixth" and the following initial /ʃ/ on "sheik's," for example. We don't get the benefit of coarticulation allowing blending of those phonemes, and we need to make a distinction between those words by pausing. The transition between the /θ/ and the /ʃ/ therefore is quite daunting. In terms of motor control, we likely don't have a motor program that handles that transition well. Considering the DIVA and the dynamical systems models of speech production, however, practice in saying that tongue-twister will likely produce great improvement!

Clinical Application

Clinical Case 11: Spastic Cerebral Palsy

1. After reading this chapter, particularly the discussion of speaking rate and coarticulation, return to this case and discuss the potential effect of dysarthria on both speaking rate and coarticulation.

2. After reading the section on output targets later in this chapter, return to this case and discuss the different types of output targets that might be incorporated into the SLP's feedback to the patient during exercises to modify speaking rate.

Clinical Case 12: Oral Motor Exercises

1. Why might oral motor exercises be a popular therapy goal, despite the lack of evidence to support its efficacy?

2. How might models of speech production, such as the DIVA and dynamical systems models, be used to support or refute the concept of oral motor exercises as representative of speech production?

11

Theories of Speech Perception Questions

Foundational Knowledge

11.2 Topics in Speech Perception (p. 429)

1. Some critical topics of speech perception research include
   A. How vowel formant patterns remain the same in different consonant contexts
   B. How humans "chunk" or encode acoustic information
   C. Whether or not the acoustic signal can be divided into separate phonemes that are perceived in isolation as single consonants
   D. Whether or not humans can ignore unnecessary information ("noise") in the acoustic speech signal

2. A contributing factor to the lack of invariance in the speech signal is
   A. Its linearity
   B. The fact that all possible phonemes are not represented in every language
   C. The difference in perception of pitch with increasing loudness
   D. Coarticulation

3. Factors that assist in perceptual normalization include

A. Familiarity with the person who is speaking

B. Liking the person who is speaking

C. Being the same age as the person who is speaking

D. Having the speaker talk loudly

4. The theory that humans have a specialized neural mechanism for perceiving speech sounds, compared to nonspeech sounds,

A. Is definitively supported by many research studies

B. Is definitively refuted by many research studies

C. Is supported by listeners' ability to perceive sharp discontinuities in a continuum of small changes in consonant-vowel syllables

D. Is supported by listeners' ability to perceive sharp discontinuities in a continuum of small changes in consonant-vowel syllables

5. The McGurk effect

A. Occurs when frequency and intensity are varied in opposite directions over the course of an utterance

B. Describes the tendency for humans to perceive acoustic features of speech based upon the linguistic content of what is being said

C. Demonstrates that incongruity in simultaneous auditory and visual perceptions of a stimulus can lead to perception of a unique stimulus

D. Has been heavily refuted by many research studies

6. In research, gating tasks

A. Can be used to assess the effect of semantic meaning on speech perception

B. Involve changing the rate of parts of an utterance to determine the effect on perception

C. Demonstrate that word identification is independent of the semantic context in which it is spoken

D. Involve using visual stimuli that is inconsistent with the semantic stimuli

7. True/False   Clear boundaries between phonemes can be identified from an utterance.

8. Identification of phoneme boundaries in the spectrogram (select one term) [always/sometimes] corresponds to the segmentation perceived by the listener.

9. The process by which the listener reduces the variability in the acoustic speech signal to better understand what is being said is called _____.

10. True/False   Although listeners use perceptual normalization to ignore speaker variability, listeners also do pay attention to that variability to help identify speaker characteristics.

11. The phenomenon of discontinuous, categorical perception is an example of the [lack of invariance/quantal perception] of speech.

12. The simultaneous perception of nonspeech and speech stimuli extracted from segments of the acoustic speech signal is called _____ perception.

13. True/False   Research data on quantal perception have been used to both support and refute the theory of specialized neural mechanisms for speech perception.

11.3 Theories of Speech Perception (p. 434)

14. The theoretical models of top-down and bottom-up address
    A. The extent to which the acoustic signal provides essential and sufficient information for perceptual recognition
    B. The extent to which perceptual information contributes to speech recognition and processing
    C. Whether listeners pay attention first to the individual phonemes or to the larger linguistic context of the phrase in processing speech
    D. The level of detail to which the listener attends

15. The theoretical models of active and passive speech perception address
    A. Whether or not perceptual processing occurs in the absence of external data
    B. The presence or absence of cognitive processing
    C. The extent to which hypothesis testing about phonetic or linguistic interpretation is used
    D. The extent to which the listener is actively participating in a conversation

16. The major features of the motor theory of speech perception are
    A. The concept of percept, analysis by synthesis, and the need for contextual or linguistic cues
    B. Biological specialization of speech perception, analysis by synthesis, and lack of invariance
    C. The assumption of actual physical movements of the articulators as the units of perception and the biological specialization of perception
    D. The use of visual, auditory, and tactile feedback in planning articulatory movements

17. The motor theory may be particularly relevant to speech perception in adverse listening conditions, such as

    A. Speech embedded in high-frequency broadband noise

    B. Speech embedded in low-frequency broadband noise

    C. Speech disorders

    D. The "cocktail party" problem

18. In the acoustic landmarks and distinct features model of speech perception, the landmarks used in the analysis of the acoustic signal are

    A. Vocalic, glide, and consonantal

    B. Vowels and consonants

    C. Vowels, stops, glides, and fricatives

    D. Vocalic, stop, and consonantal

19. A data-driven approach to speech perception is [top-down/bottom-up].

20. Speech perception theories that posit the need for contextual, linguistic, and cognitive cues are considered [top-down/bottom-up].

21. True/False   Autonomous theories of perception posit that perceptual processing occurs within a closed system.

22. The direct-realist theory of perception is based upon theories of visual perception and the concept of the _____, which is what the listener perceives and not the actual acoustic event.

23. Mirror neurons are located primarily in the

    A. Premotor cortex

    B. Motor cortex

    C. Somatosensory cortex

    D. Somatosensory association cortex

24. True/False   Strong evidence from studies of human behavior demonstrate the use of mirror neurons in cognitive process.

11.4 What Babies Can Tell Us About Perception (p. 438)

25. Research data suggest that infants begin to perceive basic contrasts in native language phonemes by approximately what age?

    A. 2 months

    B. 4 months

    C. 6 months

    D. 12 months

26. True/False   Research data on infant perception of speech indicate that infants cannot adapt to the inherent variability in the speech signal across multiple speakers.

27. The perceptual theory based upon the formation prototypes of phonetic categories based upon the listener's native language during early developmental stages is called the _____ theory.

11.5 Perception of Speaker Identity (p. 441)

28. The characteristics of speaker identity that we perceive in the acoustic signal are referred to as _____.

29. True/False   The features of speaker identity perceived by the listener in the acoustic signal are considered (select one term) [linguistic/extralinguistic] information.

30. Indexical properties of speaker identity

    A. Are judgments based upon learned behaviors

    B. Are acquired at a young age and remain invariant throughout life

    C. Are consistent across languages and cultures

    D. Are objective features of the acoustic signal

31. In regard to gender and sex

    A. Both are essentially the same for purposes of indexical information

    B. Listeners are generally more accurate in identification of speaker sex than speaker gender

    C. Listeners are generally more accurate in identification of speaker gender than speaker sex

    D. Biology determines both sex and gender

32. True/False   The semantic content of a message can influence the listener's perception of the degree of accentedness of a speaker.

33. Race (select on term) [is/is not] based on learned social factors.

Conceptual Integration

1. Theories of speech perception propose that acoustic features are perceived by the listener in "chunks" rather than in individual bits because
   A. Similar features must be grouped together in order to be perceived.
   B. Unimportant features are encoded as "chunks" and important features are encoded as individual bits.
   C. The number of acoustic features is too large and the transfer rate would have to be too fast for a listener to be able to perceive the features in individual bits.
   D. Many theories, in fact, do propose that individual bits of information are not encoded into groups or "chunks."

2. Explain the meaning of acoustic-phonetic invariance and give an example.

3. Explain the meaning of lack of segmentation of the acoustic speech signal and give an example.

4. How can accentedness be based, in part, on listener-related factors? Provide two examples of such factors.

5. How might the process of perceptual normalization help a listener's ability to understand speakers with different types of dialectical and nonnative accents of a language?

6. The ability to understand the word *dog* when it is spoken by an adult or by a young child is an example of
   A. Perceptual normalization
   B. Quantal perception of speech
   C. Categorical perception of speech
   D. Duplex perception

7. The modification of phoneme production due to coarticulation is an example of what factor that the perceptual system must deal with?
   A. Perceptual normalization
   B. Lack of invariance
   C. The McGurk effect
   D. The motor theory of speech perception

8. Systematically modulating the second formant transition for CV syllables in incremental, graded fashion to range from /b/ to /g/ as the consonant results in
   A. A perceived coarticulatory blend of the /b/, /d/, and /g/ phonemes
   B. A novel phoneme that is not quite a /b/ or a /d/ but a blend of the two
   C. Perception of /b/, /d/, and /g/ as the only defined "categories"
   D. Perception of a series of consonants that were described to be in the category of affricates

9. How does voice onset time for voiced and voiceless stop consonants provide evidence to suggest that speech perception involves unique neural processes?

10. What does the McGurk effect tell us about speech perception?

11. The ability to perceive "sinewave speech" provides some evidence for
    A. Bottom-up theories of speech perception
    B. Top-down theories of speech perception
    C. Categorical perception
    D. Duplex perception

12. This theory of speech perception posits that the listener uses their own stored knowledge of articulatory gestures for production of speech as the unit of perception.
    A. Mirror neuron theory
    B. Distinctive features theory
    C. Bottom-up theories
    D. The motor theory

13. This theory of speech perception posits that we perceive the category of "vowels" due to the spectral characteristics of the first formant.
    A. Distinctive features theory
    B. Motor theory
    C. Native language theory
    D. Top-down processing

14. How can the use of nonspeech stimuli inform our understanding of speech perception?

15. True/False   If speech was completely invariant, the formant frequencies for infants, children, and adults would be identical.

16. What is one reason for the lack of invariance in speech?
    A. Vocal tract sizes are different for different individuals such as children versus adults.
    B. Each phoneme is produced the same way, irrespective of the speaker.
    C. Each phoneme is produced the same way, irrespective of the phonetic context.
    D. The concept of motor equivalence suggests that articulator movements are equal and identical across individuals and phonetic context.

17. Why is speech perception by infants different than by adults?

18. True/False   Studies of infant perception have provided some evidence for the idea of an innate, unique mechanism for speech perception.

19. Animal studies of speech perception provide evidence that
    A. Supports the motor theory of speech perception
    B. Refutes the concept that speech perception relies on human-specific unique processing mechanisms
    C. The unit of speech perception is the phoneme.
    D. There is no "lack of invariance" problem regarding speech perception.

20. The fact that listeners will perceive a bilabial plosive as "voiceless" given a voice onset time that could vary from 40 to 100 ms or greater provides evidence for
    A. Categorical perception of phonemes
    B. The phoneme as the unit of analysis for speech perception
    C. Coarticulation in terms of speech perception
    D. Duplex perception

21. Although both the motor theory and the native language magnet theory–expanded focus on the connection between speech perception and production, how do these theories differ?

22. Why can't the speech perception system simply match acoustic characteristics to the specific phonemes of speech?

23. How is speech perception related to judgments of speaker identity?

24. Why would a pure "bottom-up" theory not adequately explain speech perception?

TRY IT!

1. Grab a listening partner (well, ask nicely), and say the phrase, "My left nose listens through shiny dust sandals." Yes, it doesn't make sense, but that's the point. See if your listener can comprehend the phrase correctly, including all correct phonemes. But make it even more challenging by saying the phrase with your hand blocking your mouth to muffle the sound. How does the lack of context and the distorted speech acoustics affect your listener's ability to comprehend the sentence or the individual phonemes? Think of a few other nonsense sentences to try. What other modifications to the speech signal could you perform, such as blocking the view of your mouth that might negatively affect someone's perception of speech?

2. The cocktail party effect refers to our ability to pay attention to speech of a single person even though it may be in the context of multiple competing speakers. The next time you're at a cocktail party (or perhaps a noisy restaurant), try to listen to a single speaker while plugging one ear with a finger. Does speech perception (and potentially your ability to pay attention to that speaker) deteriorate if you disrupt the auditory signal by blocking an ear (or even both)? What about if you eliminate the visual component of speech perception by deliberately not looking at the speaker? Which condition (disrupting the auditory signal or disrupting the visual signal) makes the listening task harder?

Clinical Application

Clinical Case 13: Visual Feedback

1. Why might visual feedback play a different role in the early stage of skill acquisition compared to later stages of retention and learning?

2. After reading about the updated motor theory of speech perception, explain how that theory might apply to use of visual feedback in learning phoneme production.

Clinical Case 14: Auditory Feedback

1. Build a short, logical argument in support of and then against the influence of perceptual training as a precursor to production training in phoneme production.

2. Review the DIVA model of speech production in Chapter 10. How does it describe the role of perception in speech production?

3. Why might the role of perceptual feedback be different in children with articulation problems compared to adults learning pronunciation of a nonnative language?

12

Instrumentation Questions

Foundational Knowledge

12.1 Introduction to Measurement (p. 452)

1. The term *instrumentation* as it is currently used in speech science refers to

   A. Any machine that can record the speech audio signal

   B. Any digital machine that can record the speech audio signal

   C. Any machine that can capture objective data about speech production

   D. Any digital machine that can capture objective data about speech production

2. Speech instrumentation is generally used in (select one term) [research/clinical/both research and clinical] settings.

12.2 Basic Principles of Measurement (p. 452)

3. The physical quantity to be measured is called the _____.

4. Which of the following statements about measurement is true?

    A. The physical quantity we want to measure dictates the instrumentation to be used.

    B. The instrumentation to be used dictates the physical quantity we want to measure.

    C. The physical quantity to be measured is independent of the instrumentation to be used.

    D. Measurement uncertainty is addressed once the physical quantity is measured.

5. The process of comparing the instrumentation's output to a known standard is called _____.

6. Measurement error

    A. Can be completely avoided if one adheres to proper measurement protocols

    B. Can occur due to variables beyond our control

    C. Occurs when a noise floor exists in the electronics of the instrumentation

    D. Is prevented with correct calibration

7. The small magnitude of noise generated by the instrumentation itself is referred to as the _____.

8. The signal to noise ratio

    A. Must be 1 to obtain valid and reliable measures

    B. Should be as high as possible to obtain valid and reliable measures

    C. Should be as low as possible to obtain valid and reliable measures

    D. Is built into the instrumentation and cannot be altered

9. The process of changing energy from one form to another is called _____.

10. The following is an example of a transducer

    A. Pencil

    B. Air

    C. Rubber band

    D. Microphone

11. A sensor
    A. Produces an output that is proportional to the magnitude of the energy received
    B. Produces an input that is proportional to the magnitude of the energy received
    C. Is dependent upon electrical energy
    D. Is a transducer

12. True/False   All sensors respond to similar types of energy.

13. The change in a signal from the input to its output is called the (select one term) [transfer/conversion] function.

14. An instrument that converts acoustic energy to electrical energy is called a (select one term) [acoustic resonator/microphone].

15. Match the term on the left with the type of energy on the right. Energy types may be used more than once or not at all.

Term	Energy
Volts	Aerodynamic
Current	Potential
Kinetic	
Alternating	
Direct	

12.3 Sensors for Capturing Speech (p. 457)

16. True/False   Microphones and pneumotachometers are both examples of sensors.

17. True/False   Pneumotachographs can measure oral airflow but not nasal airflow.

12.4 Microphones (p. 459)

18. Three types of microphones are the handheld, lavalier, and _____.

19. The two main types of microphone transducers are
    A. Battery powered and plug-in
    B. Condenser and dynamic
    C. Electret and voltage based
    D. Multi- and omnidirectional

20. The microphone transducer which is based on electromagnetic induction is a (select one term) [dynamic/condenser] type.

21. If you use a condenser microphone, you must
    A. Use an external source of power for the microphone
    B. Have a magnet for calibrating the microphone periodically
    C. Not record very loud sounds, which can ruin the microphone
    D. Remove the cover and clean the contacts periodically to prevent noise

22. True/False   The term *phantom power* refers to the external power source for the condenser microphone.

23. A circular plot showing the degree to which a microphone can capture sound is called a _____ plot.

24. A cardioid directional response pattern is also called a _____ response pattern.

25. In an environment with significant ambient noise, it is best to use a microphone with what type of directional response pattern?

26. The term *proximity effect* refers to
    A. A cardioid microphone that is too close to the speaker
    B. An omnidirectional microphone that is too close to the speaker
    C. A response pattern that emphasizes the high frequencies
    D. A response pattern that damps the high frequencies

27. When all the frequencies that a microphone is sensitive to are captured with equal amplitude, the microphone is said to have a (select one term) [full/flat] frequency response.

28. The range of frequencies to which a microphone responds best is called a _____ plot.

29. For clinical and research analysis of speech and voice production, the optimal frequency response for a microphone is
    A. Cardioid
    B. Flat
    C. High-pass
    D. Low-pass

30. True/False   A nonuniform frequency response of a microphone may be used to provide the most pleasant sound for listeners.

31. Amplified presentations such as in the theater or concert hall, as well as hearing aids, can sometimes create reamplified acoustic waves referred to as _____.

32. A microphone that has a maximum SPL of 160 dB and a self-noise level of 35 dB will have a dynamic range of how many dB?
    A. 160
    B. 195
    C. 125
    D. 35

33. True/False   A microphone with a high sensitivity means that it can respond well to high-frequency sounds.

34. The dynamic range and frequency response of a microphone should be (select one term) [greater than/similar to/less than] the physiologic range of speech.

12.5 Amplification (p. 466)

35. A preamplifier
    A. Evens the inevitable irregularities in the voltage so that it is ready to be amplified
    B. Increases the amplitude of the voltage so that it can be used by other instrumentation
    C. Steepens the cutoff frequencies of the signal so that it is ready to be amplified
    D. Measures the voltage to identify whether the signal needs to be amplified to be used by other instrumentation

36. The increase in amplitude of a signal is called _____.

37. In general, impedance refers to
    A. The ease with which electricity flows through the microphone circuits
    B. The resistance of the microphone's diaphragm to the incoming acoustic pressure wave
    C. The degree to which the microphone interferes with the flow of the acoustic pressure wave from the speaker's mouth
    D. The degree of constriction airflow through the microphone circuits

38. True/False   The impedance characteristics of a microphone must match the impedance of its preamplifier.

39. The three specifications describe the function of an amplifier
    A. Voltage, current, frequency
    B. Voltage level, maximum frequency, maximum dB
    C. Gain, frequency response, dynamic range
    D. Frequency response, dynamic range, impedance

40. A waveform that has experienced peak clipping (select one term) [can/cannot] be corrected to its original signal with careful adjustments.

41. The category of biopotential amplifiers
    A. Includes preamplifiers for microphones
    B. Is required to physically isolate wires connected to a person from the amplifier circuitry
    C. Is used only for gathering acoustic data from biological sources such as people or animals
    D. Has similar frequency and dynamic range characteristics as preamplifiers

12.6 Making the Connection (p. 469)

42. An electrical plug is referred to as a (select one term) [male/female] connector and a socket is referred to as a [male/female] connector.

43. Good-quality microphone connectors most often use what type(s)?
    A. TRS
    B. XLR
    C. Both TRS and XLR
    D. Standard three-pronged power plug

44. True/False   Connectors used for headphones and earbuds are typically TRS connectors.

45. A TRS connector is composed of a
    A. Tip, ring, sleeve
    B. 1/2 inch, 1/8 inch, 1/4 inch
    C. Base, core, tip
    D. Male, female, and base

46. A balanced configuration of an XLR connector includes
    A. Out-of-phase signal conductors
    B. In-phase signal conductors
    C. Backup signal conductors
    D. Miniature signal conductors

47. The major purpose of cables and connectors of speech and voice instrumentation is to
    A. Preserve the life of the instrumentation
    B. Prevent excessive electrical discharge
    C. Transmit the sensor's electrical signal while preserving signal integrity
    D. Power the instrumentation

12.7 Recording Environment (p. 470)

48. Unwanted noise present in the recording environment is referred to as _____ noise.

49. True/False   A sound level meter is useful before recording with a microphone to determine the presence of ambient noise.

50. Unwanted noise generated by power cords, computer monitors, cell phones, and other electronic devises is referred to as what kind of noise?
    A. Electroambient
    B. Electromagnetic
    C. Magnoelectric
    D. EMG noise

51. The alternating current (AC) from electrical outlets can be detected by analyzing the signal for extra amplitude at
    A. 12 Hz
    B. 40 Hz
    C. 60 Hz
    D. 120 Hz

12.8 Data Acquisition: Let's Get Digital (p. 472)

52. True/False   Modern instrumentation gathers signals already in digital format so conversion from analog to digital data is unnecessary.

53. To make an accurate analog to digital conversion, the analog signal must be sampled
    A. Continuously from the beginning to the end of the measurement
    B. At discrete and random time intervals
    C. At discrete and preplanned unequal time intervals
    D. At discrete and equal time intervals

54. The sampling frequency in analog to digital conversion is equal to the
    A. 1 / the number of samples to be obtained
    B. 1 / time interval between consecutive samples
    C. The duration of the signal × the number of samples to be obtained
    D. The duration of the signal × time interval between consecutive samples

55. The sampling frequency must be at least _____ the highest frequency of the original analog signal.
    A. Twice as high as
    B. Equal to
    C. One half
    D. It depends upon the storage capability of the digital medium.

56. The concept that guides the sampling frequency for digital data acquisition is called the _____ theorem.

57. The recommended sampling rate for speech signals is
    A. 44.1 Hz
    B. 44.1 MHz
    C. 44.1 kHz
    D. It depends upon the mean f_o of the voice.

58. Quantization represents
    A. The levels of digitization of the amplitude of a signal
    B. The levels of digitization of the frequency of a signal
    C. The reassembly of a digital audio signal back to analog so that it may be perceived as speech
    D. The reassembly of any type of digital signal so that it may be represented as a continuous waveform

59. A 16-bit analog-to-digital converter has what number of discrete quantization levels?

    A. 665,360

    B. 65,536

    C. 2,560

    D. 256

60. In the ADC conversion process, undersampling will result in (select one term) [aliasing/shadowing].

61. True/False   Filtering out the frequencies above twice the sampling rate can prevent distortion in the ADC conversion process.

12.9 Data Storage (p. 478)

62. A signal that is sampled at 44.1 kHz at 16-bit quantization will produce a bit rate of

    A. 44.1 kHz × 16 bits per second

    B. 44.1 kHz / 16 bits per second

    D. 44.1 kHz × 16^2 bits per second

    C. 44.1 kHz / 16^2 bits per second

63. An example of a file storage format that represents lossy data compression is

    A. .wav

    B. MP3

    C. CD

    D. High definition

12.10 Balancing Cost, Complexity, and Accuracy in Digital Data Acquisition (p. 480)

64. True/False   In general, computer and tablet applications for signal acquisition are much less expensive than higher-quality "reference grade" instrumentation but of similar quality due to the digital nature of the apps.

65. Physiologic signals such as the air pressures associated with consonant production are (select one term) [able/not able] to be captured using computer soundcards.

12.11 Best Practices in the Use of Instrumentation (p. 483)

66. In regard to clinical and research instrumentation, specifications for frequency and dynamic range should

    A. Match or exceed the expected mean values of the data to be acquired

    B. Match or exceed the expected peak values of the data to be acquired

    C. Match or exceed the expected mean frequency values of the frequency data to be acquired but not exceed the expected mean dynamic values or distortion will result

    D. Match or exceed the expected peak frequency values of the frequency data to be acquired but not exceed the expected peak dynamic values or distortion will result

67. The noise floor of the microphone should be at least how many dB lower than the lowest expected speech intensity?

    A. 5 dB

    B. 10 dB

    C. 15 dB

    D. 20 dB

12.12 Let's Wrap This Thing Up! (p. 486)

68. Most of the higher-quality instrumentation systems (select one term) [will/will not] alert the user to invalid data acquisition due to errors in sampling rate, digitization, and other potential factors.

Conceptual Integration

1. You would like to use a sound level meter app on your smartphone to accurately measure sound levels, so you compare the app's output value to the value shown on a sound level meter you know to be accurate. This is an example of

    A. Calculating signal to noise ratio

    B. Measuring the noise floor

    C. Calibration

    D. Quantization

2. How may an instrument's "self-noise" negatively affect the quality of a signal that has been captured?

3. What will the signal to noise ratio be for a signal with an amplitude of 12 V and an instrument's noise floor of 0.4 V?

    A. 0.4 / 12 = 0.03

    B. 12 / 12 = 1.0

    C. 12 / 0.4 = 30

    D. 12 * 0.4 = 4.8

4. What sources of noise contribute to the noise floor that can be seen on a captured waveform?

5. The wavelength of a sound is 4.5 feet. What is the wavelength as measured in barleycorns?

    A. 4.5

    B. 12

    C. 135

    D. 162

6. What is the frequency of the sound that has a wavelength of 4.5 feet?

7. How is the transfer function of a microphone analogous to the transfer function of the vocal tract for the production of vowels?

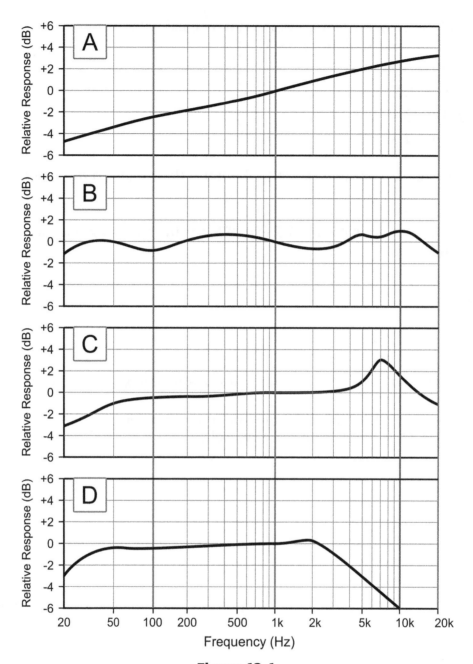

Figure 12–1

8. Figure 12–1 shows frequency response plots of four microphones. Which microphone (A–D) has the narrowest frequency range?

A. Microphone A

B. Microphone B

C. Microphone C

D. Microphone D

9. Which microphone(s) in Figure 12–1 have a frequency range that is appropriate for capturing speech?

    A. Microphone A only

    B. Microphones A, B, and C

    C. Microphones B and C

    D. Microphones A and D

10. Which of the four microphones shown in Figure 12–1 is the most appropriate for use in capturing speech for data analysis purposes?

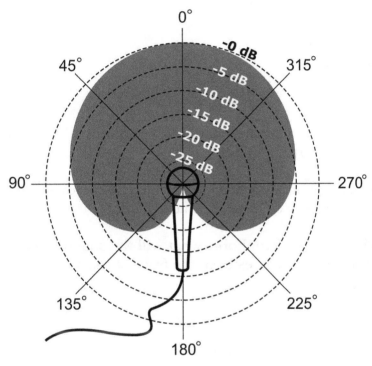

Figure 12–2

11. Figure 12–2 shows the polar plot for a microphone. In terms of directionality, what type of microphone response is shown?

    A. Cardioid

    B. Omnidirectional

    C. 180-degree directional

    D. 0-dB directional

12. Using Figure 12–2, consider a 68 dB sound approaching the microphone from 90 degrees relative to the front of the microphone. What will the sound level be as captured by the microphone?

    A. 0 dB

    C. 43 dB

    C. 62 dB

    D. 68 dB

13. Using Figure 12–2, consider a 103 dB sound approaching the microphone from 225 degrees relative to the front of the microphone. What will the sound level be as captured by the microphone?

    A. 15 dB

    B. 88 dB

    C. 103 dB

    C. 206 dB

14. What type of microphone would you pick if you wanted to be able to capture sound coming from any direction?

15. What type of microphone will produce an increase in low-frequency response if the sound source is very close to the microphone?

16. For an omnidirectional microphone, what will the sound level be if an 84 dB sound is coming at 180 degrees from the front of the microphone?

    A. 0 dB

    B. 84 dB

    C. 96 dB

    D. 168 dB

17. Fill out the following table on digital signal acquisition quantization bit depth.

Bit Depth	Number of Quantization (Amplitude) Levels
2	
4	
8	
12	
16	
20	
24	
30	

18. If the data acquisition sampling rate is set at 20 kHz, what's the highest frequency that can be captured by the system?

    A. 20 Hz

    B. 2000 Hz

    C. 10,000 Hz

    D. 20,000 Hz

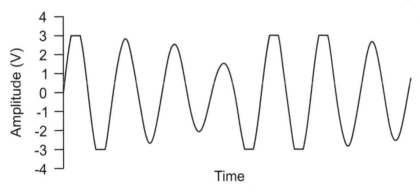

Figure 12–3

19. Figure 12–3 shows a waveform of a sound as captured by a microphone connected to a microphone preamplifier. Describe the characteristics of this waveform as shown.

20. For the signal shown in Figure 12–3, how could the microphone's preamplifier be adjusted in order to avoid clipping the captured waveform?

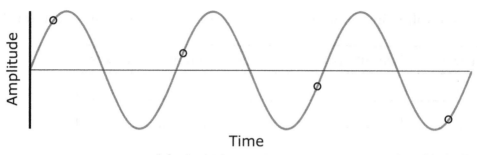

Figure 12–4

21. Figure 12–4 shows an analog waveform in the process of being converted to a digital format. The circles represent individual samples taken during digitization. What can you conclude from this figure in regard to the process of digitization?

22. For Figure 12–4, consider that the waveform is 3200 Hz. What is the minimum sampling rate necessary in order to capture this waveform in digital form?

   A. 1600 Hz

   B. 3200 Hz

   C. 6400 Hz

   D. 20,000 Hz

23. What is the highest frequency signal that can be captured by a digital data acquisition system with a sampling rate of 40 kHz, with respect to the Nyquist rate?

   A. 10 kHz

   B. 20 kHz

   C. 40 kHz

   D. 80 kHz

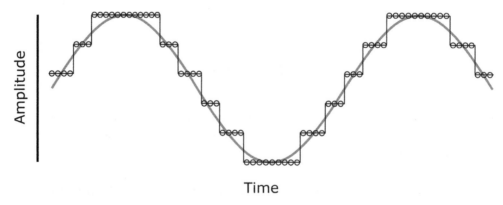

Figure 12–5

24. Figure 12–5 shows an analog waveform (gray line) that is in the process of being converted to a digital format. The circles represent individual samples taken during digitization, and the black connecting line between the circles represents the final digitized waveform. What can you conclude about the process of digitization given this figure?

25. Considering Figure 12–5, what is the apparent bit depth of the digitizer used to convert this analog waveform to digital format?
    A. 1 bit
    B. 2 bits
    C. 3 bits
    D. 6 bits

26. Considering Figure 12–5, what would produce the result of digitization that is shown?

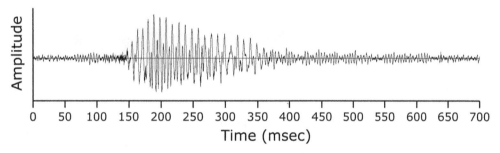

Figure 12–6

27. Figure 12–6 shows a speech waveform that begins at approximately 150 ms. What can you conclude from this figure regarding the quality of the captured waveform?

28. What recording condition(s) might have resulted in the waveform shown in Figure 12–6?
    A. A very low background noise level was present.
    B. The speech signal was of great enough sound pressure level so that the waveform nearly filled the screen.
    C. The sampling rate was too low, although the quantization bit depth was sufficient.
    D. The speech signal was very low in sound pressure level and a high level of noise (potentially including instrument self-noise, ambient noise, and electromagnetic noise) may have been present.

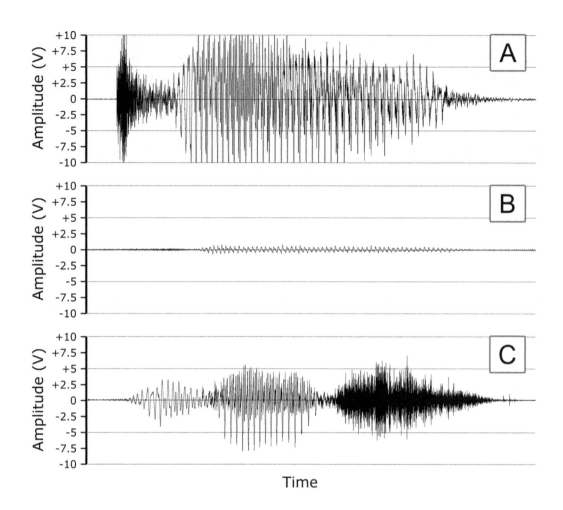

29. Figure 12–7 shows three speech waveforms. Which waveform likely has the lowest signal to noise ratio?

    A. Waveform A

    B. Waveform B

    C. Waveform C

30. If the speech signals in Figure 12–7 were all produced at the same dB level and at the same distance from the microphone, which waveform would represent the greatest amount of microphone preamplifier gain?

    A. Waveform A

    B. Waveform B

    C. Waveform C

31. If the speech signals in Figure 12–7 were all produced at the same dB level and with the same microphone preamplifier gain, but the speaker was at different distances from the microphone, which waveform would be produced with the speaker at the greatest distance from the microphone?

    A. Waveform A

    B. Waveform B

    C. Waveform C

32. Considering panel A in Figure 12–7, why does the maximum waveform amplitude equal exactly +10 volts and minimum amplitude equal exactly –10 volts for much of the waveform?

    A. The signal amplitude is too great and has exceeded the dynamic range of an instrument in the signal chain, causing clipping at +10 and –10 volts.

    B. The microphone preamplifier was adjusted perfectly so that the signal's amplitude exactly matched the maxima and minima of the dynamic range of the digitizer.

    C. The signal from the microphone consisted of exactly 65,536 quantization units, which matched the number of quantization units of the digitizer.

    D. The speaker was able to maintain a perfectly consistent amplitude of their voice (at +10 and –10 volts) throughout the utterance.

33. Considering Figure 12–7, which waveform(s) would be best suited for performing acoustic analysis and why?

34. True/False   For a USB microphone, the acoustic waveform will first be digitized by the microphone and then once again by the computer the microphone is attached to.

35. True/False   If a microphone has a frequency range of 20 Hz to 20 kHz and the microphone preamplifier has a frequency range of 20 Hz to 17 kHz, the highest frequency that a signal that has passed through both instruments will be 17 kHz.

36. True/False   The signal transduced by a microphone is an exact copy of the compressions and rarefactions of the sound wave.

37. A microphone has a maximum sound pressure level of 89 dB and a noise floor of 24 dB. What is the dynamic range of this microphone?

    A. 34 dB

    B. 65 dB

    C. 99 dB

    D. 133 dB

38. Will the above microphone (with specifications for maximum sound pressure level of 89 dB and a noise floor of 24 dB) be suitable for capturing a speech waveform? Why or why not?

39. Consider the performance specifications for the following microphones in the following table. Which microphone is best suited for capturing speech for analysis purposes?

Microphone	Frequency Range	Maximum Sound Pressure Level	Directionality	Transducer Type
A	75 Hz–20 kHz	102 dB	Omnidirectional	Dynamic
B	45 Hz–16 kHz	148 dB	Cardioid	Condenser
C	120 Hz–8 kHz	120 dB	Cardioid	Dynamic
D	40 Hz–18 kHz	150 dB	Omnidirectional	Condenser

40. True/False   To connect a USB microphone to a computer, a cable with an XLR connector is used.

41. For a microphone's cable, what type of wiring will reduce ingress of external electromagnetic noise?

    A. TRRS connection

    B. Phantom power

    C. Balanced wiring

    D. XLR connection

42. What situation can result in electromagnetic interference (electromagnetic noise) contaminating an electrical signal from a sensor such as a microphone or a pneumotachometer?

    A. High levels of ambient sound in the recording environment

    B. Signal cables running parallel to power cables

    C. High preamplifier gain

    D. Use of balanced wiring

43. Why is an MP3 file (or other compressed file formats) not suitable for storage of a captured speech waveform to be used for acoustic analysis?

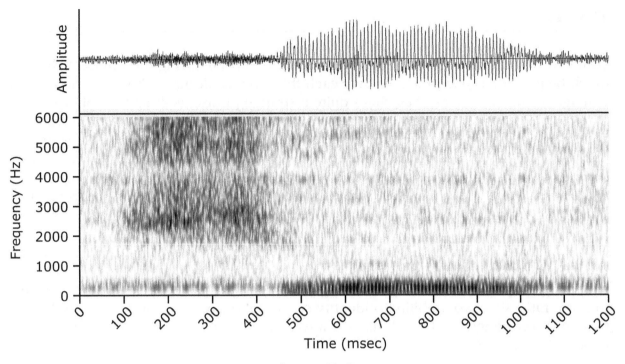

Figure 12–8

44. Figure 12–8 shows a speech waveform (top panel) and its associated spectrogram plot (lower panel). In general, what phonemes are in this speech utterance?

A. The first phoneme is a vowel and the second is a nasal.

B. The first phoneme is an unvoiced stop, the second is a glide, and the third is a liquid.

C. The first phoneme is an unvoiced fricative and the second is a vowel.

D. The first phoneme is a voiced affricate, the second is a nasal, and the third is a vowel.

45. Considering the waveform (top panel) of Figure 12–8, why is it difficult to identify the onset and offset of the phonemes in this utterance?

46. Considering the spectrogram plot (bottom panel) of Figure 12–8, why are the formants for the vowel not clearly visible?

47. What could be done in order to improve the signal integrity for the recorded speech waveform shown in Figure 12–8?

TRY IT!

Using your smartphone or your computer, record yourself saying the phrase, "That quick beige fox jumped in the air over each thin dog. Look out, I shout, for he's foiled you again, creating chaos." Yes, that's quite a strange phrase, isn't it? That phrase is an example of a phonetic pangram: It contains all English phonemes. You can record yourself using a voice recorder app or just use the video camera function on your phone if you like. After recording one try, record a second attempt but this time play some background noise (e.g., run some water in a nearby sink, turn on the TV, etc.). Finally, make a few recordings at different distances from the phone or computer (but without changing the loudness of your voice!) to explore the effect of the inverse square relationship of sound energy to distance (remember that from Chapter 3?). Now, play back your recordings and see if you can hear the effect of varying speech intensity (relative to the changing distances) and varying background noise on your speech signal. You've just changed the signal to noise ratio! How does a lower signal to noise ratio affect your ability to identify certain phonemes? What do you think that your recordings would look like on waveform and spectrogram plots? Isn't experimenting fun?

Part II
ANSWERS

Part II
ANSWERS

CHAPTER 2
Describing and Explaining Motion Answers

Foundational Knowledge

2.1 Systems of Measurement (p. 12)

1. A
2. C
3. A
4. B
5. Metric
6. 100

2.2 Describing Motion: Speed, Velocity, Acceleration, and Deceleration (p. 13)

7. C
8. D
9. A
10. Time
11. Talking
12. False

2.3 Newton's Laws Explain Motion (p. 14)

13. A
14. B
15. D
16. B

17. C
18. C
19. Inertia
20. Inertia
21. Mass

2.4 Momentum and Energy (p. 15)

22. B
23. D
24. A
25. C
26. D
27. D
28. C
29. B
30. Potential
31. False

2.5 Three States of Matter (p. 18)

32. B
33. A
34. C
35. C

36. A

37. B

38. A

39. D

40. A

41. C

42. A

43. True

Conceptual Integration

1. B

2. A

3. A

4. A

5. C

6. A

7. B

8. D

9. B

10. A

11. A

12. A

13. 15.2955

14. 1.176

15. 421.6924

16. False

17. A

18. A

19. A

20. B

21. A

CHAPTER 3
Sound Waves Answers

Foundational Knowledge

3.1 Vibration (p. 28)

1. A
2. A
3. D
4. C
5. A
6. A
7. B
8. B
9. C
10. A

3.2 The Nature of Waves (p. 28)

11. C
12. D
13. A
14. A
15. B
16. A
17. A
18. B
19. Transverse

3.3 Transfer of Energy in Waves (p. 32)

20. A
21. C
22. False

3.4 Visualizing a Sound Wave (p. 35)

23. C
24. B
25. A
26. B
27. A
28. Sinusoidal wave

3.5 Properties of Sound Waves (p. 35)

29. B
30. A
31. C
32. D
33. C
34. D

35. A

36. False

37. C

38. A

39. A

40. A

41. C

42. False

43. B

44. D

45. True

46. False

47. True

48. A

49. A

50. A

51. D

52. True

53. True

54. B

55. C

56. B

57. A

58. False

59. False

3.6 The Perception of Sound Waves (p. 46)

60. 2, 1, 2, 1, 1

61. B

62. A

63. C

64. C

65. A

66. D

67. B

68. A

69. Psychophysics

70. Difference limen

71. Audiometric zero

72. Less

73. More

74. Sone

75. Nonlinear

76. Acoustic, psychoacoustic

77. False

78. False

3.7 Pure and Complex Tones (p. 52)

79. True
80. B
81. D
82. B
83. C
84. A
85. A
86. B
87. False
88. C
89. C
90. A
91. C
92. False
93. True
94. D
95. A
96. C
97. B
98. A
99. B
100. True

3.8 Behavior of Sound Waves (p. 56)

101. A
102. C
103. A
104. True

3.9 Resonance (p. 59)

105. B
106. B
107. True
108. True
109. D
110. A
111. B
112. True
113. A
114. True
115. B
116. C
117. True
118. False

Conceptual Integration

1. A
2. A
3. C
4. A
5. A
6. B
7. B
8. A

9. B

10. C

11. A

12. Density

13. True

14. False

15. True

16. C

17. A

18. B

19. A

20. False

21. D

22. A

23. B

24. C

25. B

26. C

27. C

28. B

29. C

30. D

31. True

32. Waveform

33. Power spectrum

34. C

35. B

36. D

37. B

38. D

39. A

40. True

41. B

42. A

43. A

44. B

45. D

46. A

47. A

48. C

49. A

50. A

51. C

52. C

53. A

54. A

55. C

56. D

57. C

58. C

59. A

60. C

61. False

62. True

63. A

64. D

65. C

CHAPTER 4
Breathing Answers

Foundational Knowledge

4.1 Introduction (p. 72)

1. B
2. A
3. C
4. Speech breathing
5. Inspiration, expiration
6. C
7. A
8. C
9. A
10. B
11. C
12. D
13. B
14. Cranial nerves
15. Pathway
16. Fight or flight, rest and digest
17. Neurotransmitters
18. Final common pathway
19. Reticular formation

4.2 Respiration (p. 76)

20. A

21. A
22. Carbon dioxide

4.3 Balloons or Boyle's Law? (p. 76)

23. B
24. D
25. A
26. D
27. A
28. Front to back (or anteroposteriorly)
29. Lesser
30. Positive
31. Increase

4.4 Anatomy of the Lower Airway (p. 78)

32. C
33. B
34. D
35. A
36. C
37. A
38. B

39. Trachea, bronchial tree

40. Air, tissue

41. Diaphragm

42. In unison

43. Generation

44. Alveoli

45. C

46. Pascal's

47. Subglottal or alveolar

48. B

49. A

50. Motor unit

51. Greater

52. C

53. A

54. Ten

55. Passive

56. Isotonic

57. Muscle lengthens, eccentric

    Muscle shortens, concentric

    Length remains unchanged, isometric

58. D

59. Antagonist

60. Agonist

61. B

62. True

63. C

64. C

65. A

66. B

67. Diaphragm, external intercostals

68. Internal intercostals

69. Convex, flattens downward

70. Elevated, upward and outward

71. Equivalence

72. True

73. True

4.5 The Biomechanics of Breathing (p. 87)

74. A

75. B

76. C

77. B

78. A

79. B

80. A

81. B

82. D

83. Linkage between the lungs and thoracic cavity (or pleura)

    Restorative forces (or elastic recoil forces)

84. Visceral

85. Potential

86. Elastic recoil

87. Contract

88. Equilibrium

89. Expiratory

90. 12 to 15

91. False

92. True

93. False

94. D

95. True

96. C

97. A

98. B

99. D

100. A

101. B

102. A

103. 15

104. Residual

105. Resting lung

106. 38, 40

107. True

108. False

109. A = external intercostals, B = internal intercostals

110.

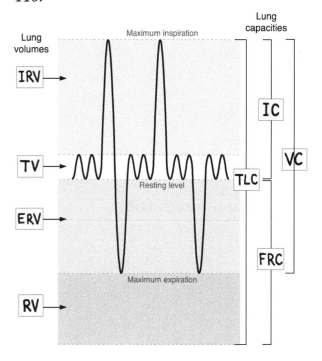

4.6 The Biomechanics of Speech Breathing (p. 95)

111. Negative

112. B

113. Transthoracic

114. 38%

115. 60%

116. Inspiratory checking

117. D

118. 40%, 10%, 60%, 90%

119. Exhalation

120. False

121. A

122. False

123. B

4.7 The Work of Breathing (p. 106)

124. A

125. Diaphragmatic

126. C

127. Driving

128. Viscosity

129. B

130. False

4.8 Instrumentation for Measuring Breathing Kinematics (p. 110)

131. Electromyography

132. A

Conceptual Integration

1. B

2. A

3. C

4. True

5. D

6. A

7. D

8. Inverse, volume and pressure

9. D

10. A

11. D

12. C

13. D

14. D

15. Exhalation

16. A

17. B

18. A

19. C

20. A

21. A

22. D

23. B

24. D

25. B

26. B

27. A

28. C

29. B

30. A

31. B

32. A

33. True

34. True

35. C

36. A

37. B

38. A

39. D

40. B

41. A	55. B
42. A	56. B
43. D	57. C
44. D	58. C
45. D	59. D
46. D	60. D
47. A	61. A
48. B	62. C
49. B	63. C
50. B	64. D
51. A	65. B
52. B	66. True
53. B	67. False
54. A	68. True

Clinical Application

4.9 Clinical Application: Disorder Related to Breathing

1. B

2. True

3. A

4. A trade off often exists between articulatory accuracy and rate of articulation. When a person speaks in a rushed manner because of concerns about dyspnea, it often happens that the articulators do not move as accurately and precisely as necessary to fully produce the necessary phonemes. Therefore, listeners may experience increased difficulty in understanding the speaker.

Clinical Case 1: Breath-Holding Speech

1. Inspiratory checking action is the use of inspiratory thoracic muscle contraction to counteract the relaxation pressure of the lungs when the lung pressure is greater than what is required to sustain speech. The lungs remain expanded,

slowing the rate of exhalation to support speech. Excessive use of inspiratory checking can become fatiguing because it requires excessive muscle contraction.

2. Air flows from greater to lesser pressure. As the driving pressure is decreased, airflow will decrease. Therefore, decreased airflow means that the driving pressure (lung pressure) has decreased. Decreased lung pressure will generally result in decreased intensity.

   Intensity is the acoustic correlate of loudness. Loudness is a perception that corresponds roughly (but not exactly) to the amount of intensity of the acoustic pressure wave.

3. Her speech likely would fall within the normal area of the relaxation curve for speech breathing—between 38% and 60% vital capacity. However, clinically, it is suggested that the range she uses for speaking would be a smaller percentage of vital capacity within that range because of the excessive inspiratory checking and that she does not exhale to 38% vital capacity as often as she should to achieve relaxed breathing.

4.

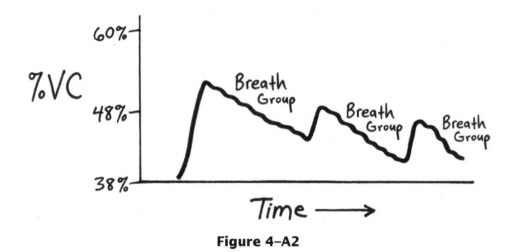

Figure 4–A2

Figure 4–A2 shows an example of how the change in lung volume may appear over a few cycles of speech breathing. Note that, due to the excessive braking action ("breath holding"), Seleena does not return to resting expiratory level at the end of each breath group.

5. Knowledge of relaxation pressures, checking action, and the speech breathing inspirator-inspiratory cycle is necessary to understand Seleena's speech breathing behaviors and the therapeutic goals that will help her to address her symptoms.

CHAPTER 5
Phonation I: Basic Voice Science Answers

Foundational Knowledge

5.1 Overview (p. 121)

1. Phonation
2. False

5.2 Anatomy of the Larynx (p. 122)

3. A
4. Hypopharynx
5. B
6. True
7. Cricoarytenoid
8. C
9. Extrinsic
10. C
11. A
12. Extrinsic = thyrohyoid membrane, thyroepiglottic ligament, cricotracheal ligament, cricothyroid membrane, hyoepiglottic ligament

    Intrinsic = quadrangular membranes, aryepiglottic folds, the vocal ligament, conus elasticus
13. Ventricular, aryepiglottic
14. False
15. Supraglottic
16. A

17. Intrinsic
18. Opening, closing
19. Posterior cricoarytenoid
20. Relaxor, tensor, tensor, abductor
21. Rotates muscular process of arytenoids forward and inward

    Pulls arytenoids forward

    Pulls thyroid cartilage downward

    Rotates vocal process of arytenoids laterally

    Draws thyroid cartilage forward

    Pulls apex of arytenoids medially

    Tenses vocal folds

    Glides arytenoids together
22. D
23. False
24. Depressor, elevator, elevator, depressor, elevator and depressor, elevator, depressor
25. Thyroarytenoid
26. True
27. Reinke's space
28. More
29. Disorganized and loosely arranged elastin fibers, densely distributed, organized elastin fibers, tightly packed collagen fibers

30. False

31. Basement membrane zone

32. A

33. B

34. C

35. Cricothyroid

36. B

37. C

38. A

5.3 Neural Control of Phonation (p. 142)

39. Opposite

40. B

41. External, superior

42. D

43. A

44. D

5.4 Theories of Voice Production (p. 145)

45. B

46. C

47. Bernoulli

48. Myoelastic-aerodynamic theory

49. Cannot

50. Passive

51. Excised

52. True

53. False

54. False

5.5 Biomechanics of Vocal Fold Vibration (p. 150)

55. B

56. B

57. A

58. A

59. A

60. D

61. A

62. A

63. C

64. A

65. D

66. C

67. 2, 4, 1

68. A

69. D

70. Prephonatory

71. Do not

72. Shear

73. Momentum

74. Vertical out-of-phase

75. Compression

76. Time

77. Vocal folds

78. Phonation threshold pressure

79. True

80. True

81. False

82. True

83. False

84. True

85. False

86. True

5.6 Biomechanical Stress-Strain Properties of Vocal Fold Tissues (p. 160)

87. A

88. B

89. Unit area

90. Stretched or lengthened

91. False

5.7 Physiology of Phonatory Control (p. 162)

92. A

93. C

94. D

95. Does

96. C

97. B

98. C

99. A

100. D

101. A

102. 3, 6, 2, 5, 1, 4

103. Stiffness

104. Increases, decreases

105. Increase

106. Lung pressure or subglottal pressure

107. Increased

108. Decrease

109. Increased

110. Lombard

111. False

112. True

113. True

114. False

115. False

116. True

117. True

118. False

119. False

5.8 Voice Quality (p. 174)

120. B

121. Voice quality

122. True

Conceptual Integration

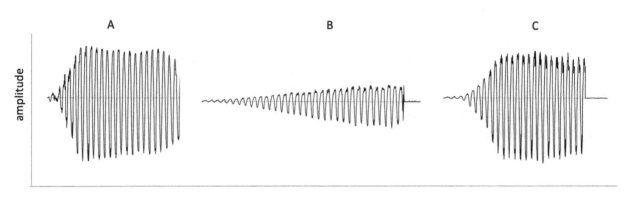

1. A = hard onset, B = breathy onset, C = soft onset

2. Valving refers to opening and closing action of the vocal folds. For phonation, the opening and closing occurs very rapidly and is accomplished in an out-of-phase waving motion occurring from inferior to superior. For airway protection, the valving is achieved by a single, forceful closure of the vocal folds to allow for buildup of subglottal pressure to expel a foreign object in the larynx; for stabilization of the thoracic cavity, the vocal folds close and remain closed for a brief moment while the lifting or other postural action is achieved.

3. A

4. A

5. C

6. D

7. B

8. Indirectly, directly, directly

9. Transglottal pressure

10. A

11. D

12. A

13. On average, compared to women, vocal folds in men have greater mass. Mass per unit length is one factor that regulates f_o, with greater mass per unit length resulting in slower vibration (e.g., lower f_o).

14. Contraction of cricothyroid pulls the thyroid cartilage forward and downward, causing the vocal folds to be elongated. The stretch results in a decrease in mass

per unit length as the vocal folds are thinned and an increase in stiffness. Both of these characteristics result in increased f_o. The increased length of the vocal folds is meaningful only in that the stretching results in decreased mass and increased stiffness,

15. In the prephonatory phase, the arytenoid cartilages rock and, to a lesser extent, slide toward one another, which approximates the vocal folds. (The vocal folds may adduct completely or may only be brought very closely together—it depends upon the type of vocal onset being used.) As air pressure builds up subglottaly, the vocal folds are pushed upward and outward and oscillation begins. However, the arytenoid cartilages do not move open and closed—they remain together. Once phonation ceases, the arytenoid cartilages rock and slide apart to abduct the vocal folds and allow for inhalation.

16. 1, 4, 2, 3

17. A

18. C

19. To initiate phonation, the aerodynamic force must be sufficiently great to overcome the inertia of the nonmoving vocal folds. Once the vocal folds are vibrating, aerodynamic force is assisted by momentum.

20. Stiffness refers to the amount of force required to displace an object. Increased vocal fold stiffness means that greater aerodynamic force is required to abduct the vocal folds (move the vocal folds laterally away from equilibrium). As a result, greater restorative force is built up in the vocal folds, and thus the vocal folds will spring back to midline more quickly. This increased speed of movement results in increased f_o.

21. First, the vocal folds vibrate open and closed to generate compressed puffs of air that vibrate upward through the glottis. The string of an instrument does not act as a valve. Instead, it vibrates freely in the air. Second, to increase the rate of vibration of the vocal folds, the longitudinal tension is increased through elongation of the vocal folds, which thins their mass per unit length and increases their stiffness. To increase the rate of vibration of a musical string, the length remains the same but the stiffness is increased and mass per unit length is decreased by increasing the longitudinal tension through turning a key to "tighten" the string.

22. A

23. D

24. C

25. A

26. C

27. C

28. B

29. C

30. C

31. B

32. C

33. B

34. A

35. B

36. C

37. A

38. B

39. C

40. C

41. A

42. A

43. A

44. B

45. True

46. True

47. B

48. B

49. A

50. C

51. A

52. False

53. D

54. C

55. False

56. D

Clinical Application

Clinical Case 2: Running Out of Breath

1. A lung pressure of approximately 2 to 3 cmH_2O is required to sustain soft phonation, and greater lung pressure is required for louder phonation. The longer the breath group, the greater the amount of air that is expended. Braking action (maintenance of contraction of the inspiratory muscles) is used to maintain a stable lung pressure during the phrase breath group. As lung pressure becomes insufficient to maintain phonation below resting expiratory level, speech becomes quieter and more effortful to maintain.

2. Christine's phrase groups were noted to be quite lengthy. Likely she has insufficient lung pressure to maintain modal phonation at a conversational-level intensity. Vocal fry is often achieved with decreased vocal fold stiffness and lower lung pressures.

3. In Clinical Case 1, Seleena was using excessive braking to limit expiratory airflow. In Clinical Case 2, Christine was using excessively lengthy phrase groups, making it difficult to maintain sufficient lung pressure for phonation. Both speech breathing patterns require increased muscular effort and are therefore inefficient.

Clinical Application: Disorders Related to Voice Production

1. An elementary school teacher might have a phonotraumatic voice problem. Phonotrauma arises from excessive mechanical stress to the vocal folds for prolonged periods of time. A grade school teacher might have to talk loudly to her class each weekday, which could cause excessive stress to the vocal fold tissues. (Other jobs might be mother of young children or someone who works on a noisy factory floor or works in a call center.)

2. The right recurrent laryngeal nerve innervates most of the right-sided intrinsic muscles of the larynx, including those that rock and glide the right arytenoid cartilage to allow the right vocal fold to adduct. Increased loudness requires firm glottal closure to allow for buildup of lung pressure below the vocal folds. If the right vocal fold cannot move and so phonatory glottal closure cannot be achieved, sufficient lung pressure cannot build up.

3. The voice quality of breathiness is associated with air escaping upward through the glottis during phonation due to incomplete phonatory glottal closure. The escaping air prevents buildup of lung pressure below the vocal folds, thus limiting loudness.

4. Communicative activities of daily living are those activities that an individual participates in during their daily life that require speaking. It is important for a therapist to understand the patient's vocal use so that he or she may help the patient to adjust their voice use and their vocal behaviors to meet their daily vocal needs.

CHAPTER 6
Phonation II: Measurement and Instrumentation Answers

Foundational Knowledge

6.1 Measurement of f_0 and Intensity (p. 187)

1. D

2. True

3. A

4. Maximum performance

5. Maximum frequency range

6. Narrow, lower

7. C

8. Jitter

9. D

10. True

11. Jitter percent, jitter factor, jitter ratio, relative average perturbation, pitch perturbation quotient

12. False

13. A

14. Voice range profile

15. A

16. Intensity

17. A

6.2 Measurement of Phonatory Aerodynamics (p. 193)

18. Pneumotachograph

19. True

20. B

21. Glottal efficiency, vocal efficiency

22. C

23. Z, S

24. A

25. Maximum phonation time

26. B

27. D

28. Phonatory glottal closure

29. B

6.3 Instrumentation for Exploring the Dynamics of the Vocal Folds (p. 199)

30. A

31. B

32. C

33. B

34. D

35. A

36. 4, 1, 3

37. 3, 5, 1, 4

38. C

39. Glottography

40. Contact microphone, electroglottograph

41. High-speed imaging

42. Good, poor

43. Quantal

44. False

45. True

46. False

47. True

6.4 Vocal Registers (p. 210)

48. 3, 1, 4

49. Fundamental frequency

50. False

51. True

52. False

Conceptual Integration

1. Both reading and spontaneous speech contain volitional changes in f_o and intensity. (We don't read or speak in a monotone!) Thus, it would be very difficult to determine what portion of the variability was due to purposeful changes compared to unintentional irregularity.

2. A

3. C

4. D

5. A

6. C

7. A

8. A

9. C

10. B

11. B

12. C

13. A

14. At the lowest frequencies, it is difficult to achieve significantly increased intensity because the vocal fold cover must remain lax to achieve the slow rate of vibration. Yet the overall resistance to the airflow must be increased to withstand the increased lung pressure necessary for increased intensity. In summary, these two factors constrain dynamic energy at the lowest frequencies. At the highest frequencies, a similar relationship exists in balancing lung pressure with vocal fold tension. To achieve high-frequency phonation, we know that the vocal folds must be quite tense, which would then increase their resistance to the airflow, which would in turn require high lung pressure to maintain phonation. Such high levels of lung pressure would, of course, result in greater intensity.

15. The high lung pressure required for greater intensity also requires that the vocal folds are able to withstand the greater pressures. In general, that increased resistance is achieved with greater vocal fold stiffness, which in turn raises f_o.

16. Incomplete phonatory glottal closure results in extra airflow through the glottis that is not converted to harmonic energy.

17. False

18. Research data do not necessarily support the assumption that /s/ and /z/ should be able to be sustained for equal durations. It may be that the target s/z ratio could be less than 1, because the /z/ might normally be sustained for greater duration than the /s/ due to the increased resistance to the airflow associated with vibration of the vocal folds. Second, several compensatory behavioral maneuvers can be used to achieve normal or near-normal values. For example, excessive inspiratory checking (maintenance of excessive contraction of the inspiratory muscles while phonating) can be used to maintain lung expansion, decreasing expiratory flow (in lieu of the resistance to the airflow that would be offered by the adducted vocal folds in normal phonation) and thereby helping to maintain longer voicing. Also, excessive constriction of the supraglottal musculature, particularly the ventricular folds, can help to achieve increased resistance to the airflow, again slowing down the rate of egressive flow and helping to maintain longer phonation.

19. Use of compensatory strategies such as squeezing of the supraglottis may influence the phonatory duration to yield a normal value, yet the squeezing itself is not desirable. In addition, the instructions provided by the person eliciting the measure can strongly influence the results. For example, providing a lot of encouragement to continue phonating can produce longer phonation times than if no encouragement is provided.

20. Note: Check your answer with Figure 6–6 (A) in the textbook. Your marks may start at a different point in the cycle. That's okay. The main idea is to show that the light flash and resulting visual representation of vocal fold movement (your dashed line) represents an average of multiple cycles, not the actual vibratory cycles!

21. Keep in mind that stroboscopic imaging is composed of very brief glimpses of moments selected from different glottal cycle. Small irregularities that exist in the rate of vibration and in movement of the vocal fold mucosal tissue from cycle to cycle, and so the sampling of images obtained by the strobe as blended together by the observer's brain is less than a perfect representation of the true vibration. The more irregular the actual vibration of the vocal folds, the less accurate the representation by the stroboscopic images.

22. False

23. Open quotient = (B-A)/(D-A)

    Speech quotient = (B-A)/(C-B)

    Closed quotient = (D-B)/(D-A)

24. A = Maximum glottal opening

    B = Contact of the upper margin of the vocal folds only

    C = Complete closure of the glottis

    D = Separation of the lower margins of the vocal folds only

    E = Initial complete separation of the upper and lower margins of the vocal folds

25. A

26. B

27. A

28. B

29. C

30. B

31. True

32. C

33. A pressure sensor connected to a small plastic tube is placed in the mouth as the speaker says the syllable /pa/, measuring intraoral pressure. Pascal's law states that pressure changes are transmitted equally and rapidly in an enclosed chamber; therefore, as the respiratory system is closed at the lips for the production of the plosive /p/, the intraoral pressure is equal to the lung pressure.

34. The estimation of lung pressure based on measurement of intraoral pressure requires the respiratory system to be a closed air chamber, considering Pascal's law. If lung pressure is to be estimated by measuring intraoral pressure, the lungs must be part of that closed air chamber, and thus the vocal folds need to be open as occurs during the production of an unvoiced plosive. Also, given that /p/ is a bilabial plosive, relatively easy access is provided for the intraoral pressure sensor to be placed inside the closed air chamber, just behind the closed lips.

35. A

36. A

37. C

38. D

39. C

40. A

41. B

42. True

43. B

44. A

45. A

46. B

47. High-speed laryngeal imaging uses a high-speed camera to capture video of vocal fold vibration. Playback of the video will show a true slow-motion view of the movement of the vocal folds during phonation in which each sequential vibration cycle is shown in its entirety. Therefore, high-speed laryngeal imaging will not be negatively affected by highly irregular vocal fold vibratory movements, unlike stroboscopy.

Clinical Application

Clinical Case 3: Camp Voice

1. Loud speech or shouting across distances and within noisy environments on a frequent basis are activities that could increase shear and collisional stresses on the vocal folds and contribute to dysphonia.

2. Incomplete phonatory glottal closure would allow extra turbulent air to escape up through the glottis, adding noise and decreasing the intensity of the harmonics. These features would decrease overall vocal intensity and increase perception of breathiness. Irregular mucosal wave vibration could cause decreased excitation of the air molecules within each puff of air that escapes upward through the glottis with each vibratory cycle, resulting in increased jitter, contributing to the perception of roughness (lack of "clear" voice).

Clinical Case 4: Persistent Falsetto

1. Mean speaking f_o (see Table 5–5 in the textbook) for boys around 10.5 years is 220 Hz. By age 14, mean speaking f_o descends to approximately 170 Hz and continues to drop over the next few years. Alexei's mean speaking f_o pre- and posttherapy was approximately 260 Hz and 124 Hz, respectively.

2. Yes, these characteristics would be expected. Alexei's f_o was elevated pretherapy. To elevate f_o, the vocal folds are elongated to increase longitudinal tension so that mass per unit length is decreased and stiffness is increased.

3. The increased stiffness of the vocal folds at high f_o often results in decreased phonatory glottal closure: The mucosa is thinned and amplitude of mucosal wave vibration is generally reduced. Intensity is mainly regulated by lung pressure. With incomplete glottal closure, it is harder to maintain a buildup of lung pressure, and thus intensity is often reduced.

CHAPTER 7
The Production and Perception of Vowels Answers

Foundational Knowledge

7.1 Introduction (p. 226)

1. Phoneme

2. False

3. Phonetic, phonemic, phonetic, phonemic, phonetic

4. Allophonic

5. A

7.2 Acoustic Theory of Speech Production (p. 227)

6. C

7. True

8. D

9. Acoustic resonator

10. Frequency

11. B

12. IS

13. A

14. D

15. A

16. B

17. True

18. D

19. Lower

20. $(18 \times 4) = 72$ cm

$34,000 / 72 = 472.2$ Hz = first resonance

$(472.2 \times 3) = 1,416.7$ Hz = second resonance

21. False

22. C

23. False

7.3 Vowels (p. 237)

24. B

25. A

26. False

27. C

28. A

29. Lowered

30. B

31. D

32. A

33. C

34. D

35. A

36. B

37. D

38. A

39. /ə/ (the schwa)

40. C

41. D

42. True

43. Far apart, close together

44. B

45. True

46. A

47. Vowel space

48. Greater

49. B

50. C

51. Monophthong

52. B

53. A

54. Onglide, offglide

55. B

56. Reduction

57. A

58. B

59. D

60. B

61. XII, hypoglossal

62. C

7.4 Language and Dialect Influences on Vowel Production (p. 259)

63. D

64. /ɔ/

65. A

66. False

67. Dialects

68. B

7.5 The Vocal Tract as a Regulator of Intensity (p. 260)

69. B

70. A

71. C

72. Raised

73. Formant tuning

74. Harmonic

7.6 Acoustic Filters (p. 265)

75. 2, 4, 1

76. D

77. A

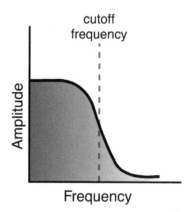

78. Low-pass

79. Decrease, frequency

80. Center

81. Bandwidth

82. Half-power point

83. Bandpass

7.7 Instrumentation for Measuring Vocal Tract Acoustics (p. 268)

84. A

85. C

86. A

87. B

88. D

89. A

90. C

91. A

92. A

93. B

94. Narrowband

95. Closer together

96. Cannot

97. Formants

98. Long-term average spectrum

99. Harmonics to noise ratio

100. Cepstral analysis

101. True

102. True

103. False

104. False

105. True

106. True

107. False

108. False

109. False

7.8 Vocal Tract Imaging: Current Research and Future Trends (p. 279)

110. C

111. False

Conceptual Integration

1. A = Wideband, B = Narrowband

The wideband spectrogram smears the harmonics and shows broad bands of dark gray in the frequency location of the formants. The wideband spectrogram also shows vertical striations that correspond to glottal pulses. The narrowband spectrogram shows the individual harmonics clearly. The location of the formants is suggested by the darkness (energy) of the harmonics.

2.

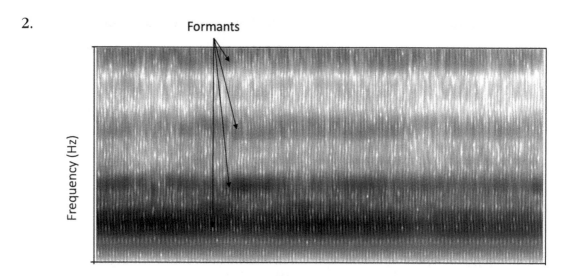

Formants

Frequency (Hz)

Time (s)

3.

f_o 6th harmonic above the f_o

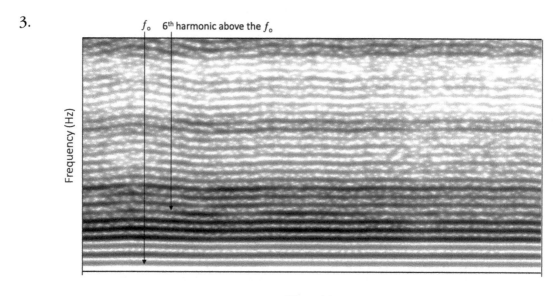

Frequency (Hz)

Time (s)

4. The harmonics in the region of the formants will have greater energy than harmonics farther away from the frequencies of the formants. Energy in the spectrogram is shown by the grayscale, with darker harmonics indicating greater energy.

5.

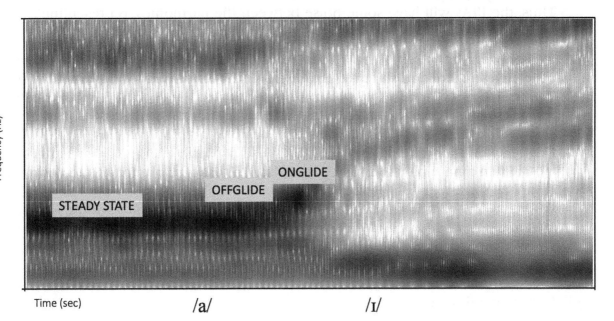

Note that the offglide of the /a/ and the onglide of the /ɪ/ are continuous with each other.

6. The steady-state portion of the initial vowel (/a/) is much shorter in the diphthong, with the transition to the second vowel occurring more rapidly. Compared to separately produced sequential vowels, diphthongs are produced with rapid movement from one vowel to the next.

7. B

8. C

9. D

10. Spectrum (a) on the left is most likely derived from a woman's voice and spectrum (b) on the right is most likely from a man's voice. In general, men's f_0s are lower than those of women. Keeping in mind the harmonics are integer multiples of the f_0, the higher f_0 will result in a greater number of frequencies separating the harmonics compared to the man's voice. (For example, an f_0 of 220 Hz will produce harmonics at 440 Hz, 660 Hz, 880 Hz, and so on. An f_0 of 120 Hz will produce harmonics at 240 Hz, 360 Hz, 480 Hz, and so on.) Thus, the peaks representing the energy at each harmonic will be spaced farther apart in the spectrum from the woman's voice compared to the man's voice.

11. Vocal fold vibration is not perfectly periodic. The voice signal is nearly periodic. For example, approximately 1% jitter is commonly observed in the vocal signal. Thus, the LTAs will have some noise between the harmonics, representing oscillatory variability.

12. Each vowel is represented by a vocal tract articulatory posture, in which areas of relative constriction shift depending upon the movement of the articulators. The formants are areas of resonant frequencies that are specified by the relative constrictions and the size and cross-sectional area of the acoustic resonating cavities that they create. When the frequency of a harmonic is close to the frequency of the formant, the vocal tract resonates the energy of that harmonic well. When a harmonic frequency is far from a formant frequency, the vocal tract dampens the energy of the harmonic. Therefore, as the speaker phonates each vowel, the formant frequencies change and so some harmonics will be resonated well and others poorly and those resonatory characteristics will change for each vowel. Thus, harmonics seem to appear and fade.

13. B

14. Larynx, vocal tract

15. Harmonics are integer multiples of the f_0 and describe the sound source. Formants are resonating characteristics of the vocal tract and describe the acoustic filter.

16. Lip rounding extends the length of the vocal tract. The longer the vocal tract, the lower the formant frequencies.

17. The greater the energy, the greater the displacement of air particles. Therefore, air particle displacement is greatest at frequencies that have the greatest intensity. The source spectrum has a 12-dB per octave energy roll-off, which means that the f_0 and lower harmonics have greater intensity than the higher harmonics. At the boundary between the lips and the atmosphere, the atmosphere offers greater resistance to the lower frequencies, associated with larger particle displacements, than the resistance offered to the higher frequencies with their smaller particle displacement. In other words, the radiation characteristics at the lips *favor* the high-frequency components.

18. A small degree of vocal tract constriction at various locations along the vocal tract must occur in order to specify a given vowel. The location of the relative constrictions and the degree of the constrictions can be used to predict, or specify, the acoustic output of all vowels of American English. Constrictions of the vocal tract are achieved by movement of the tongue, jaw, and lips, and, to a lesser extent in English, contraction of the muscles of the pharyngeal wall. These constrictions alter the cross-sectional area of the vocal tract in different locations, which specifies the resonant characteristics (formants) of the vocal tract. These constrictions result in a characteristic spectral envelope (formant frequencies that emphasize or dampen different harmonic frequencies). We interpret the spectral envelope as a given vowel.

19. The tongue is a large muscle, connected at its base to the hyoid bone. It is also an incompressible structure, which means that retracting the tongue tip, for example, will cause the portion of the tongue in the oropharynx to be affected as well. Movements of the mandible similarly will affect the base of the tongue. And movement of the base of the tongue will influence the relative constriction of the pharynx, which has an effect upon the acoustic representation of a vowel. Furthermore, although the tongue and mandible often move together, they also can easily move independently of one another. Front vowels also have important resonating cavities in the back of the mouth, and back vowels also have important resonating cavities in the front of the mouth. Thus, describing vowel quality by the resonating cavity is more accurate than tongue position.

20. Refer to Figure 7–16 in the textbook to check the accuracy of your drawing.

21. Specifying vowels in terms of tongue height and advancement is not completely accurate. Tongue height and tongue advancement are not completely uniform with regard to the high and low vowels and the front and back vowels, respectively. Use of the phrase "vowel height" refers to the frequencies of the first and second formants and are thus more accurate in the description of the quadrilateral.

22. The air contained in the neck of a bottle is an acoustic resonator. When air is blown across the top, it exerts a downward pressure on the air in the bottle neck. When the air in the neck is pushed downward, it compresses the air inside the body of the bottle. Restorative forces cause the compressed air to expand, pushing the air in the neck upward. The air will move beyond equilibrium due to momentum, thus rarefying the air within the bottle, which causes the pressure to drop and sucks the air in the neck back into the bottle. The upward and downward oscillation of the air in the bottle neck continues until frictional forces cause the oscillation to come to rest. The rate of the oscillation is dependent upon the size of the resonating cavity, which can be altered by selecting different-sized bottles or taking several similar-sized bottles and filling up each one to a different capacity with water.

23. B

24. B

25. The natural resonant frequencies of the vocal tract vary depending upon the vocal tract posture. These postures result from movement of the articulators, which create different acoustic resonating spaces. These spaces are variable in that they can change with movement of the articulators.

26. Phonate a series of three vowels at a constant f_0 and intensity. The f_0 and intensity represent voice source characteristics. The vowels represent vocal tract resonances. As you change the vowel, the source remains the same. Thus, the source and filter are functioning (somewhat) independently.

27. She could round her lips, which would lower F2 while maintaining the tongue position for /i/.

28. The formants of the vocal tract are located at the same frequencies whether you provide energy from the glottal sound source or not. The vocal tract filters the energy with which it is supplied. In a voiceless whisper, you have supplied the vocal tract with turbulent, aperiodic airflow instead of complex harmonic structure of a voiced sound. The vowel is not as distinct, but you can still hear the vowel quality because changes to the spectral characteristics of the source do not change the characteristics of the vocal tract transfer function.

29. The shape of the vocal tract is not uniform in diameter along its length, and vocal tract shape changes dynamically with each change in articulatory shape required to produce the phonemes of speech.

30. C

31. C

32. A

33. B

34. A

35. C

36. C

37. The shape of the vocal tract changes greatly with different phoneme productions, therefore altering the resonant characteristics (and frequencies) of the vocal tract as a series of connected tubes.

38. B

39. C

40. D

41. B

42. A

43. C

44. A

45. B

46. C

47. C

48. A

49. C

50. A

51. B

52. A

53. D

54. D

55. C

56. B

57. B

58. A

59. B

60. A

61. D

62. B

63. B

64. B

65. C

66. C

67. D

Clinical Application

Clinical Case 5: Accent Management

1. The frequencies of F1, F2, and F3, and the relationship among those formants, are important cues for perception of vowel identity in English. The inherent duration of a vowel is also an important acoustic cue for vowel perception in English. In Spanish, it is expected that formant frequencies are equally important to vowel perception, although the specific frequencies will be different for Spanish vowels compared to those of American English. In addition, some research suggests that vowel duration is a less important acoustic cue in Spanish compared to English.

2. Movements of the articulators create constrictions in the vocal tract, which specify the length and cross section of the various acoustic resonating spaces in the vocal tract. These resonating spaces specify the frequencies of the formants, which in turn specify the vowel quality.

3. A wideband filter setting would be most appropriate to identify spectrographic features of vowel production. The wideband filter reveals broad bands of energy—the spectral peaks—that are associated with vocal tract formants. The spectrograms of Jaime's vowel productions would likely show formant frequencies at different locations compared to the displays created by the SLP's speech.

4. A vowel adjacent to a nasal consonant will typically carry some of the nasalization of that consonant, because the velopharyngeal port does not open and close as rapidly as the sequence of phonemes is produced.
   The SLP could help Jaime focus on production of the nasal consonant without addressing nasal coarticulation, which would happen naturally.

5. Stressed syllables tend to be longer in duration than unstressed syllables and produced with greater intensity and higher pitch than are unstressed syllables. The SLP could help Jaime focus upon one or more of these cues to achieve greater distinction between stressed and unstressed syllables.

6. The SLP must determine whether therapy goals should address voice source or vocal tract resonance features. Because the accent management plan would address the oral articulatory postures of consonant and vowels production, the focus was upon vocal tract resonance rather than voice source characteristics.

Clinical Case 6: Ataxic Dysarthria

1. Vowel quality is defined by the frequencies of the formants, which are specified by the resonance shapes—the shape of the vocal tract and locations and degree of constrictions. The resonance spaces are formed by movement of the

articulators; in a disease such as Friedreich's ataxia, the resonance spaces are continually changing. Thus, the vowel quality is also changing.

2. Paul does not have full control of the muscles of the vocal folds and other muscles that control the larynx due to the disease. Therefore, control of vocal fold stiffness and mass per unit length are impaired, resulting in abnormal vocal qualities. Given that both the voice source and the vocal tract resonance features are impaired, this disorder would be characterized as one of voice and speech.

3. The f_o contour is controlled by changes in vocal fold stiffness and mass per unit length. Syllabic stress is achieved through a combination of changes in f_o, intensity, and duration. Since these variables are not well controlled due to the brain damage in this disease, which decreases control of muscles contractions, impairments in f_o contour and syllabic stress would be impaired. Similarly, rate changes require the ability to control muscle contractions of rapidly sequenced articulator movements, and they too would be impaired.

CHAPTER 8
The Production and Perception of Consonants Answers

Foundational Knowledge

8.1 Introduction (p. 295)

1. Nearly periodic, turbulent

2. Upstream

3. B

4. A

5. Pharyngeal constrictors

6. Velum

7. D

8. A

9. C

10. Lowering

11. False

8.2 Three Sources of Speech Sounds (p. 298)

12. /s/ = B, /z/ = A, B, /b/ = A, C, /r/ = A, /m/ = A, /p/ = C

13. Backward

14. B

15. A

8.3 Phonetic Description of Consonants (p. 299)

16. B

17. False

18. Refer to Table 8–1 in the textbook for the completed chart.

19. D

20. A

8.4 Acoustic Representation of Consonants (p. 301)

21. Plosives

22. B

23. Voice bar

24. True

25. Bilabial = B, Alveolar = A, Velar = D

26. Longer

27. Aspiration

28. C

29. B

30. Voice onset time

31. C

32. A

33. Prevoicing

34. C

35. Voiced, voiceless, voiced

36. False

37. Longer

38. B

39. A

40. C

41. True

42. C

43. B

44. A

45. C

46. D

47. A

48. A

49. B

50. C

51. B

52. D

53. A

54. D

55. A

56. B

57. D

58. A

59. Frication noise

60. Downstream

61. Sibilants

62. Upstream

63. Obstruents

64. Are not

65. Semivowels

66. Dark, light

67. Nasal murmur

68. Velar pinch

69. Not very helpful

70. Homorganic

71. True

72. False

73. True

74. False

75. False

76. False

77. True

78. False

8.5 Clinical Application: Speech Sound Disorders (See Clinical Application Questions Section)

8.6 Language and Dialect Influences on Consonant Production (p. 342)

79. A

80. 24

81. True

82. C

8.7 Instrumentation and Measurement of Vocal Tract Aerodynamics (p. 344)

83. B

84. A

85. C

86. B

87. Posterior

88. Higher

89. False

90. True

91. False

8.8 Instrumentation for Measuring Articulation (p. 347)

92. A

93. C

94. X-ray microbeam

95. Electromagnetic midsagittal articulography

96. Pseudopalate

97. True

98. False

Conceptual Integration

1. C

2. Stops and fricatives are considered obstruents because they obstruct the airflow partially or completely. A phonemic voicing distinction means that a fricative that is voiced is a different phoneme than the same fricative that is unvoiced. For example, /s/ and /z/ are both produced with the same articulatory positions. The only difference is that the former is unvoiced and the latter is voiced. This difference results in two distinct phonemes.

3. Less variability of consonant production is permitted compared to vowels. Regional dialects influence vowel quality more than consonant production. Thus, slight variations in vowel production will generally not alter the meaning (phonemic distinction) of the word. Variations in consonant production, however, are more likely to alter the meaning of the word.

4. For any given target phoneme, the phoneme immediately preceding and following the target phoneme will influence production. The vocal tract posture for a given phoneme is carried over to the target phoneme, and the vocal tract posture for the following phoneme is anticipated. Therefore, coarticulation is both the influence of and simultaneous articulation of surrounding phonemes.

5. The articulatory posture of the vocal tract shifts as the speaker moves from the vowel to the stop. For both the voiceless and voiced stops, the speaker does not wait until the vocal tract is in the optimal posture for producing the stop. Stop production begins while the vowel is still being articulated. The frequency of the vowel formants therefore will shift (formant offglides) during this transition quite rapidly. Because the articulatory postures of the stops differ (bilabial, linguadental, etc.), the formant shifts will be specific to each manner of stop articulation.

6. A transglottal pressure drop is necessary to maintain voicing (vocal fold vibration). During the closed portion of the /b/, the vocal tract is completely sealed by the closed velopharyngeal port and the sealed lips. Thus, the supraglottal pressure quickly becomes equal to the subglottal pressure when voicing during the closed portion of the /b/. During production of the /m/, although the oral cavity is sealed by the lips, the velopharyngeal port remains open and air can continue to flow out of the nose. In that case, duration of voicing is limited only by available lung pressure.

7. A range of durations of VOTs have been found for the distinction of voiced and voiceless plosives. As the VOT approaches the 20- to 40-ms range (from short to long lag), other acoustic cues contribute to the perception of voicing. Four secondary cues include (1) duration of the closure, which is longer for voiceless stops; (2) presence of aspiration, which is generally present in voiceless stops; (3) f_o, which tends to go downward prior to the stop closure; and (4) the vowel preceding the stop closure tends to be longer for voiced stops.

8. Hypernasal speech, compared to normal oral or oral + nasal resonance, has less radiated acoustic power because the nasal antiformants dampen energy. The presence of nasal turbulence can also contribute noise to the acoustic signal. Also, airflow through the nose results in less intraoral pressure, so that articulation of oral consonants results in less acoustic energy and, therefore, the acoustic cues for the oral consonants are decreased.

9. The waveform shows change in amplitude over time. Greater intensity is represented by larger amplitude. VOT is measured from the release of the stop closure to the onset of voicing. In voiceless stops, the closed portion will show as almost no change in amplitude in the waveform. In voiced stops, the closed portion will show minimal change in amplitude. The VOT can be seen as a rapid onset of a small change in amplitude prior to the large change in amplitude associated with the subsequent vowel.

10. A

11.

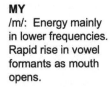

MY
/m/: Energy mainly in lower frequencies. Rapid rise in vowel formants as mouth opens.

FLY
/f/: Broadband frication noise.
/laɪ/: gradual change in formants from /l/ to vowel

SPY
/s/: Higher frequency frication noise.
/paɪ/: stop gap of voiceless plosive, then burst and rapid transition to vowel formants

TIE
/t/: Small burst, then broadband aspiration noise.
/aɪ/: formants of vowel

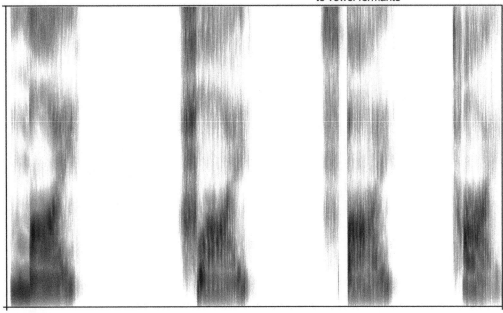

Time (s)

12. A distinct downward movement of F2 and F3 is observed as the vowel transitions into the consonant, and an upward movement is observed in the onglide in the VC transition. The downward movement into the consonant and the upward movement out of the consonant suggest that the consonant is producing a smaller cross section of the vocal tract (increased constriction) compared to the vowel. However, the transitions to and from the consonant are smooth without abrupt changes, minimal high-frequency noise is noted, and formant structure is clearly present throughout the consonant, dominantly in the lower frequencies. Therefore, we can guess that the consonant is a /w/ or /r/.

13.

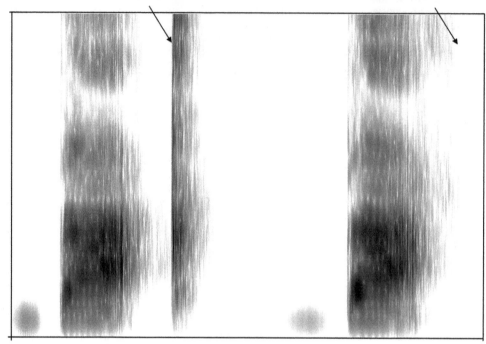

Released /k/
Burst noise followed
by aspiration noise.

Unreleased /k/
Silence of stop gap

Time (s)

14.

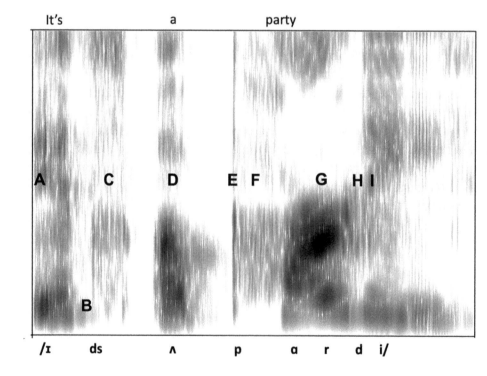

It's   a   party

A = 3, B = 6, C = 1, D = 7, E = 4, F = 8, G = 2, H = 9, I = 5

15.

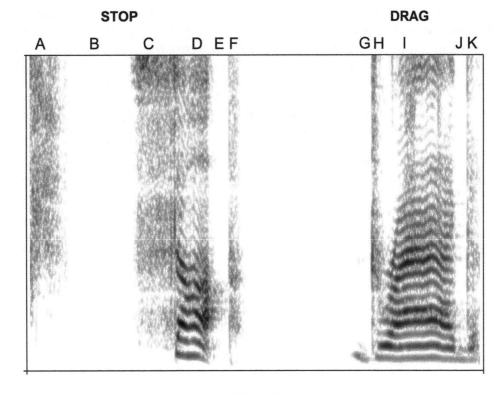

A = High-frequency frication noise of /s/

B = Stop gap of /t/

C = Aspiration noise of release of /t/

D = Harmonic energy of vowel

E = Stop gap of /p/

F = Aspiration noise of release of /p/

G = Release burst of /d/

H = Aspiration noise after release of /d/

I = Harmonic energy of /r/ transitioning smoothly to vowel

J = Stop gap of /g/

K = Release burst with aspiration of /g/

16. B

17. A

18. C

19. A

20. All vowels only have one sound source: phonation. Some consonants have more than one sound source. For example, voiced fricatives such as /z/ and /v/ and /ð/ are produced by forcing air through a tight constriction to produce frication noise while the vocal folds are simultaneously vibrating to produce phonation. The sound energy from each of the two sound sources adds together.

21. With complete closure of the lips, bilabial plosives /p/ and /b/ as well as the nasal /m/ phonemes can be produced.

22. Blowing air through each tight constriction at locations "c" and "e" will generate similar turbulent airflow that we will hear as frication noise. However, the "tube" of the vocal tract is longer for the frication noise produced at location "e," and it will therefore resonate at a lower frequency than for frication noise produced at location "c." The filtered frication noise created at location "e" will sound lower in pitch than the frication noise created at location "c."

23. C

24. The phoneme will show frication noise but also evidence of formants representative of a vowel due to the acoustic energy of the frication noise being applied to the entire vocal tract.

25. B

26. C

27. The resonating tube for dental and labiodental fricatives is very short and is essentially only the distance from the teeth to the lips in each case. This short resonating tube yields a very high resonant frequency that is similar for both dental and labiodental fricatives.

28. Consider the resonating tube defined by location "c" to the lips as a tube open at both ends. Such a tube will function acoustically as a half-wave resonator, and the lowest resonant frequency will have a wavelength of twice the length of the tube and the formula frequency = C / 2L, where C = the speed of sound and L = tube length. For this example, the resonant frequency = 340 / 2*0.04 meters = 4,250 Hz.

29. The sonorant consonants are produced similar to the vowels, with phonation as the sound source and being filtered by the formants of the vocal tract. Voiced obstruent consonants also utilize phonation as a sound source, although this may be in conjunction with frication and transient noise generated in the vocal tract. The frication noise generated by many obstruent consonants may be filtered in the vocal tract due to resonant frequencies of the vocal tract as an acoustic resonating tube in a similar way that formants filter the acoustic energy of phonation for vowels and sonorant consonants.

30. Formants are resonant frequencies of the vocal tract and will result in selective amplification of the harmonic frequencies that are at or near to the formant frequencies. As a result, we hear the amplified phonation harmonics to a greater

extent than those harmonics that do not produce resonance in the vocal tract. Antiformants produce selective attenuation of the harmonic frequencies that are at or near the antiformant frequencies, resulting in a loss of acoustic energy. Perceptually, the frequencies that are attenuated by the antiformants become very quiet relative to frequencies that are produced by phonemes that do not generate antiformants.

31. C

32. The voice onset time is approximately 60 ms as measured from the start of the aspirated burst at approximately 20 ms to the end of the burst at approximately 80 ms. A voiceless stop is characterized by a voice onset time of longer than approximately 30 ms.

33. B

34. A

35. B

36. D

37. C

38. A

39. D

40. C

41. C

42. Based on the abrupt onset of frication noise and the frication noise without a voice bar, the consonant in the first syllable is likely an unvoiced stop. Based on the more gradual onset and greater intensity and duration of frication noise, the consonant in the second syllable is likely an affricate. As there is no voice bar present for the consonant in the second syllable, the affricate must be the unvoiced /tʃ/.

43. C

44. C

45. Based on the spectrogram plot, the consonants for both syllables show long duration of frication noise and a relatively similar concentration of energy and frequency range of the frication noise. Also, a voice bar is evident for the consonant of the second syllable but not for the first syllable. The waveform also shows a gradual onset of each syllable. Taken as a whole, this information suggests that the consonants are cognate pairs of fricatives. Here, the consonant in the first syllable is /s/ and the consonant in the second syllable is /z/.

46. The first (left) phoneme shows a concentration of acoustic energy that is much higher in frequency as compared to the second (right) phoneme, indicative of a shorter resonating tube and therefore a closer relationship between the location of turbulent airflow producing frication noise and the end of the tube at the lips.

47. A

48. C

49. D

50. C

51. This is a voiced continuant consonant as evidenced by the long duration of the phoneme (from approximately 50 to 200 ms) and the presence of a voicing bar on the spectrogram plot. Additional support for the presence of "voicing" is the periodic nature of the waveform during this time period. Frication noise is evident in the spectrogram plot, although it is very weak in intensity due to it being a weak fricative as well as the attenuating effect of voicing on the amplitude of the frication noise.

52. The stop gap starts at approximately 270 ms, and the burst release occurs at approximately 300 ms. During the stop gap, the waveform shows continual periodicity, which indicates continual voicing. In addition, the aspiration following the burst release appears to have a duration of approximately 20 ms prior to initiation of voicing for the following vowel, and thus the voice onset time is approximately 20 ms. These characteristics suggest a voiced stop.

53. Immediately prior to the stop consonant, formant 2 rises and formant 3 lowers in frequency. The pattern reverses following the burst release of the stop. The narrowing of the frequency range between formant 2 and formant 3 is evidence of the "velar pinch" characteristic of vowels that surround a velar stop consonant. In conjunction with the characteristics suggesting a voiced stop (see previous question), the velar pinch indicates that the stop is the /g/ phoneme.

54. For nasal consonants as well as the liquid /l/, the airstream is divided into two pathways, causing resonance in two air chambers simultaneously. For nasal phonemes, the air chambers include the oral and nasal cavities. For the liquid /l/, the air chambers consist of two lateral chambers formed in the oral cavity. The acoustic resonance formed in two separate air chambers simultaneously interacts to attenuate frequencies, resulting in areas of low intensity as seen on a spectrogram plot.

55. To generate the salient acoustic characteristics for stop phonemes, positive air pressure must be created behind the closure of the airway by the articulators. The subsequent rapid release of the air pressure causes the transient burst noise. For affricates and fricatives, air pressure is also built up and released, producing turbulent airflow and resulting in frication noise as the air is forced through a narrow opening. However, the release of the air is over a much greater time period for fricatives as compared to affricates.

Clinical Application

Clinical Case 7: Facial Nerve Trauma

1. Because he had difficulty sealing the oral cavity to build up intraoral pressure, the phonemes that are produced with high intraoral pressure would be most impaired: the plosives and fricatives. He also would likely have difficulty producing other consonants that require significant lip rounding, such as /r/ and /w/.

2. For the plosives, the VOT, burst noise, aspiration, and poststop vowel formant transitions would be altered. For the fricatives, the intensity and spectrum of the frication noise would be altered. Because these cues contribute substantially to perception of the phonemes, the listener would likely have some difficulty understanding the phonemes that Sean is trying to produce.

3. Exaggerated movements of the mandible for closure and opening of the oral cavity would assist in replacing the lip movement necessary for impounding and releasing the air pressure in the oral cavity for stop production. Thus, the acoustic cues would be closer to those of normal plosive production. However, lip closure and opening can occur more rapidly than mandibular movement, and thus the timing of the opening and closure would be different.

4. Vowels that require significant lip retraction (/i/—high front vowel) and lip rounding (the back vowels) would be difficult to produce with impaired lip movement.

5. Constriction at the lips lowers all formant frequencies. Thus, without the ability to constrict the mouth opening, formant frequencies would likely be higher than normal. Similarly, lip puckering extends the vocal tract, which lowers formant frequencies, so again, the formant frequencies would be higher with unpuckered lips.

6. Research shows that listeners use visual cues of lip movement to assist in interpretation of auditory cues. The lack of lip movement could further confuse the listener for vowels and consonants that typically demonstrate lip rounding and lip seal.

7. Nonspeech oral-motor exercises may help to facilitate return of nerve function to the lips and thus help improve articulatory movements.

Clinical Case 8: Articulation Errors

1. The acoustic evidence for the place of articulation for fricatives is (1) the frication noise generated from the turbulent airflow and (2) the formant transitions in the CV and VC contexts.

2. Because of the significant constriction for /s/ and /ʃ/, these sibilants have a lot of high-frequency frication noise. The fricative /ʃ/ has slightly less constriction

than the /s/ and a slightly more posterior point of constriction. Thus, the /ʃ/ has a broader band of frequencies from high- to midfrequency range and is perceived to have a slightly lower pitch than /s/.

3. To make the sounds /s/ and /ʃ/, we have to place the front of our tongue very close to the roof of our mouth so that when we breathe out, the air must flow through a very narrow channel. For the /s/, we put our tongue tip right up behind our front teeth and make a very narrow gap for the air to flow. This makes a very high-pitched hissing sound. For the /ʃ/, we move our tongue tip a little farther back but still against the roof of our mouth, and we use a little bit more of our tongue to make the narrow gap, so that it still creates a hissing sound but it isn't quite as high-pitched compared to the /s/. If we don't make the gap the right size or put our tongue in the right place, the sound changes.

Speech Sound Disorders

1. B

2. A

3. D

4. False

5. It is important for the clinician to be familiar with the typical age of acquisition of phonemes. For example, a 3-year-old child would not be expected to produce rhotic sounds with consistent accuracy, because that group of phonemes is often not fully acquired until a slightly later age. Therefore, such an "error" would not be treated in a child of that age.

6. Obligatory

CHAPTER 9
Prosody Answers

Foundational Knowledge

9.1 Introduction to Prosody (p. 363)

1. A

2. Suprasegmental

3. Cannot

4. False

9.2 Basic Building Blocks of Prosody (p. 363)

5. B

6. 3, 4, 1

7. C

8. D

9. B

10. C

11. Intonation

12. Fundamental frequency declination

13. Duration, juncture

14. Sonority

15. Do

16. True

17. False

18. True

19. False

9.3 Syllabic Stress and Prominence (p. 370)

20. C

21. D

22. A

23. True

24. True

25. False

9.4 Speech Rhythm (p. 374)

26. A

27. D

28. A

29. Pairwise Variability Index (PVI)

30. Standard deviation

31. False

32. True

33. True

9.5 Accentedness and Prosody (p. 376)

34. C

35. True

9.6 In Summary of Prosody (p. 376)

36. B

Conceptual Integration

1. The basic acoustic features of fundamental frequency contour, intensity contour, and duration and juncture are achieved by applying these features to the vowels and also by some of the consonants, particularly the continuants. For example, to place syllabic stress on the first syllable of the word *syllable*, the phonemes /s/, /ɪ/, and /l/ are all lengthened and produced with a higher frequency and greater intensity than are the phonemes of the second syllable in the word. Thus, the prosodic or *supra*segmental feature is achieved through manipulation of the segments.

2. Syllabic stress adheres to the rules of a given language. Changing the stress of the syllable can make the word difficult to understand or it can alter the meaning of the word. Phrase prominence is the use of the basic elements of prosody to emphasize a component of a phrase to communicate meaning as determined by the speaker. Example: The second syllable of the word *umbrella* must always receive stress to be correctly pronounced. However, the speaker may elect to increase the stress of the second syllable, through perhaps increased duration and intensity of the vowel, to place greater prominence on that word within the phrase.

3. The basic building blocks of prosody are the perceptual features of intonation and changes in timing and loudness. These perceptual features are correlated with (although not equivalent to) the acoustic features of fundamental frequency contour, duration and pause, and intensity contour, respectively. These basic building blocks are used together in variable ways to emphasize syllables within a word (syllabic stress) and across a phrase (phrase prominence). Syllabic stress is the (primary and secondary) emphasis placed upon one or more syllables in a word. Phrase prominence is the emphasis placed upon syllables and words within a phrase to communicate speaker intent. Syllabic stress is a language-defined feature, and phrase prominence is a speaker-defined feature. All of these components together create speech rhythm, a complex pattern of syllabic stress and phrase prominence that incorporates variable types of syllable structures and amounts of vowel reduction in unstressed syllables.

4. B

5. C

6. Three prosodic features of the command utterance, compared to the citation utterances, are noted in Figure 9–3. First, the f_0 is higher. (Note: The f_0 is labeled in the diagram because it can sometimes be difficult to observe differences in f_0 in a spectrogram, particularly when the resolution is on a scale of 0 to 5000 Hz. Without the labels, you can still observe differences in the f_0 in two ways. First, recall that harmonics are integer multiples of the f_0. Therefore, the spacing between the harmonics is greater when the f_0 is higher. Second, because of the integer multiples, the differences between the frequencies of the harmonics of the citation and command utterances increase as the harmonics increase in frequency. Therefore, compare the fourth or fifth harmonic of the citation and command utterance to more easily see the difference in the frequencies.)

The second prosodic feature evident from the spectrogram is the greater intensity in the command utterance. The gray of the higher harmonics is darker in the command utterance, signifying greater energy.

Third, the duration of the vowel is greater in the command utterance. Frequency, intensity, and duration can all be used to signify syllabic stress and phrase prominence.

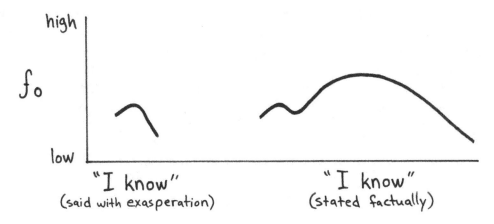

Figure 9–A1

7. Figure 9–A1 depicts an example of the two contours. Note that yours might be a little different because people might say these phrases with slightly different prosody. However, the major differences between the two curves that should be included in your drawing are the shape of the curves and the duration of the final syllable. The second curve, representing exasperation, has a wider curve (greater range). The emphasis placed on the second syllable ("know") is achieved with an upward and then downward pitch movement, as well as prolonged duration of the syllable.

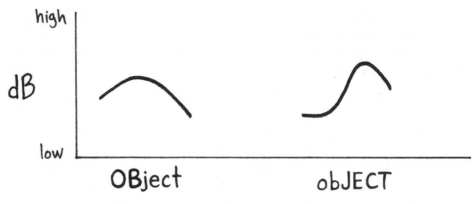

Figure 9–A2

8. In this example, we selected the word *object* said as a verb *OBject* and as a noun *obJECT* to demonstrate contrastive syllabic stress. Figure 9–A2 depicts how the intensity contour might change as a function of syllabic stress. Keep in mind that your intensity contour might look different, even for the same pair of words. The major feature is the increased intensity for the stressed syllable and probably also a bit longer duration for that syllable as well.

9. The phrase prominence appears to have been placed upon the words "so hard." The acoustic evidence in the waveform is the greater amplitude of those words compared to the rest of the phrase, representing increased intensity. The increased duration of the vowels in those words also appears to suggest emphasis. Similarly, in the spectrogram, the prominence of the higher frequency harmonics in those words suggests increased intensity, and the increased duration of the vowels in those words suggests increased duration.

TRY IT!

1. EXAMPLES: CONtent and conTENT, OBject and obJECT

2. EXAMPLES: surprise, sadness, uncertainty, and sarcasm

3. EXAMPLES: [big grip, big rip] [red eyes, red dyes] [his older brother, his soldier brother]

Clinical Application

1. Prosody is the use of the fundamental frequency contour, the intonation contour, and duration and juncture to convey linguistic, paralinguistic, and nonlinguistic information. This information is not an inherent feature of the phonemes but instead is applied to the phonemes to convey speaker intent and increase

intelligibility. These functions require an awareness of the needs of the listener as a communicative partner and thus are based upon the rules of social interaction, a deficit of the child with a pragmatic disorder.

2. Speech requires the motor coordination for production of the individual phonemes together in rapid succession, together with the management of the respiratory and phonatory systems. Recall that a synonym for prosody is the suprasegmental level of speech production. Therefore, management of prosody requires coordination of an additional level of speech production, necessary changes in fundamental frequency, intensity, and duration and juncture. If an individual has apraxia and struggles to coordinate the segmental level of speech production, then adding management of the coordination of the suprasegmental level may be quite difficult.

Clinical Case 9: Parkinson's Disease

1. The SLP addressed intensity contour and phrase prominence in English and pitch contour in Mandarin. The SLP did not address duration or syllabic stress.

2. Because Mandarin is a tonal language, changes in f_0 contour play a more critical role than they do in English. Therefore, pitch changes were the focus of the therapeutic approach for Mandarin. In English, intensity contour can be used to identify prosodic intent with syllabic stress and phrase prominence.

3. Intensity is regulated primarily by lung pressure. Therefore, inhaling to a higher percentage of vital capacity can provide the necessary additional air supply required to speak loudly. Intensity is also regulated by resonance characteristics of the vocal tract. Widening the vocal tract through greater mouth opening will decrease the amount of acoustic energy reflected back down the vocal tract and increase the amount of energy radiated outward.

4. The acoustic theory of speech production tells us that speech is composed of voice source and vocal tract resonance features. In the case of Parkinson's disease, impairments are noted in both voice source characteristics (decreased intensity and decreased change in f_0) and vocal tract features (decreased intensity, decreased clarity of articulation).

Clinical Case 10: Gender-Diverse Speech and Voice

1. The major acoustic characteristics that contribute to gender identification include mean speaking f_0, intensity, voice quality (particularly breathiness and resonance), differences in F2 vowel formant frequency, and prosody.

2. Differences in pitch patterns across an utterance and also rate of speech can be different in men and women. Length of utterance may also vary from men to women. Although prosody can help identify gender, the prosodic characteristics associated with maleness or femaleness are linguistically and culturally bound.

CHAPTER 10
Theories and Models of Speech Production Answers

Foundational Knowledge

10.1 Introduction (p. 386)

1. Spatial, temporal

10.2 Theories and Models (p. 388)

2. A
3. False
4. False
5. Occam's razor

10.3 Theoretical Issues for Consideration (p. 390)

6. Potential
7. False
8. C
9. Articulatory gesture
10. B
11. True
12. D
13. D
14. True
15. B
16. B
17. C
18. D

19. D
20. Motor program
21. Sensory feedback
22. Closed
23. Rotational/translational
24. Coarticulation

10.4 Models of Speech Production (p. 404)

25. C
26. A
27. False
28. C
29. Can
30. Dynamical systems
31. Spatiotemporal
32. Spatiotemporal index
33. A

10.5 Investigational Considerations (p. 408)

34. A
35. B
36. Perturbation

10.6 Motor Learning Principles (p. 413)

37. Motor learning

38. True

39. Large, variable, random, external target, complex target

40. Knowledge of results, lesser frequency, delayed

10.7 Language and Speech (p. 415)

41. A

42. Articulatory or gestural phonology

Conceptual Integration

1. Temporal

2. A

3. D

4. A

5. A

6. C

7. The Directions into Velocities of Articulators model is a computational-neuroanatomical model of speech production that describes a complex interaction of different regions of the brain that regulate planning, execution, and processing of speech sounds to enable the acquisition and production of speech.

8. In the early babbling acquisition phase, articulatory movements are directed by the auditory and somatosensory feedback. A map (a region of neurons) of target speech sounds has not yet been established. In the imitation learning, basic maps of the articulatory targets have been developed, based upon a map of speech sounds, and the acquired auditory and somatosensory feedback systems are used to correct errors.

9. The learning, or acquisition phase, represents the stage during which an individual is acquiring a new motor behavior. During this stage, the individual will most likely be unable to demonstrate the skill in a novel context. The performance phase represents the stage at which the individual has retained the new behavior and is able to transfer it to novel contexts.

10. Speech is a unique motor activity because it involves language centers. The articulatory motor commands are tied to meaningful units of sound. Therefore, movements such as walking, sports, and musical instrument–specific activities may have different training and feedback requirements.

11. C

12. A hypothesis is a tentative hypothesis that is based on observed data from research and is often described as an "educated guess." The scope of a hypothesis is narrow and limited to a single testable question. A scientific theory typically is generated by establishing numerous related data-driven hypotheses, and theories are refined with additional research knowledge. Theories function to provide an

explanation of more complex phenomena than a single hypothesis. A model is a type of simulation that may be computer based or physical and typically serves to explain a complex phenomenon in more simplistic terms. A model does not typically simplify all of the complexities of a comprehensive theory, however.

13. C

14. B

15. True

16. True

17. A

18. A

19. Studies in which the oral structures are anesthetized or auditory feedback is blocked provide evidence that sensory information is not crucial for speech production, suggesting that feedback control is not required for production of ongoing speech and providing support for feedforward control mechanisms. However, perturbation studies have shown that the articulators can produce compensatory movements in response to unanticipated sensory disturbance during speech production. These results provide support for feedback control during ongoing speech.

20. Coarticulation effects extend further than a single phoneme, reflecting a continuity of movement across multiple phonemes in running speech. The continuous movement generated suggests that the speech motor system is likely controlling events that are greater than a single phoneme and are perhaps at the syllable or phrase level.

21. A

22. False

23. A

24. B

25. Varying patterns of muscle contraction can produce the same outcome in terms of the acoustic output for speech. Consider that numerous synergistic muscles act on each articulator; thus, changes to the timing or amount of muscle contraction of a muscle may still result in the same outcome if those changes are matched by reciprocal changes to synergistic muscles.

26. C

27. A

28. C

29. While models of speech production have placed greater or lesser emphasis on certain output targets such as the acoustic output, evidence suggests a role for the speech production mechanism in controlling each of these targets (acoustic output, articulator positioning, and aerodynamic monitoring). Sensory deprivation and perturbation studies have provided evidence that all three output targets are controlled by the speech production mechanism. Further, models such as the DIVA model of speech production have shown that targeting just one factor (the acoustic output for the DIVA model) can produce simulated speech patterns (including disruptions of speech) that are highly similar to real speech.

30. A

31. The speech production system of the DIVA model uses the acoustic output as the primary output target. The model does not dictate how muscles will contract to achieve that output target. Instead, any pattern of temporal and spatial parameters of muscle contraction (and resulting articulatory kinematics) that yield the acoustic output target is acceptable. This is especially evident when considering how the DIVA model explains speech development in infants.

32. Experimental paradigms that rely on explicitly controlling the speech task typically create an artificial experience in terms of speech production. These experiments typically use speech stimuli that are very simple in construction, such as "CVC" syllables. Running speech is highly dynamic in terms of word and phrase construction (recall the discussion regarding the potential units of analysis of speech), and the kinematics of running speech are likely much more complex than are produced with simplified and limited speech stimuli.

33. Coarticulation shows that we don't produce isolated phonemes or syllables. Instead, we blend phonemes together for both anticipatory and carryover coarticulation in terms of the acoustic output as a direct result of the underlying articulatory movements. The articulatory movements, therefore, are also not produced in isolation. The dynamic nature of articulatory movements and the resulting coarticulatory blending of those movements are reflected in an articulatory "gesture" instead of a "posture."

34. A

Clinical Application

Clinical Case 11: Spastic Cerebral Palsy

1. Individuals tend to have a preferred speaking rate, and research suggests that changing that rate may increase variability or irregularity of articulatory movements. In the case of dysarthria, it may be necessary for a speaker to slow down, for example, to maintain accuracy of articulation and clarity of speech.

In healthy speakers, phonemes before and after the target phoneme will influence the production of the target phoneme. In the case of dysarthria, fine motor skills may be impaired so that coarticulation increases and accuracy of phoneme production decreases as the speaker tries to compensate for the loss of motor control while still trying to maintain a "normal" speaking rate.

2. Visual feedback could be used in the form of an external timing mechanism, such as the therapist's hand movements.

   Auditory feedback could be used by having the therapist model the target speaking rate and then the patient tries to match the rate that he heard. Auditory feedback can also be used by having the patient aurally monitor his own rate. Kinesthetic feedback could be used by asking the patient to focus upon articulating in a slightly exaggerated fashion and feeling the articulators move in a larger range of motion. This feedback may have the indirect effect of slowing rate of speech.

Clinical Case 12: Oral Motor Exercises

1. SLPs and clients are familiar with the concept of physical therapy and exercising muscles to increase strength and range of motion. Thus, it is easy to make the inference that such exercises would also help articulation. Furthermore, they are relatively straightforward to enact and do not require the time investment to create word lists or other speech material and tasks for practice.

2. The DIVA model posits that specific regions of the brain regulate the acquisition and production of speech and that planning and execution of speech movements involve areas of the brain that are not involved in nonspeech movements such as simple tongue protrusion. The dynamical systems model proposes that groups of muscles work together in a coordinative structure and that the timing of the movements is based upon the articulatory target. Therefore, both models specify speech production as an intrinsic component of articulation. Oral motor exercises do not include speech targets and, thus, it may be that those exercises may not address the underlying mechanisms involved in speech production.

CHAPTER 11
Theories of Speech Perception Answers

Foundational Knowledge

11.2 Topics in Speech Perception (p. 429)

1. B
2. D
3. A
4. C
5. C
6. A
7. False
8. Sometimes
9. Perceptual normalization
10. True
11. Quantal perception
12. Duplex
13. True

11.3 Theories of Speech Perception (p. 434)

14. A
15. C
16. B
17. D

18. A
19. Bottom-up
20. Top-down
21. True
22. Percept
23. A
24. False

11.4 What Babies Can Tell Us About Perception (p. 438)

25. A
26. False
27. Native language magnet

11.5 Perception of Speaker Identity (p. 441)

28. Indexical information
29. Extralinguistic
30. A
31. B
32. True
33. Is

Conceptual Integration

1. C

2. An invariant feature means that the feature does not change with different contexts. A phoneme is not always characterized by a set of unchanging acoustic features in a variety of phonetic environments. Coarticulation, prosody, and speech rate, among other factors, can alter the temporal and spectral characteristics of a phoneme's features. For example, formant patterns in the offglide of a fricative will change depending upon the following vowel. Duration and energy of the voice bar in the closed portion of a voiced stop depends upon the syllabic stress within which the phoneme resides.

3. Although an utterance is composed of separate phonemes, when an attempt is made to divide up the acoustic signal into individual phoneme segments, those segments do not necessarily represent the actual phonemes. For example, in the utterance "I don't know what he said to you," although the listener can identify each word, if the acoustic signal is segmented into phonemes, the listener would not hear a recognizable representation of each phoneme. Coarticulatory changes to the phonemes allow us to recognize the words in the utterance, but many of the individual phonemes cannot be isolated.

4. Accentedness is the listener's perception of how nonnative a speaker sounds. Listener-related factors that can influence that perception include the language background of the listener and the experience of the listener with the native language of the speaker, as well as the ambient noise level and the semantic context of the message. Personal preferences/biases about nonnative languages may also influence the listener's perception of accent.

5. Perceptual normalization refers to the process of simplification by smoothing out variability or "noise" in the acoustic signal to capture better the essence of a signal. A large amount of variability occurs within an individual speaker and across different speakers, particularly speakers with an accent different from that of the listener. By normalizing the signal, the listener is able to focus upon the critical features necessary for understanding.

6. A

7. B

8. C

9. In Chapter 8, we learned that stop consonants produced with a long lag (greater than 40 ms) between the burst release and the onset of voicing results in the perception of an unvoiced stop. A voice onset time of less than about 25 ms is associated with perception of a voiced stop. Therefore, a voice onset time of 50 ms or a voice onset time of 80 ms would be associated with the characteristic of "unvoiced," while all voice onset times from 0 ms (and even negative voice onset

time that indicates prevoicing) to 25 ms indicates "voiced." Although there is a range of voice onset times that indicate both "voiced" and "voiceless," there is a quantal perception of the characteristic of voicing instead of a graded perception of voice onset time. This is an example of categorical perception.

10. The McGurk effect provides evidence that both the visual and auditory systems are used for perception of speech. When a viewer/listener is exposed to a visual stimulus of an individual producing a /ga/ syllable but heard the syllable /ba/, the perception was of the syllable /da/. In other words, the speech event with incongruous visual and auditory information resulted in a perception that did not match either the true visual or auditory information. Perception in this situation, therefore, is dependent on both visual and auditory information.

11. B

12. D

13. A

14. Researchers have used nonspeech acoustic stimuli to explore whether or not speech perception relies on unique neural mechanisms. For example, the stimuli for sine wave speech are three time-varying sinusoid waves that simulate the formant frequencies. Other studies have inserted nonspeech waveforms into running speech, such as replacing a phoneme with the sound of a cough.

15. True

16. A

17. Unlike infants, adults have extensive experience with speaking and language and therefore have the ability to utilize contextual cues (relating to syntax, semantics, and pragmatics) in regard to speech perception. Infants, therefore, are challenged to perceive speech without the benefit of experience.

18. True

19. B

20. A

21. The motor theory of speech perception suggests that there is a biological basis for speech perception based on comparison of acoustic information with knowledge of invariant articulatory gestures. While this theory does provide an explanation for categorical perception, it is limited in explanation of the development of speech perception as it predicts that knowledge of speech production would precede speech perception. In contrast, the native language magnet theory–expanded posits that sensory learning in the form of "perceptual magnets" precedes speech production abilities. In this theory, the ability to produce speech (including language-specific phonemes) is related to the exposure to the speech acoustic signal.

22. Factors such as variance of production across speakers, allophonic variation, and coarticulation show that there is not a fixed relationship between the phoneme and the associated speech acoustics.

23. Listeners make judgments of a speaker's identity (e.g., age, sex, gender identity, race, and ethnicity) based on acoustic characteristics of speech that may include voice fundamental frequency, formant frequency variables, voice quality, and nasal resonance, among others. These characteristics may influence how the listener interacts with the speaker, but listener judgments of speaker identity based on speech acoustics are not always accurate.

24. A "bottom-up" approach to speech perception assumes that all relevant information is carried by the acoustic waveform itself without regard to context or linguistic cues. Many studies have shown that context (of the phoneme within a syllable or word or of the word within a phrase, for example) has a strong role in speech perception, providing support for top-down processing. Other studies have indeed provided evidence for the role of acoustic features (consider the distinctive features theory, for example) in speech perception. Both bottom-up and top-down strategies have roles in terms of speech perception, therefore.

Clinical Application

Clinical Case 13: Visual Feedback

1. In the early stage of skill acquisition, it may be helpful to obtain feedback information via multiple sensory inputs. However, in later stages of retention and learning, the speaker has begun to form motor patterns and internal cueing. Therefore, visual feedback may not play as important a role.

2. The updated motor theory posits that speech perception uses the motor commands of the speech production system as the units of perception. The listener accesses his or her own knowledge of how sounds are produced and then uses that reference to process the perception of sounds produced by another individual. Visual feedback might be used to teach the speaker how the target phoneme is produced, which then can be used as a reference for further learning.

Clinical Case 14: Auditory Feedback

1. For: If an individual cannot hear a difference between two phonemes, they won't be able to produce the two phonemes differently because auditory targets are an integral component of speech production. Steven's model of speech perception incorporates formant frequencies as targets that drive articulation. Formant frequencies must be heard to be used as feedback.

Against: Articulatory postures of the vocal tract can be used as targets of speech production, and thus, perceptual training is not a necessary precursor to phoneme production. One could use visual feedback from a spectrogram, for instance, to guide production of a phoneme without prior perceptual training.

2. The DIVA model posits that the target of the neural commands is a configuration of the area of the vocal tract relevant for the phoneme production. This target provices the necessary auditory and oral-sensory (proprioceptive and tactile) information to produce the formant values and vocal tract constrictions used to achieve the phoneme. Thus, speech production consists of motor commands (the feedforward control system) and auditory and somatosensory maps (the feedback control system).

3. The cause of the articulation problem is unknown, but it could reflect a disturbance in the feedforward and feedback circuits used to develop correct phoneme production. In the case of an adult learning a new language, we assume that the mechanisms of speech production and perception are normal and, thus, perceptual feedback would proceed normally.

CHAPTER 12
Instrumentation Answers

Foundational Knowledge

12.1 Introduction to Measurement (p. 452)

1. D
2. Both research and clinical

12.2 Basic Principles of Measurement (p. 452)

3. Measurand
4. A
5. Calibration
6. B
7. Noise floor
8. B
9. Transduction
10. D
11. A
12. False
13. Transfer
14. Microphone
15. Volts = potential, current = kinetic

12.3 Sensors for Capturing Speech (p. 457)

16. True
17. False

12.4 Microphones (p. 459)

18. Head-worn or headset
19. B
20. Dynamics
21. A
22. True
23. Polar
24. Unidirectional
25. Cardioid (unidirectional)
26. A
27. Flat
28. Frequency response
29. B
30. True
31. Feedback
32. C
33. False
34. Greater than

12.5 Amplification (p. 466)

35. B
36. Gain
37. A
38. True

39. C

40. Cannot

41. B

12.6 Making the Connection (p. 469)

42. Male, female

43. B

44. True

45. A

46. A

47. C

12.7 Recording Environment (p. 470)

48. Ambient

49. True

50. B

51. C

12.8 Data Acquisition: Let's Get Digital (p. 472)

52. False

53. D

54. B

55. A

56. Nyquist

57. C

58. A

59. B

60. Aliasing

61. True

12.9 Data Storage (p. 478)

62. A

63. B

12.10 Balancing Cost, Complexity, and Accuracy in Digital Data Acquisition (p. 480)

64. False

65. Not able

12.11 Best Practices in the Use of Instrumentation (p. 483)

66. B

67. C

12.12 Let's Wrap This Thing Up! (p. 486)

68. Will not

Conceptual Integration

1. C

2. A very low-amplitude signal may not be much greater than the self-noise generated by the electronic instruments, producing a very low signal to noise ratio. If the signal and the instruments' self-noise are the same amplitude, the signal to noise ratio will be 1.0, which is very low and unsuitable for performing data analysis on the signal.

3. C

4. The noise floor consists of all sources of unwanted noise that may be present. This includes self-noise from electronic instruments, electromagnetic noise from nearby electronic equipment that is not part of the signal chain, and ambient sound in the recording environment. The combination of all of these noise sources adds up to be the overall noise floor.

5. D

6. We can calculate this with the barleycorn figure, but let's be more conventional and accurate with our measurement units. As you recall, the formula for frequency if you know wavelength is frequency = velocity of sound / wavelength. Here, we can convert 4.5 feet (162 barleycorns) into 1.372 meters, giving the formula 343 m/sec ÷ 1.372 m = 250 Hz.

7. A transfer function is the representation of how a signal (or a sound) is changed after it passes through a system such as an electronic instrument or an acoustic resonator. For the vocal tract, the formants amplify certain phonation harmonic frequencies while attenuating others. Similarly, a microphone's frequency response plot shows how it will respond relatively better to certain frequencies and while attenuating others.

8. D

9. C

10. The microphone shown in panel B is the most appropriate for use in capturing speech. Although the microphone shown in panel A has a frequency response that appears to be less variable (due to the straightness of the line) than the other microphones, it has a large amount of attenuation in the low frequencies and a relatively large increase in response at the higher frequencies. The microphone shown in panel C has a "flat" response except for a large peak at around 7 kHz that has a greater than 2-dB variation from 0 dB. The microphone shown in panel D also has a "flat" response, but this microphone's frequency range ends at approximately 5 kHz, with significant attenuation of higher frequencies. Although the response of the microphone shown in panel B appears to be more varied

than that of the other microphones, the variability of its response is less than 2 dB across its frequency range, and its frequency range is wide enough to fully cover the frequency range for speech.

11. A

12. C

13. B

14. Omnidirectional

15. Cardioid

16. B

17.

Bit Depth	Number of Quantization (Amplitude) Levels
2	4
4	16
8	256
12	4,096
16	65,536
20	1,048,576
24	16,777,216
30	1,073,741,824

18. C

19. This waveform has variable amplitude of waveform cycles, but the highest-amplitude cycles have been "clipped," as evidenced by the squared-off peaks and valleys. The dynamic range of the microphone's preamplifier appears to be from −3V to +3V, and it appears that the largest-amplitude cycles have exceeded the dynamic range.

20. The gain of the preamplifier should be reduced so that the captured signal doesn't exceed the dynamic range of the preamplifier.

21. The sampling rate for this waveform is too low, as there are fewer than two samples taken per waveform cycle. With such a low sampling rate, this waveform will not be converted to a digital form, but an aliased waveform of lower frequency will be created.

22. C

23. B

24. The sampling rate for this signal is high enough to accurately capture the temporal characteristics (and therefore frequency) of the waveform, but the amplitude representation of the digitized waveform is highly inaccurate. There are only six quantization levels evident on this digitized waveform. Such a small number of quantization levels will produce a large amount of error in amplitude measurement of this waveform.

25. C

26. Either use of a very low bit depth quantizer (e.g., a 3-bit quantizer) or use of a very small percentage of the digitizer's total dynamic range will result in a small number of quantization levels applied to the waveform. A digitizer that has a bit depth of 16 bits, for example, will have 2^{16} or 65,536 potentially useful quantization levels. However, if the captured signal is very low in amplitude and only covers 0.1% of the dynamic range of the digitizer, effectively only 65 quantization levels will be applied to the digitized waveform.

27. The captured waveform is not much greater in amplitude than the noise floor, yielding a relatively low signal to noise ratio. The noise floor is evident as the waveform energy present prior to the start of the speech, approximately 150 ms. With such a low signal to noise ratio, it is not possible to clearly identify the end of the speech waveform.

28. D

29. B

30. A

31. B

32. A

33. Waveform A was captured at a level that exceeded the dynamic range of some component of the signal chain. As such, the waveform has been clipped and is not suitable for performing acoustic analysis. Waveform B was captured at a very low amplitude level, perhaps due to the speaker being too far from the microphone or the gain of the microphone preamplifier being too low. This resulted in a very low-amplitude signal and a very low signal to noise ratio. The low amplitude of the signal means that only a fraction of the available quantization levels was utilized to capture the waveform, yielding a high amount of quantization error. Waveform C was captured at an amplitude level that uses most of the dynamic range (and quantization levels) of the digitizing system without exceeding the dynamic range. Waveform C is the only waveform that would be appropriate for taking valid measurements and performing acoustic analysis.

34. False

35. True

36. False

37. B

38. The microphone described here is quite sensitive and therefore has a relatively low maximum sound pressure level of 89 dB. This gives it a dynamic range of 65 dB (based on a noise floor of 24 dB), which would only be suitable for capturing quiet to fairly high-amplitude speech but not loud or shouted speech or singing. A microphone with a higher maximum sound pressure level would be required to capture very loud speech and singing.

39. D

40. False

41. C

42. B

43. MP3 and other compressed file formats rely on a reduced bit rate, which is achieved by lowering the sampling rate and/or the number of quantization levels for the stored waveform. While this does decrease the file size, it reduces the fidelity of the stored waveform data and may negatively affect speech analysis results.

44. C

45. The signal to noise ratio is very low in this captured speech signal, and as such, the amplitude of the first phoneme is comparable to the amplitude of the noise (i.e., the noise floor).

46. Due to the very low signal to noise ratio for this captured speech signal, the amplitude of the formants is comparable to the amplitude of the noise. For the spectrogram plot, the large amount of gray reflects the relatively high amplitude of the noise. The voice bar is still evident for the vowel, however, as the first harmonic of phonation in this case was relatively high in amplitude.

47. If this waveform has been captured and saved (recorded) to a data file, nothing can be done to improve the signal to noise ratio. However, future recordings could be improved by (1) reducing ambient noise in the recording environment, (2) reducing potential electromagnetic interference, and (3) increasing the amplitude of the captured speech signal by moving the microphone closer to the speaker (if possible) and increasing the gain of the microphone preamplifier.